# Interpreting macroeconomics

*Interpreting Macroeconomics* explores the different ways in which the history of macroeconomic thought can be written. Three historiographical chapters criticise both relativism and constructivism, arguing instead for an eclectic, pluralistic approach. The remaining chapters demonstrate the advantages of this, by adopting a range of approaches to the history of macroeconomic thought.

The ideas of pre-Keynesian economists are analysed from the perspective of modern economic theory. The story of macroeconomics since Keynes is told in three ways: a history innocent of methodology; a methodological appraisal of Keynesian economics; and a Lakatosian rational reconstruction in which monetarism and Keynesianism are viewed as part of the same research programme. Rhetorical analysis is applied to the work of Milton Friedman, John Muth and Axel Leijonhufvud. The message of the book is that these very different perspectives all have something to contribute – that the history of economic thought has many dimensions, and that different methods are needed to uncover them all.

**Roger E. Backhouse** is Reader in the History of Economic Thought at the University of Birmingham. He is the author of *A History of Modern Economic Analysis* (1985), *Economists and the Economy* (1994) and two macroeconomics textbooks. He is also a co-editor of *Economics and Language* (1993) and the editor of *New Directions in Economic Methodology* (1994).

# Interpreting macroeconomics

## Explorations in the history of macroeconomic thought

Roger E. Backhouse

**London and New York**

339
B12ι

First published 1995
by Routledge
11 New Fetter Lane, London EC4P 4EE

Simultaneously published in the USA and Canada
by Routledge
29 West 35th Street, New York, NY 10001

Printed in Great Britain by Mackays of Chatham PLC, Chatham, Kent

*British Library Cataloguing in Publication Data*

*Library of Congress Cataloguing in Publication Data*
Backhouse, Roger.
    Interpreting macroeconomics: explorations in the history of macroeconomic
thought/Roger E. Backhouse.
        p.    cm.
    Includes bibliographical references and index.
    ISBN 0-415-12709-2
    1. Macroeconomics. 2. Macroeconomics–History. I. Title.
    HB172.5.B33    1995
    339–dc20                                                            94–40703
                                                                              CIP

# Contents

# List of figures and tables

**FIGURES**

**TABLE**

# Acknowledgements

Chapter 3 was previously published as 'How should we approach the history of economic thought: fact, fiction or moral tale?' *Journal of the History of Economic Thought* 14(1), 1992, pp. 18–35; Chapter 4 as 'History's many dimensions: a reply to Weintraub', *Journal of the History of Economic Thought* 14(2), 1992, pp. 277–84; Chapter 2 as 'Perspectives on the history of economic thought', *Scottish Journal of Political Economy* 35(1), 1988, pp. 97–104; Chapter 6 as 'F. A. Walker's theory of "hard times" ', *History of Political Economy* 19(3), 1987, pp. 435–46; Chapter 5 as 'J. A. Hobson as a macroeconomic theorist', in *Reappraising J. A. Hobson*, edited by M. Freeden (London: Allen and Unwin, 1990), pp. 116–36; Chapter 10 as 'The neo-Walrasian research programme in macro-economics', in *Appraising Economic Theories: Studies in the Methodology of Research Programmes*, edited by N. B. de Marchi and M. Blaug (Aldershot: Edward Elgar, 1991), pp. 403–26; and Chapter 9 is an English version of a paper previously published in Polish as 'Ocena metodologiczna economii keynesistowskiej', in *Współczesny Keynesizm: Studi I Materialy*, 42 (Warsaw: Poltext, 1993), pp. 93–110. I am grateful to the publishers for permission to reprint this material.

Chapters 1, 7, 8, 11 and 12 are published here for the first time.

# Chapter 1

# Methodology, rhetoric and the history of macroeconomic thought

## METHODOLOGY, RHETORIC AND HISTORIOGRAPHY

Once upon a time (to inject the appropriate fairy-tale element into the story) historians of economic thought believed that they knew how to do their subject. The question 'Why?' might have been difficult to answer in a way that persuaded other economists, but between them historians of economic thought such as Viner, Schumpeter, Robbins, Bowley, Black, Hutchison and Blaug had established, by example as much as by explicit arguments, how the subject should be approached. The subject was represented in a number of surveys that have since become classics, notably Hutchison (1953), Schumpeter (1954) and Blaug (1968/85).[1] For these economists the history of economic thought had a number of characteristics.

1  It dealt with the way in which economic ideas had changed over time.
2  These ideas were to be explained and understood against the appropriate historical background, this including (a) cultural background; (b) sociological factors; (c) policy requirements; (d)

---

[1]  The books by Schumpeter and Blaug are acknowledged classics. The inclusion of Hutchison's book may be a little more surprising. I include it because it exemplifies what might be termed the 'mainstream' approach to the subject, perhaps better than the books of either Schumpeter or Blaug, each of which is in some ways (brilliantly) idiosyncratic.

developments in other disciplines; (e) biographical information on the economists concerned.

3 Ideas were to be appraised for (a) their logical consistency, (b) their compatibility with evidence either available at the time or subsequently discovered and (c) their implications for future developments in the subject.

Past economic theories might be appraised from the perspective of modern economic theory and the results of such appraisals might be used in explanations of why theories had succeeded or failed. This was, however, not the whole story. It was widely accepted that to explain why economic ideas had developed in the way they had, it was necessary to go beyond this – 'external' factors had to be taken into account. Most historians of economic thought were, therefore, absolutists in the sense outlined by Blaug (1968/85, p. 2). Understanding the historical context was necessary to explain why economic thought evolved as it did, but historical context did not justify the ideas, except in the sense that it might suggest that, given the information and techniques available to them, economists might have been justified in drawing the conclusions they did. It was as though they accepted the distinction emphasized by Popper between the contexts of discovery and justification.

To this extent, therefore, the history of economic thought was eclectic and pluralist. This pluralism arose from a recognition that though the appraisal of past theories in terms of modern theory was a valid, and important, exercise, there were other questions that needed to be answered. To explain the dominance of the Marshallian school, or the international transmission of economic ideas, sociological stories were told; Jevons's approach to economics was explained by locating it in the context of his views on the nature of science; Ricardo's views were illuminated by exploring the nature of his relationship with his mentor, James Mill; and so on. Different questions necessitated different methods of inquiry.

But this situation did not continue happily ever after. The first blow came with the entry of Kuhnian and later Lakatosian philosophy of science into the history of economic thought.[2] Economists interested in methodology turned to the history of economic thought as a testing ground for philosophical ideas. Kuhn's picture of science developing through a series of paradigms and periods of normal science offered a way of making sense of the apparent unevenness in the growth of economic knowledge. Though their conceptions of science were very different, Kuhn's concept of a paradigm was used to make sense of Schumpeter's 'classical situations' and the accepted habit of seeing the history of economic thought in terms of classical, neoclassical and Keynesian economics.

This idea that the history of economic thought should be used as a testing ground for philosophical ideas was taken a stage further with Lakatos's methodology of *historical* research programmes. This involved the idea that the way to test a methodology was to provide a rational reconstruction of the history of science – writing history as though science had developed in accordance with the methodology. If the rational reconstruction accounted for the main features of the actual history, without any need for recourse to 'external' factors (factors not part of the methodology) then this was evidence in favour of the methodology. The significance of this for our purposes is that it involves a conscious attempt to write the history of science (or economics) in a way that is influenced by philosophy.[3]

This use of history of economic thought as an adjunct to methodology had the benefit of making it clear why the history of economic thought was necessary. There were, however, costs. The main one was that Lakatosian rational reconstructions were seen as valuable exercises only as long as the philosophy on which they were based was considered useful. In the late 1980s Lakatosian methodology was called into question, to the extent that by the end of the decade support for it was very limited indeed (see Backhouse, 1994c). One reason for this loss of interest in Lakatos was the critique of 'Methodology' by McCloskey

[2]   See the Introduction to Backhouse (1994b).
[3]   For a list of such studies, see de Marchi's 'Introduction' to de Marchi and Blaug (1991). Perhaps the classic work in this genre is Weintraub (1985). A more recent use of Lakatosian ideas is Vint (1994).

(1983, 1986). McCloskey's claim that 'Methodology', a 'modernist' notion involving an indefensible presumption that methodologists could tell economists how better to do science, should be replaced by the study of rhetoric – of how economists persuade each other. To support this argument he produced a number of case studies in the rhetoric of economics. Though not presented as history of economic thought, they can be seen as contributions to it, for they provided new readings of important episodes. If McCloskey is right, historians of economic thought should be aiming to explain how economists have persuaded each other.

The other cost of such philosophically informed history of economic thought was that it appeared, by some standards, 'thin' and un-historical. Taking up an idea proposed by McCloskey (1988), and inspired by work on the history of science, the sociology of scientific knowledge and literary criticism, Weintraub (1991a) argued that we should be writing 'thick' histories which recount the way in which economic ideas were negotiated within specific communities. Our standards should, he contended, be taken from history, not philosophy. Similarly Mirowski (1990) has been very critical of much writing on the history of economic thought, focusing instead on the underlying metaphors on which economic ideas are, he contends, dependent.

Rather different, though equally critical of 'standard' history, is Brown's (1993) critique of 'canonizing' discourses. These are writings that present history as a unilinear progression towards modern theory, suppressing dissenting voices. We should, instead, she argues, be writing 'decanonizing' histories, sensitive to the variety of voices within our sources. This is a view strongly influenced by literary theory, critical of the notion that in searching for the meaning of a text we should be trying to find what was the original author's intention. Like Weintraub she sees meaning as located in communities' readings of texts.

Between them, these various ideas about how one should approach the history of economic thought have resulted in the subject looking very different from the way it looked up to, say, the mid-1970s. However, and this is one of the main themes of this book, it can be argued that, at least as regards the history of macroeconomics,[4] the 'traditional' pluralistic approach to the history of economic thought is quite compatible with bringing to the subject insights obtained from areas such as methodology and rhetoric. This is argued explicitly in the three chapters in Part I.

The opening chapter tackles the issue of relativism through reviewing a book that adopts an extreme relativist stance. Dasgupta's argument is that successive theories belong to different epochs, each characterized by the asking of a new set of questions. As a result, he claims, successive theories are independent of each other. It is impossible to speak of progress. The main response to this thesis is that when considering theories we need to consider the different levels at which a theory can be specified, ranging from, for example, general statements about the pursuit of self-interest leading to the coordination of economic activity to specific, numerical models of equilibrium in specific economies. At the former level it is hard to sustain the relativist argument, whilst at the latter level it is much easier. The other response is that there is enormous continuity in the history of economic thought, both in the questions asked and in the way in which economists sought to answer them. This is not to say that there are no discontinuities – clearly there are. But these discontinuities must not be exaggerated.

Dasgupta's argument against what others have termed 'Whig' history is a practical one – that the nature of economics is such that a 'Whig' approach makes no sense. In contrast, recent critics of such history provide a philosophical argument in support of their case. This argument is the subject of Chapter 3, which takes up the charge, made most forcefully by Weintraub (1991a), that the constructedness of history undermines any basis for 'Whig' history (by this he means histories such as those written by Hutchison, Schumpeter and Blaug, that ask whether past theories were right or wrong). History should, he claims, be written as history, free from any philosophical baggage – free from the notion that theories might be progressing towards the truth. A

[4]   I add this qualification simply because I shall not be discussing other areas of economics, not because I wish to suggest that macroeconomics is different. Not everything can be done at once.

useful way of tackling this problem is through the typology developed by Rorty (1984). In this typology the most significant distinction is between rational reconstructions, which read past ideas from the perspective of present-day ideas, and historical reconstructions, which understand past ideas in the context of their own times. Though he does not cite Rorty, Weintraub's critique of 'Whig' history has much in common with Rorty's arguments in favour of historical reconstructions. In particular, both are based on the notion that the constructedness of knowledge severely limits what we can say about truth, undermining epistemology.

The main argument against this critique of 'Whig' history, it is argued in Chapter 3, is that we are not faced with a choice simply between foundationalist epistemology and social constructivism. Once this is recognized, the Rorty–Weintraub case collapses. It is further undermined by two additional arguments. The first is that the distinctions Rorty draws between various types of history are blurred. It is never possible totally to escape from our current concerns in order to view the past on its own terms. There is thus always an element of rational reconstruction, or Whiggishness, in any history. Even Weintraub's view that one should be writing histories that recreate the way in which ideas were negotiated within specific communities – 'thick' history – reflects a specific philosophical position. The second is that to abandon the notion of standards is to abandon the notion of appraisal. This means that the history of economic thought can no longer play a critical role within economics. The Rorty–Weintraub case is very conservative.

Chapter 4 explores further the idea of 'thick' history used by McCloskey and Weintraub. It distinguishes between the philosophical case for such history, discussed in Chapter 3, and the 'historian's' argument that history is too complex to fit into any simple scheme. The problem with the latter is that it relies on an unanalysed notion of historical sensibility. Neither argument is persuasive. The conclusion is drawn that history is written for a variety of purposes, different purposes calling for different approaches to history.

## MACROECONOMICS

Keynes is, arguably, central to any history of macroeconomics in the sense that contemporary macroeconomics emerged out of the debates initiated by Keynes's *General Theory of Employment, Interest and Money* (1936).[5] This is not to say that macroeconomics did not exist before Keynes – it did. Rather it is that the impact of the Keynesian revolution was such that previous approaches were, with a few exceptions, neglected in favour of a way of thinking about macroeconomic problems that originates in the debate over Keynes's book.

Macroeconomics, as the subject is now understood, has a number of characteristics, of which the following are perhaps the most important.

1 It deals with aggregates, such as GDP, consumers' expenditure, investment, employment, unemployment, and so on, most of which have generally accepted definitions.[6]
2 Behavioural relations do not necessarily take the same form as those that describe the behaviour of individual agents in the economy, even if they are derived from aggregating the behaviour of individual, possibly optimizing, agents.

The paradigm case of a macroeconomic model is thus determination of the equilibrium level of national income using the consumption function and the condition that in equilibrium saving equals investment. Such analysis makes sense only once it has been accepted that 'national income' is a meaningful variable to model and that categories of saving and investment have been defined. The consumption function is a macroeconomic law that need not have a direct parallel at a microeconomic level.

The chapters in Part II discuss four pre-Keynesian economists: Hobson, Walker, Mitchell and J. M. Clark. What they have in common is that they all tackled the 'Keynesian' problem of persistent

---

5   Note that this does not say that the subject was created by Keynes. Though Keynes was clearly the dominant influence, the wording leaves open the issue of how far contemporary economics has been faithful to Keynes's ideas. See Chapters 8, 9 and 10.

6   Arguably the aggregate over which there is least agreement as to the precise definition is unemployment.

unemployment. Though these economists are in no sense 'typical' pre-Keynesian economists (if there is such a thing) discussing them illustrates some of the important changes that differentiate macroeconomics after Keynes from much of what went before.[7] One of the major changes is the development of concepts and techniques. For example, since the Keynesian revolution the terms saving and investment have acquired fixed meanings. The stock/flow distinction is clearly understood to such an extent that it is hard to see how serious economists could confuse them. For earlier generations, however, this was not the case. Associated with this increase in conceptual precision, however, there has also been a narrowing of focus: phenomena that do not fit within the accepted theoretical framework are usually ignored or deemed to be of minor importance.

The first economist to be considered (in Chapter 5) is J. A. Hobson. Hobson's writings on economics were published between 1889 and 1933, but his work in many ways reflects the conceptual framework of classical economics, notably that of J. S. Mill. The 'Keynesian' strand in his work is his belief that unemployment (the term was coined by Hobson, who defined it in the modern way as involuntary leisure) was caused by underconsumption – by a deficiency of aggregate demand. In holding this belief he was following the widespread consensus amongst businessmen and popular writers. He sought to show how underconsumption might arise, contrary to the arguments of the classical economists using a theoretical framework that had much in common with theirs. The most prominent classical feature of Hobson's theory is his treatment of the quantity of money as a flow, not a stock. This led to great misunderstanding when he discussed the ideas of Fisher, who defined the money supply unambiguously as a stock. Linked to this was Hobson's complete failure to allow for the possibility of hoarding – failing to conceive of the notion of a demand for a stock, he failed to see a whole range of issues in monetary economics. Finally, Hobson failed to see the need to distinguish between saving and

---

[7] These changes are not due entirely to Keynes. Much of the work that led to the refinement of the concepts of saving and investment, for example, dates from the 1920s and 1930s and involved many economists other than Keynes.

investment, seeing saving as involving more than simply not consuming. This meant that his theorizing, whilst in some ways along Keynesian lines, led him in a somewhat different direction.

Unlike Hobson, F. A. Walker, the subject of Chapter 6, rejected the idea that what he called 'hard times' were caused by under-consumption. For him the problem was a low level of production which in turn caused a low level of demand. He saw clearly that production might get stuck at a low level – low production and low demand reinforced each other. To break out of this situation required a revival of what Keynes later called 'animal spirits'. The problem was one of co-ordination failure. Yet, as with Hobson, Walker's analysis was not Keynesian. He was working in a framework that was shared by the classical economists and, before them, by Hume and Cantillon.

The examples of Hobson and Walker show very clearly the difference between much late-nineteenth-century thinking on unemployment (from the perspective of Keynesian economics they were, arguably, two of the best writers on the subject) and that which underlies modern macroeconomics. Contemporary macroeconomics is based on a specific set of accounting concepts of which the most important relate to national income, but also including stock-flow distinctions and related identities. From modern national income accounting it is but a short step to derive the multiplier. Neither Hobson nor Walker had such a framework available to them. Without it, the multiplier hardly makes sense.

Chapters 5 and 6 combine elements of, to use Rorty's terminology (see Chapter 3), rational and historical reconstructions. They could never have been written were it not for the use of modern macroeconomic concepts. Hobson and Walker are both appraised according to the standards of contemporary theory and found wanting. Yet at the same time these two chapters represent attempts to make sense of Hobson and Walker on their own terms. Hobson's arguments are taken seriously in Chapter 5 in a way that they were not taken seriously by most of his more orthodox contemporaries (for example Keynes – see page 87). Similarly the message of Chapter 7 is that, despite using language that at first sight suggests a similarity with Keynes's writing on uncertainty, Mitchell and J. M. Clark were analysing the problem from within a very different theoretical framework from Keynes. As a result what they wrote on uncertainty had a very different significance. To that extent the chapters in Part II can be regarded as historical reconstructions. They contain no discussion of the details of the way in which meanings and understandings were negotiated within the relevant communities, but they nonetheless ask important, historical questions. There are other questions that can be asked, but that is no problem.

## METHODOLOGY AND RHETORIC

The chapters in Part III tackle the question of what methodology can contribute towards our understanding of the history of macroeconomics. This is done by juxtaposing three accounts of the evolution of macroeconomics since Keynes. Chapter 8 presents an account that is innocent of the philosophy of science, pointing out two ways in which the history can be viewed. The first view runs in terms of the progressive removal of what Lucas has termed 'free parameters' – parameters not grounded in maximizing behaviour. The second view is in terms of an ongoing debate between Keynesianism and monetarism. The conclusion is that, whilst the latter story captures much of what went on, especially at the level of policy prescriptions, it misses important key elements that were common to both Keynesian and monetarist economics, the main one being the attempt to explain more and more in terms of rational, maximizing behaviour.

Chapters 9 and 10 provide methodological appraisals of this history. Chapter 9 starts with a summary of some of the reasons why one might wish to undertake a methodological appraisal, taking Keynesian economics as the example, and then outlines how one might perform such an appraisal using three sets of criteria: *a priorism*, naive falsificationism and Lakatos's methodology of scientific research programmes. Its conclusion is that only the latter comes anywhere near providing an explanation of the changing fortunes of Keynesian economics (and, implicitly, of monetarism) during the half-century since

Keynes. Chapter 10 then uses Lakatos's MSRP to explore the other view outlined in Chapter 8, the drive towards models based on rational behaviour.

This chapter provides a rational reconstruction of the history discussed in Chapter 8 as though that history had developed in accordance with Lakatos's MSRP. The story is told in terms of the establishment and development of a neo-Walrasian research programme in macroeconomics, the neo-Walrasian research programme being defined in substantially the same way as in Weintraub (1985).[8] Essentially it is a research programme defined by a particular modelling strategy, centred on markets, rational behaviour and formal modelling. The conclusion is that macroeconomics fits into this programme remarkably well. The rational reconstruction has much in common with the removal-of-free-parameters story told in Chapter 8.

Both the formal Lakatosian appraisal in Chapter 10 and the slightly less formal appraisal in Chapter 9 show that Lakatos's MSRP can be used to make sense of much (though not all) of the history of post-war macroeconomics. There are, however, reasons for caution, these relating mostly to problems with Lakatos's concept of a research programme.[9]

1 There are some features of the story that do not fit into the 'neo-Walrasian' story, of which the main example is Milton Friedman. The neo-Walrasian research programme is one into which Friedman's work emphatically does not fit (see Chapter 11).
2 If the interpretation in terms of Keynesian and monetarist research programmes is accepted, there arises the problem of how one makes sense of the evident common features in the evolution of the two programmes.
3 The fact that it is plausible to tell the story in ways that involve differently defined research programmes raises doubts about whether Lakatosian methodology does provide the best possible way to divide up economics into units of appraisal. There is more to the

8    There are minor differences in the way Weintraub and I specify this programme, but these differences are not ones of substance.
9    This argument is outlined in more detail in Backhouse (1994c).

structure of macroeconomics than can be captured using Lakatos's concepts of the hard core and heuristics.

However, whilst the similarity of the methodologically informed accounts in Chapters 9 and 10 with the methodologically 'naive' account in Chapter 8 can be read as providing evidence in support of the methodology, it is equally possible to interpret this as raising the question of what methodology has to contribute. The most general answer to this question is that having an explicit philosophical framework forces us to ask questions that might otherwise have remained unanswered. Most importantly, it directs attention to the question of appraisal: how is the drive to base theories on rational behaviour justified? Lakatos's methodology directs us to look for successful predictions of novel facts – to look for theoretical and empirical progress. In finding successful predictions of novel facts we are providing a possible explanation of why economists found this research strategy attractive. Of course, it may be that this Lakatosian interpretation is wrong and that some alternative methodology provides a better explanation, but that is no argument against bringing in methodology: it is just an argument for appraising macroeconomics in terms of other methodologies, or of seeking to find some methodology implicit in what macroeconomists have been doing. In addition, the appraisal in Chapter 10 forces us, in a way that the story told in Chapter 8 does not, to confront other issues such as the difference between the Keynesian research strategy and the research strategy that has dominated macroeconomics since then, and the methodologically idiosyncratic nature of Friedman's contribution to post-war macroeconomics.

One of the most widely canvassed alternatives to methodology (and Chapters 9 and 10 are clearly exercises in what McCloskey condemns as Methodology, with a capital M) is rhetoric. Rhetorical analysis is used in the two chapters in Part IV, which take up two of the claims McCloskey has made for rhetoric. Chapter 11 takes up McCloskey's claim that we should be more concerned with the 'unofficial', or 'implicit', rhetoric of economics than with the 'official' rhetoric that is found in economists' methodological pronouncements. An analysis of

Friedman's rhetoric is used to support the claim that understanding an economist's rhetoric does not dispense with the need to understand his or her explicit methodology. Even with someone as distinctive in style as Friedman, rhetorical analysis provides no more than hints that are open to a variety of interpretations. Equally important, there are *three*, not just two, aspects of economists' work that need to be taken into account: (a) explicit statements on methodology, (b) rhetoric and (c) practice. Implicit methodology can be inferred from either rhetoric or practice, but rhetoric and practice are not the same and must not be confused. To make sense of an economist's work it is necessary to consider all the evidence. Rhetorical analysis may be revealing, but it should not be privileged above all else.

One of McCloskey's most attractive case studies in *The Rhetoric of Economics* (1986) is his chapter on Muth in which he translates Muth's jargon-ridden prose into ordinary English. Two points he makes in that chapter that are potentially relevant to understanding the history of economic thought are that the success of Muth's work owed much to the rhetorical devices he employed and that the article took a long time to be recognized because it was badly written. Chapter 12 considers these claims in the context of a comparison with Leijonhufvud. Leijonhufvud's main work was also published in the 1960s but, despite initial success, its influence waned rapidly. In both respects Muth and Leijonhufvud are very different. Any history of macroeconomic thought since the 1960s has to be able to explain the very different fates encountered by these two authors' ideas. If McCloskey is right, rhetoric should be important. However, whilst rhetorical analysis of the way these two economists argue does reveal important differences, it is not clear that it has much to do with the way in which economists responded to their ideas. The missing element in McCloskey's thesis is a failure to explain why economists find certain ideas persuasive. Methodology may be inadequate or incomplete as an explanation of why economists choose certain ideas over others, but it represents a serious attempt to answer this question.

## CONCLUSIONS

Interpreting the history of macroeconomic thought is a large and complicated task. The essays in this book appraise and provide examples of different ways in which this task might be approached. Though others may wish to write different types of history because they have different questions they wish to answer, the theme of this book is that the traditional, pluralistic approach – in which appraisal in terms of modern standards is combined with a recognition that historical context is indispensable for answering certain questions – is still defensible. There are good reasons for using philosophy of science and methodological ideas to sharpen up our analysis at certain points: even though 'rational reconstructions' may in themselves be inadequate as historical accounts we can nonetheless learn from them. Similarly, rhetorical analysis has much to offer even though it cannot be a substitute for other forms of analysis. But these are not alternatives, either to each other or to other ways of approaching the history of economic thought. The claim that we should dismiss as 'Whig' history or 'doxography' the type of history in which historians of economic thought have traditionally been interested, is unjustified. To understand the history of macroeconomics a range of different techniques needs to be employed.

# Part I

# Historiography

# Chapter 2

# Relativism in the history of economic thought

## EPOCHS OF ECONOMIC THEORY

The purpose of Dasgupta's *Epochs of Economic Theory* (Dasgupta, 1985) is, in the author's own words, 'only to suggest a perspective for viewing the development of economic theory' (Dasgupta, 1985, p. 7). Despite the modesty of this aim, however, Dasgupta's thesis raises a number of very important issues concerning both contemporary economics and its history, and it is important that these are addressed. The remainder of this introduction outlines Dasgupta's main claims, and the following sections discuss some of the issues raised.

*Epochs of Economic Theory* opens with the claim that economic theories are relative, the reason given for this being that,

> Economists deal with a universe where data are freakish and not valid universally, and where phenomena emerge which were not only not known before but had not existed before. It is of the nature of economic science that it involves events and phenomena which not only change complexion from time to time but do not also occur at all places. Problems that emerge as crucial at one time may turn out to be totally irrelevant at another time in the same economy, and those that are relevant in the context of one economy may well be irrelevant elsewhere. *In economics old theories do not die. And they do not die not because one is built on the other, but because one is independent of the other.*
>
> (Dasgupta, 1985, emphasis added)

Dasgupta thus objects to the notion that there is continuity in the development of economic science (Dasgupta, 1985, p. 1), though he does admit the possibility that 'there is often progress from a lower to a higher level of abstraction in a particular line of analysis', citing as an example the passage from Adam Smith's concept of the division of labour to the modern theory of increasing returns (Dasgupta, 1985, p. 4).

Given this position of extreme relativism, Dasgupta proceeds to argue that the history of economic thought should be analysed in terms of a series of what he, using terminology introduced by Gide and Rist (1909), calls 'epochs'. Different epochs are characterized by economists asking different questions, the economic theory of one epoch being independent of that of other epochs. Though these epochs have something in common with Kuhnian paradigms, Dasgupta claims that the implied breaks in the history of economic thought 'have not at any stage brought about anything like a revolution' (Dasgupta, 1985, p. 5). When it comes to identifying the main epochs in the history of economic thought Dasgupta finds three, which he labels 'classical', 'marginalist' and 'Keynesian', these being concerned with the problems of growth, resource allocation and stagnation respectively.

Though *Epochs of Economic Theory* opens with the argument that economic theories are of necessity relative because of the non-uniform and changing nature of the world they are seeking to explain, Dasgupta explains the shift of interest associated with the transition from the classical epoch to the marginalist one in terms of ideology. Putting on one side, for the moment, the implications of this for Dasgupta's concept of epochs, it raises serious doubts about the value of much contemporary economic theory. Furthermore, both Dasgupta's relativism, and his 'Marxist–Post Keynesian' interpretation of the place of marginalist economics within the history of economic thought are arguments which have been used to similar effect by other economists who are critical of much of contemporary economics. Dow (1985), for example, has defended a position which, though significantly different from Dasgupta's, is similar in these important respects.

The remainder of this paper examines four of the main issues raised by *Epochs of Economic Theory*: (1) the idea that it is changes in the questions asked, not progress in economic theory, that results in economic theories being abandoned in favour of new theories; (2) the concept of epochs in the history of economic thought; (3) the status of marginalist economics; and (4) the emphasis placed on the theory of value.

## THE OBSOLESCENCE OF ECONOMIC THEORIES

There are several elements in Dasgupta's thesis concerning the obsolescence of economic theories that are unquestionably correct and important. The world does change, and there are important differences between different economies at any one time, as many economists have long since recognized (e.g. Richard Jones, 1833). In addition there have been important changes in emphasis, economists being concerned with different questions at different times. Dasgupta's characterization of classical, marginalist and Keynesian economists as having, respectively, emphasized growth, resource allocation and stagnation is a generally accepted view. Furthermore, such shifts of attention, along with any associated developments in the economy, can fruitfully be used to explain the way in which economists' ideas have evolved. The clearest example of this is perhaps the way monetary theories have had to change as monetary institutions have developed from ones dominated by simple metallic currencies to more complicated credit systems (see, for example, Hicks, 1967). In more recent times the evolution of macroeconomics is clearly impossible to understand without knowing something of the changing nature of the issues confronting economists and economic policy-makers.[1] Finally, it is perfectly justifiable to claim that theories are sometimes abandoned because economists' interests have changed. Pre-Keynesian theories of unemployment and the trade cycle, for example, contained numerous insights which were neglected in the aftermath of Keynes's *General Theory*.[2]

Dasgupta, however, takes the argument far beyond this, arguing, as the quotation above shows, that there is no such thing as progress in

1    See Backhouse (1985, Chapter 26); or Blaug (1985, Chapter 16).
2    See, for example, Backhouse (1985, Chapter 16); or Casson (1983).

economic theory. Two responses can be given to this. (1) It can be argued that the reason old theories do not die is not that they are independent of each other, but that economic theories are extremely difficult to falsify. Even when a theory has been abandoned, as was classical economics in the 1860s, it will still retain adherents. (2) It is a large, and unjustifiable, step from showing that the history of economic thought involves (Kuhnian) losses as well as gains, to the conclusion that there is no comparability *at all* between different economic theories. As soon as there is some comparability Dasgupta's thesis collapses and we can speak of progress, even if only limited progress, in economic theory.

How can we reconcile these different elements? The answer would seem to be that we have to distinguish more carefully between different types, or levels, of economic theory. In particular, the susceptibility of an economic theory to obsolescence depends crucially on its precision (or falsifiability). Consider the theory of supply and demand. There are several levels (ranked in order of falsifiability) at which such a theory could be formulated: (1) it could be asserted that economic equilibrium is the outcome of men and women pursuing their own self-interest, interacting with each other through markets; (2) we could postulate a general theory of supply and demand in competitive markets, with consumers maximizing utility and firms maximizing profits; (3) specific assumptions could be made concerning the properties of utility and production functions, to obtain a model which yields definite, but qualitative, predictions; (4) numerical data could be attached to the parameters, to yield a model which gives quantitative predictions. If we were to confine our attention to level 4, it would be easy to defend Dasgupta's relativist position. Even if economists were able always to work out the correct model to describe the economy at any time, their theories would change simply because of changes in the real world. There would be no progress, merely new models applicable to different circumstances.

It could be argued, however, that a new set of parameter values does not constitute a new economic theory. If we accept this we have to decide what changes would constitute a new theory. If we have changes at level 3, for example, (suppose diminishing returns set in where returns had previously been constant) does this constitute a new theory? In one sense it does, but in another sense it is a minor change. The lesson to be drawn from this is that where one draws the line between changes that constitute changes in economic theory, and those that do not, is to some extent arbitrary.

This has important implications for Dasgupta's relativist thesis, for the extent to which economic theories change in response to events (the extent to which they are subject to obsolescence) depends on the theoretical 'level' being considered. In the example above, theories at level 1 are unlikely to become obsolete as long as a capitalist, market-oriented economy exists. Theories at levels 2 and 3, on the other hand, will become obsolete much more easily as the result of either institutional or technological changes within a capitalist economy. At level 4 there will be continual change due to obsolescence.

The theoretical systems we deal with when we consider the history of economic thought comprise many levels of theory, and the fates of these are very different. Consider as an example classical economics. Classical theory formulated at level 3 used the Malthusian theory of population, and the assumption of diminishing returns in agriculture to produce very definite predictions concerning capital accumulation and the course of distributive shares (admittedly formulated as laws of tendency). At this level the theory undoubtedly became obsolete and was abandoned for reasons quite compatible with Dasgupta's thesis. Classical theory, however, contained much more than simply this model. The labour theory of value, for example, is logically independent of the Ricardian theory of distribution (Sraffa, 1960) and the reasons for its demise were very different. Furthermore, much of the classical theory was based on neither the Ricardian theory of distribution, nor on any labour theory of value, but simply on a more basic theory of supply and demand. At this level classical theory never became obsolete. Thus whether we find continuity, and hence scope for theoretical progress, or whether we find obsolescence and a succession of independent theories, depends crucially on which aspects of classical economics we choose to look at.

## THE CONCEPT OF EPOCHS

Dasgupta uses the term epoch in a way which is very hard to define. It has a temporal connotation, but it does not denote simply the economics of a certain time period. Consider the classical epoch. If we were to define the term so as to include all the economists writing between, for example, 1776 and 1848, the classical economists would include many demand and utility theorists. For his thesis to be sustainable Dasgupta has to exclude these precursors of marginalist economics, with the result that his epoch becomes much more like a Kuhnian paradigm: it includes all those economists who work within a certain framework. When we adopt such an interpretation of the term epoch we are immediately confronted with the question of just what aspects of, say, classical theory an economist has to subscribe to if his work is to be considered classical: what is the paradigm (i.e. framework) within which classical economists work (is it supply and demand, or is it the Ricardian edifice)? The result is that Dasgupta's epochs are defined in such a way that parts of his thesis become almost tautological.

For all the criticisms of Kuhn's paradigms (see Kuhn, 1970), and many of these apply to Dasgupta's epochs, Kuhn's paradigms have the important merit of forming part of a larger theoretical structure. When we ask whether or not a certain piece of scientific history can be regarded as a Kuhnian paradigm we are directed, because it occupies a well-defined place in a larger theoretical structure, to ask certain questions about the historical evidence. This process can thus be revealing, even if the concept of a paradigm turns out to be of limited use. In contrast, it is hard to see the concept of an epoch as being of any use. It leads us to ask no new questions, and it is so elastic that it can always be made to fit.

The significance of this is that the use of concepts such as Dasgupta's epochs makes it easier to tell the history of economic thought in a very misleading way. The use of the concept of epochs could be described, using Leontief's (1937) term, as 'implicit theorizing': the concept is used as part of an important argument, yet because it is not defined explicitly it is impossible to refute. Consider, for example, the treatment of classical economics. Dasgupta's use of the term epoch means that 'classical' economists who can by no stretch of the imagination be fitted into a Ricardian mould (Dasgupta cites Samuel Bailey and Mountifort Longfield, but we might add J. B. Say) can be considered as not belonging to the classical epoch. Compare this with the alternative approach of, for example, O'Brien (1975). This is to define the classical economists as a well-defined sociological group of economists working at a specific time – O'Brien's definition, contrary to what Dasgupta (1985, p. 11) asserts, is not simply chronological. Bailey, Say and Longfield were classical economists because they were members of a particular scientific community, the background to whose work was Adam Smith's *Wealth of Nations*. Given such a definition we can test the hypothesis that classical economics was synonymous with Ricardian economics, and establish that it was false. The concept of classical economics, defined in O'Brien's way, proves useful, enabling us to produce testable hypotheses concerning this phase of the history of economic thought.

Such an approach can also be applied to other aspects of the history of economic thought. For example, it is possible to analyse it in terms of sociologically defined schools, such as those of Marshall or Schmoller (see, for example, Coats, 1967). Alternatively, national characteristics can be investigated (see Perlman, 1980). Such a sociologically-based approach has its limitations, and does not produce the simple, grand schemes that seem to be favoured by many Marxists and Post-Keynesians, but it is nonetheless an important exercise, with considerable potential (see Coats, 1984).

Alternatively we might evaluate the discontinuities in the history of economic thought in terms of concepts taken from a larger theoretical structure. Kuhn's paradigms, mentioned above, have been used by many economists to examine episodes in the history of economic thought.[3] Of even more use has been Lakatos's framework of scientific research programmes (Lakatos, 1970). Lakatos's concept of the 'hard core' of a research programme, for example, does, for all its inadequacies, provide a framework within which to think about what

[3]   See, for example, Coats (1969) or Blaug (1985).

are the really important features of a set of economic theories (see, for example, Remenyi, 1979).

In contrast, a term so loosely defined as Dasgupta's epochs cannot be used in this way. It neither contributes to the formation of testable hypotheses, nor results in the asking of useful questions.

## MARGINALIST ECONOMICS

Dasgupta sees marginalism as an interlude in the development of economic theory, distracting economists from the important questions confronted by both classical and Keynesian economists (Dasgupta, 1985, p. 142). He claims, quoting Joan Robinson, that the marginalists 'drove economic science into a system of "arid formalism" and turned it away from problems that are actually interesting'. He goes on to cite with approval Joan Robinson's contention that

> Economic analysis, serving for two centuries to win an under-standing of the Nature and Causes of the Wealth of Nations, has been fobbed off with another bride – a Theory of Value.
>
> (Dasgupta, 1985, p. 142)

To achieve this the marginalists are said to have focused attention on the static problem of resource allocation: economic theory came to be viewed 'chiefly as an enquiry into the conditions of maximisation under given constraints' (Dasgupta, 1985, p. 77). This is, he claims, in marked contrast to the classical concern with dynamics. This approach colours the whole marginalist approach to economics, consumption rather than production being seen as the mainspring of economic activity, and distribution becoming 'a species of value – a problem of factor prices rather than one of class relations'.

Two reasons are adduced for this changed perspective. Developments in the economy were rendering the classical approximations invalid (Dasgupta cites the subsistence theory of wages, the assumption of fixed factor proportions, and the homogeneity of the labour force – 1985, pp. 92–3). In addition, the marginalists considered the implications of Ricardian theory, in which there was an inverse relation between profits and wages, unacceptable. Though Smith and Ricardo had been able to draw *laissez-faire* conclusions from it, once the classical model's implications concerning class conflict had been seen, as was the case by the 1870s, it had to be abandoned and an alternative defence of liberalism had to be found (Dasgupta, 1985, pp. 94–8).

There is, amongst these arguments, much that is justified. (1) Marginalist economics did place less emphasis on growth and distribution than had the classical economists, and there was a correspondingly greater emphasis on resource allocation. (2) There was a greater stress on demand. (3) It is possible that developments in the economy were making the Ricardian simplifications even more clearly inadequate (though it is important to note that severe problems with the Ricardian assumptions were evident well before 1870 – see Blaug, 1980, p. 75).

Where then does Dasgupta go astray? He asserts not only that interest in the classical issues waned, but that it was 'suppressed' (Dasgupta, 1985, p. 76) through the employment of a 'static' method in which 'the economy is assumed to be stationary by hypothesis' (Dasgupta, 1985, p. 78). For part of their work, such a working hypothesis was certainly made by the marginalists, but it is going much too far to suggest that dynamics were neglected. Marshall is so clearly an exception that Dasgupta has no problem in excepting his work from the marginalist canon. Marshall, however, was far from alone amongst the marginalists in investigating growth and dynamics. Walras's dynamics, described by Harrod (1956) as 'pure Ricardo', are essential if his work is to be understood properly (see Morishima, 1977, or Backhouse, 1985, Chapter 8).

Another marginalist who is misrepresented by Dasgupta is Jevons. (1) Jevons's *The Coal Question* (1865), written before his *Theory of Political Economy* (1871), but after the main ideas in his theory of value had been presented to the British Association, is very much in the classical tradition: it is concerned with the Ricardian question of the prospects for growth in the face of a given scarce resource. For Jevons the scarce resource was coal, not cultivable land, but he and Ricardo were nonetheless concerned with similar issues. (2) Jevons saw deductive theory as comprising merely a *part* of economics. As his *The Coal*

*Question* shows, Jevons treated the problem of growth inductively: he did not neglect or suppress it. Indeed, amongst the general public it was his work on coal for which he was best known. Such a position, treating distribution and exchange as amenable to deductive inquiry, and production as amenable to inductive inquiry, was also the view of Sidgwick (1883, pp. 30–4).

Another of the leading marginalists who must be mentioned here as laying great stress on dynamics was J. B. Clark (see, for example, Backhouse, 1985, pp. 108–9). Clark analysed dynamics in terms of adjustment to a constantly shifting static equilibrium, but he emphatically did not neglect them. Given the interest in the classical question of growth shown by so many of the leading marginalists, it is therefore hard to claim that the issue was suppressed. New areas of inquiry were discovered, and as a result growth was placed in a different position within the discipline, but this is a very different perspective from that presented by Dasgupta.

The charge that marginalism was motivated by a desire to provide a new defence of *laissez-faire* is also easy to answer. Though there were of course marginalist economists committed to *laissez-faire*, it is misleading to portray this as the purpose of marginalist analysis (see, for example, Hutchison, 1978, pp. 94ff. and 257ff.). Of the pioneers, Walras proposed a scheme of land nationalization (to which he attached enormous importance) for which the Ricardian elements in his theory were crucial, for it was based on the assumption that growth raised land values. Jevons, after his early commitment to *laissez-faire*, supported extensive intervention in the economy. Furthermore the movement away from the classical assumptions towards marginalist theories led, as Hutchison (1978, p. 257) has pointed out, to (1) opening up the question of poverty; (2) the case for progressive taxation; (3) concern with unemployment as a cause of poverty and the justification for relief works; and (4) a superior analysis of monopoly.

Thus it seems hard to maintain either that the marginalists sought to suppress the issue of growth that had concerned the classical economists, or that the theoretical developments concerned were primarily a means of supporting *laissez-faire* ideology. There is also the problem that Dasgupta's thesis fails to explain the process by which the transition to marginalist ideas took place. Marginalist ideas were not the reason for the decline in English classical political economy. By the 1860s confidence in English classical political economy had already been shaken (see Hutchison, 1953 and 1978, Chapter 3). Though much of the credit for this is due to the criticism of those who wanted a more historical approach, a major reason for this decline was problems within the classical theory itself. When we consider developments outside Britain, the picture is again different from that suggested by Dasgupta, Ricardian economics never having taken root (see Hutchison, 1978).

## THE THEORY OF VALUE

In *Epochs of Economic Theory* much attention is paid to the theory of value and distribution as distinguishing classical and marginalist economics. There is of course a sense in which this is right: an understanding of value and price is fundamental to any understanding of an exchange economy. This emphasis can, however, give rise to a distorted picture, for in many areas of economics it is impossible to discern any discontinuity between the classical and marginalist periods. In monetary economics, for example, there is no break whatsoever. With the theory of international trade there are changes, but these do not correspond to the transition between classical and marginalist economics. Marshall and Edgeworth clearly built on foundations laid by Ricardo and Mill. Even when we look at the theory of growth, to which Dasgupta gives so much attention, we find considerable continuity. Despite all the differences in the details, all classical and marginalist theories of growth have had at their centre the relationship between capital accumulation, labour force growth and increased production. Various economists may have tried to go beyond this to explain technical progress and changes in the quality of the inputs, but no one has succeeded.

If the theory of value is so fundamental, why do we not see large changes in these applied fields? One reason would appear to be that for all the different types of value theory (labour, cost of production, utility) it is, for many purposes, sufficient to argue in terms of supply and demand. The precise details of what underlies supply and demand schedules is not always very important. In trade theory, for example, comparative advantage can be formulated in terms of comparative labour values, or in terms of more widely defined costs of production. The other reason is that much classical economics was based, not on a labour theory of value, but on a more general supply and demand theory influenced by Smith rather than Ricardo. When this is taken into account the changes in value theory, though still significant, appear much less important than when only Ricardian theory is considered. Thus it is necessary to pay considerable attention to these applied fields if a distorted picture is not to be created.

## CONCLUSIONS

The perspective from which Dasgupta invites us to view the history of economic thought has three main features: (1) the notion that there is no progress in economic theory, merely changes in the questions; (2) that the history of economic thought should be seen as comprising a series of epochs; and (3) a vision of marginalist economics as constituting an interlude in the history of economic thought, classical and Keynesian economics standing together against it. Though this last point is presented as an interpretation of history, it is reasonable to see it as a claim that marginalism *should* be consigned to the past, as a detour, much as Jevons viewed Ricardian economics.

In my opinion the case for this perspective has not been substantiated. Though there is clearly an unevenness in the history of economic theory, there is also *enormous* continuity, and there is plenty of evidence for the subject having made substantial progress since the time of Adam Smith. Furthermore, if Dasgupta's case is to be substantiated, surely it is necessary to examine *contemporary* marginalism: there is, in addition to Keynesian economics, a great deal of fundamental importance, which has happened to economic theory in the twentieth century, and this cannot be neglected (see Backhouse, 1985). To give one example, modern theories of competition and monopoly are unquestionably more powerful than were those of Adam Smith: classical theory did not even provide a framework within which issues such as market structure could be discussed.

There is also a serious methodological error involved in attempts, such as Dasgupta's, to attack contemporary marginalist theory by examining its past (cf. Hutchison, 1978, Chapter 8). That this is Dasgupta's intention is clear from his concluding chapter in which he argues that the questions of relevance to developing economies are those relating to mass poverty and stagnation. He claims that whilst the writings of Smith, Malthus, Ricardo and Marx are full of insights relevant to such situations, marginalist economics 'does not provide any answer' (Dasgupta, 1985, p. 144). This may or may not be true, but to establish it, it is pointless to look at the reasons why the pioneers of marginalist economics impelled the subject in the direction they did. The appropriate procedure is rather to compare the economic analysis of Ricardo with that of contemporary marginalism: to look not at Jevons's *Theory of Political Economy* (1871), but at works such as, to choose two at random, Newbery and Stiglitz's *The Theory of Commodity Price Stabilization* (1981), or Bliss and Stern's *Palanpur: the Economy of an Indian Village* (1982).

This is not to say that marginalist economics does not involve a set of blinkers. It does, in that problems are repeatedly forced into a framework of individuals choosing their most preferred options from a set of well-defined alternatives. This is, using Lakatosian terminology, part of the 'positive heuristic' of the marginalist research programme.[4] These blinkers should be judged according to whether they enable us to unearth hidden structures amongst the diverse economic problems which confront us, and according to whether the research programme of which they form a part remains progressive, predicting new facts.

[4]    This is discussed in detail in Chapter 10.

# Chapter 3

# Fact, fiction or moral tale? How should we approach the history of economic thought?*

## INTRODUCTION

For students of my generation, the classic statement of alternative views on how to approach the history of economic thought was the first chapter of Mark Blaug's *Economic Theory in Retrospect* (1985). The crucial choice, he argued, was between relativism and absolutism.

> The relativist regards every single theory put forward in the past as a more or less faithful expression and reflection of contemporary conditions, each theory being in principle equally justified in its own context; the absolutist has eyes only for the strictly intellectual development of the subject regarded as a steady progression from error to truth. Relativists cannot rank the theories of different periods in terms of better or worse; absolutists cannot help doing so.
>
> (Blaug, 1985, p. 2)

* Parts of this chapter were contained in a paper presented to the ESRC Political Economy Study Group in May 1990; and to the History of Economic Thought Conference at the University of East Anglia in September 1990. I am grateful to participants in both meetings for useful comments and advice. I also wish to thank Mark Blaug, Richard Davies, Chris Hookway, Philip Mirowski, Mary Morgan, Denis O'Brien, Donald A. Walker, Roy Weintraub, Donald Winch and three anonymous referees for helpful comments on various versions of this chapter. The usual caveat, absolving them from all responsibility for any remaining inadequacies, applies.

Faced between the choice of Stark (1944) and Rogin (1956) on one side, or Blaug and Schumpeter (1954) on the other, there was no contest! The notion that the history of economic thought was concerned with evaluating ideas received a further boost from the spate of research influenced, directly or indirectly, by Lakatos's methodology of scientific research programmes with its fascinating hypothesis (his methodology of *historical* research programmes) that one might look at the history of science in order to decide amongst competing methodologies.

From this perspective, suggestions such as those recently made by Donald Walker concerning the way in which we should approach the subject seem unproblematic. We should judge the works of past economists according to the standards of modern economic theory; we should ask whether the writings of the economists we consider were original, influential and logically consistent; we should criticize economists for claiming to have shown things which they did not show; and we should praise writers for explaining reality well (Walker, 1988, pp. 101–2).

This viewpoint, however, has recently come in for strong criticism. What makes it important to take recent criticisms seriously is the fact that they represent not merely a reworking of old ideas, but involve the introduction of new ideas taken primarily from philosophy and literary criticism.[1] These criticisms may sound very much like the relativism that Blaug discussed in the passage quoted above, but they are not the same. The main argument concerns the idea that knowledge is socially constructed, knowledge-claims being the property of specific discourse communities, making little sense outside those communities. The clearest statement of such a position is that of Weintraub, who is concerned, in his *Stabilizing Dynamics* (1991a), to take seriously the notion that knowledge is constructed, not found. This observation, he explains, applies at two levels: at one level it means that 'the work of the

---

[1] The descriptions 'new' and 'old' refer to newness within the history of economic thought. Many of the ideas have a long history in other fields. For example, the view that we should take 'conversation' as our model goes back at least to Oakeshott and probably a long way before him. Even within the history of economic thought it can be argued that some of these ideas came in via Kuhn's *Structure of Scientific Revolutions* (1970).

economist is not well-understood as the work of an explorer and finder, a creator of theories and assembler of facts'; at another level it means that 'histories of economics are constructed, not chanced upon' (1991a, pp. 3–4). Such a perspective, claim its proponents, leads to an approach to the history of economic thought that is significantly different from those advocated by Blaug and Walker.

A different line of argument about how the history of economic thought should be studied has been taken up by Schabas (1992), who has argued that historians of economics 'should learn to embrace their historical sensibilities', leaving the task of modelling to economists, and reducing their reliance on philosophy. Though her focus is on the appropriate institutional affiliation for historians of economic thought, completely avoiding the methodological questions that Weintraub addresses, her appeal to develop a greater historical awareness implies a certain criticism of the way the subject is usually approached. It has much in common with Weintraub's claim that 'the most subversive feature of *More Heat than Light* [Mirowski, 1990] is its historiographic stance, one which denies the separate disciplinary status of the history of economic thought' forcing 'economists to become historians first, economists second' (1991a, pp. 1–2).[2]

Weintraub's purpose is to argue for a particular way of doing history, his inspiration coming from the sociology of science and, above all, from literary criticism. His argument about knowledge being the product of specific discourse (interpretive) communities has, however, much in common with Rorty's views on how the history of philosophy should be written. Rorty's position is worth considering here for two reasons. The first is that although it is based on arguments similar to those used by Weintraub, Rorty takes the argument significantly further, providing a more comprehensive critique of certain types of

---

2    On reading such remarks one wonders whether it was prescience that caused Bernard Corry (1975, p. 252) to write the following paragraph; 'Rumour has it that somewhere out West (Mid?) there is a township of Econsville which announces to the visitor "Abandon Hope All Ye That Enter Herein". The story further has it – although even I doubt the substance – that a bit further on we hit Hopesville, which proclaims (although few listen) "Abandon Economics All Ye Who Enter Herein".'

history. The second is that Rorty's classification of four genres has been taken up by Mirowski (1987) and Blaug (1990, 1991a), but has not received adequate critical attention.

The purpose of this chapter is to provide a critical examination of these claims.

## THE CASE FOR 'CULTURAL' HISTORY[3]

### The constructedness of economic knowledge

Economic knowledge is, like any other knowledge, socially constructed – it is produced by specific communities. Thus Weintraub takes as his starting point 'the fact that economics is a social activity and it is carried out, is done, in communities' (1991a, p. 6). Quoting the literary critic Stanley Fish, he argues that such interpretive communities are made up of 'those who share interpretive strategies, not for reading but for writing texts, for constituting their properties' (Fish, 1980, p. 14; quoted in Weintraub, 1991a, p. 6). The significance of this definition is that it marks out a position in which meaning is neither subjective (where the reader is free to determine the meaning of a text) nor objective (where meaning is inherent in a particular text). The community creates meaning, for it is the community which determines the rules according to which texts are written and interpreted. Continuing Weintraub's quotation from Fish,

> [Interpretive] strategies exist prior to the act of reading and therefore determine the shape of what is read rather than, as is usually assumed, the other way round. ... [But] an interpretive community is not objective because as a bundle of interests, of particular purposes and goals, its perspective is interested rather than neutral; but by the same reasoning the meanings and texts produced by an interpretive community are not subjective because they do not proceed from an isolated individual but from a public and conventional point of

---

[3]   The term 'cultural history' is being used in Passmore's sense, discussed below. The precise term used here is not important: the terms 'historical reconstructions' (Rorty, 1984), 'thick history' (McCloskey, 1988) could equally well have been used.

view. ... [M]embers of the same community will necessarily agree because they will see (and by seeing, make) everything in relation to that community's assumed purposes and goals; and conversely, members of different communities will disagree because from their respective positions the other 'simply' cannot see what is obviously and inescapably there.

(Fish, 1980, pp. 14–16; quoted in Weintraub, 1991a, p. 6)

In place of the dramatic choice posed by Blaug, Weintraub, following Fish, seems to have found a third way.

This view of knowledge as being constructed by particular communities' interpretive strategies has, it has been claimed, implications for the way we view economics, for different economists see the economy in different ways: thus 'Where Marx "saw" a falling rate of profit, Clark "saw" a marginal product of capital. ... Where Solow "sees" a market failure, Lucas "sees" rational competitive activity' (Weintraub, 1991a, p. 150). Claims about economic phenomena (such as that the economy is in a stable equilibrium) can be understood only as imposing a discursive order on phenomena. When an economist makes such a claim he or she is simply inviting others 'to participate in a (Wittgensteinian) language game to be played according to a particular set of rules' (ibid.). It thus makes no sense for us to be falsificationist in our economic methodology.[4]

**Implications for the history of economic thought**

If we adopt such a perspective on economic knowledge, it has enormous implications for the way we study the history of economic thought. As Weintraub puts it, *'If we are not falsificationist in our conceptualization of economics, we are under no compulsion to remain falsificationist about our histories of economics'* (1991a, p. 4, italics in original). Like the economics which forms their subject-matter, histories of economics are constructed – they are not there to be found:

---

[4] This claim is explored in detail in Backhouse (1992). In that paper it is argued that there are ways in which methodology, even falsificationist methodology, can be defended against these criticisms.

We must accept that history is not presented to us raw, as a neutral case or data source, upon which we may perform tests of our methodological theories or how scientific knowledge is gained. History is not 'out there' waiting to answer our questions or corroborate our hypotheses. History is not found. Instead, history is written, and is itself as much a creative enterprise as is the 'theory' it is often 'meant' to describe.

(Weintraub, 1991a, p. 4)

The notion that everything we see is constructed extends even to historical texts themselves. Texts are not 'fixed', for they cannot be read without being interpreted. This carries the implication that even relatively straightforward issues, such as the attribution of priority, involve interpretive acts on the part of the historian: 'historians construct by providing reinterpretations of apparently "fixed" texts. So too "priority" is constructed, not discovered and then awarded' (Weintraub, 1991b, p. 385).

There is, therefore, no basis for 'Whig' histories, as advocated by Samuelson (1987) and Walker (1988) in which 'history must be a moral exemplar showing how scientists came to get it right, eventually, where the right stuff is called Truth' (Weintraub, 1991a, p. 149). Not only is it not possible to know what is the Truth, but even the notion of Truth is problematic. Truth, Weintraub argues, can be seen only in terms of faithful representation of the true state of the economy, but all we can possibly have is constructions. Referring to economists' seeing different things in the economy (see above), he claims

Such 'seeing' is a construction, not a representation in the sense of a discursive act that is closer to the truth than any other construction. For me, I cannot confidently appreciate what such an idea of 'representation' might mean.

(Weintraub, 1991a, p. 150)

### Taking history seriously

The conclusions Weintraub draws for the history of economic thought are straightforward. He argues that the constructedness of all economic knowledge implies that it makes no sense to view the history of economic thought through methodological spectacles: the only way to write history is to treat appraisal as a complex process.

> We have to ask more complex questions of a theory and its interpretations: How was it developed? How was it presented? What do its terms mean? Who was its audience? We seek to understand the way the interpretive community has read the economy text, and what makes the community more likely to respond to one interpretation rather than another.
>
> (Weintraub, 1991a, p. 7)

In his history of the analysis of stability of general equilibrium, therefore, he is concerned not with documenting progress, in the sense of the achievement of better, more general or more rigorous proofs, but with questions such as how economists' understanding of concepts such as equilibrium and stability evolved over time. Appraisal, understood in falsificationist terms, is not on the agenda.

This approach is similar to that of Dorothy Ross, who describes herself as writing

> that kind of intellectual history which seeks to reconstruct the discourse within which social scientists worked. I understand discourse as conversation, developed over time, centring around certain problems, setting the terms of discussion for those who enter into it, and at the same time responding to the different intentions of participants.
>
> (Ross, 1991, pp. xviii–xix)

In such a historical reconstruction or cultural history, it is clearly *vital* to take account of developments outside economics, whether these are doctrines of American exceptionalism (Ross, 1991) or energetics (Mirowski, 1990).[5] It explains Weintraub's appraisal of Mirowski's accomplishment as being '*nothing less than a redefinition of what might constitute a convincing account of some feature, or other, of economic analysis*

---

5    Whether *More Heat than Light* is best viewed as historical or rational reconstruction is a moot point, beyond the scope of this paper.

(1994, p. 302, italics in original). To borrow an expression from McCloskey, Weintraub is saying that after Mirowski, the old stories do no longer have satisfactory endings (McCloskey, 1990).

Historians of economic thought, argues Weintraub, have been 'looking for love in all the wrong places' (1991a, p. 11). Accepting the constructivist position, he claims, means that we can afford to lose interest in methodology, and that we should 'give up the wish for approval from philosophers of science'. Similarly, Schabas (1992) criticizes historians of economics for persisting in a 'longlasting love affair with Kuhn, Lakatos and Popper' long after mainstream historians of science have turned their attentions elsewhere. She attributes this partly to 'Physics envy' but also to a preoccupation with modelling and theory. Her conclusion is that we should embrace our historical sensibilities, leaving the task of modelling to economists, and that we should 'break away' from economics: the benefits of self-sufficiency (perhaps in the company of historians of science) would be worth the cost.[6]

## RORTY'S CASE AGAINST DOXOGRAPHY

### Four genres in the history of philosophy

Mirowski (1987) and Blaug (1990, 1991a) have urged us to think of the history of economic thought in terms of Rorty's four genres (Rorty, 1984): (i) historical reconstructions, (ii) rational reconstructions, (iii) *Geistesgeschichte* and (iv) doxography. This classification is, however, similar to one proposed nearly two decades earlier by John Passmore (1965), who distinguished between (i) polemical, (ii) cultural and (iii) elucidatory histories, subdividing the last of these into three sub-types: (iiia) doxographical, (iiib) retrospective and (iiic) problematic

---

[6]    There are also institutional factors underlying this suggestion that historians of economics should break away from economics departments. Here, however, we are concerned only with the intellectual case. It is worth noting at this point that Weintraub argues that historians of economics should not jump out of the arms of philosophers into those of historians of science. As this sentence implies, Schabas is non-committal on the question, though she clearly sees advantages in cooperation with historians of science.

histories. Though our main focus is on Rorty, reference to Passmore's more precise classification helps clear up some of the ambiguities in Rorty's definitions, particularly in his catch-all category of doxography.

*Historical reconstructions* or *cultural histories* are accounts of the work of dead philosophers which set them in the context of their own times. This is what McCloskey (1988) describes as 'thick' history. Though they might dissent from some of the details of Rorty's account, the type of history advocated by Weintraub and Ross fits in here. *Rational reconstructions* or *retrospective histories* are accounts of past philosophers' ideas which view them in the context of contemporary philosophy. *Geistesgeschichte*[7] are larger, more sweeping stories than either historical or rational reconstructions. They are concerned with problematics rather than with solutions to problems, being histories which seek 'to justify the historian and his friends in having the sort of philosophical problems which they have' (Rorty, 1984, p. 57). They seek to justify particular views of what philosophy is, and are concerned with questions such as, 'Why should anyone have made the question of — central to his thought?' or 'Why did anyone take the problem of — seriously?'[8]

*Doxography* is defined by Rorty as 'the attempt to impose a problematic on a canon drawn up without reference to that problematic, or, conversely, to impose a canon on a problematic constructed without reference to that canon' (ibid.). It is, he argues, 'exemplified by books which start from Thales or Descartes and wind up with some figure roughly contemporary with the author, ticking off what various figures traditionally called "philosophers" had to say about problems traditionally called "philosophical" ' (Rorty, 1984, p. 62).

[7] The nearest we can get to an English translation is 'histories of the spirit'. The word '*Geist*' refers to Hegel, whose work is paradigmatic of this genre (Rorty, 1984, p. 56).

[8] Although we equated Passmore's 'retrospective history' with Rorty's 'rational reconstruction', it has something in common with *Geistesgeschichte*, for 'retrospective histories' fit everything into a continuous pattern 'as if a particular philosophy had been from the beginning of time the "one far-off divine event, to which creation moves"' (Passmore, 1965, p. 23). Though it can be used with care, the distinction between rational reconstructions and *Geistesgeschichte* is not clear cut.

As defined by Rorty, however, doxography would seem to cover *three* of Passmore's categories. *Polemical histories* use a discussion of historical figures to make certain philosophical points. They arise out of a particular tradition in the teaching of philosophy, and are neither histories nor attempts to advance our knowledge of the history of philosophy (cf. Passmore, 1965, p. 7). *Doxographical histories* 'are concerned to "tell us what actually happened" within philosophy' (Passmore, 1965, p. 18). In them,

> the major conclusions of philosophers are concisely set out, generally to the accompaniment of a certain amount of biographical detail. The chronological framework is provided by the idea of a 'succession', or a school, alleged to indicate a line of influence.
>
> (Passmore, 1965, p. 19)

They contain basic information but give us no understanding.

(Passmore, 1965, p. 22)

*Problematic histories* are Passmore's favoured genre. Philosophers, he argues, do not set out to construct systems: they set out to solve problems. Thus, to understand a philosopher's work we must retrace the steps by which he or she solved, or sought to solve, certain problems. The history of philosophy can thus be seen as a series of attempts to solve particular problems.

### The critique of doxography in the history of philosophy

Rorty considers history not as an end in itself, but rather as serving particular purposes. Historical reconstructions make us aware of the contingency of human ideas. Rational reconstructions enable us to see progress in history. The latter may be anachronistic, but that is acceptable provided that we are aware of what we are doing. *Geistesgeschichte* tell us what is important in philosophy and who are the important philosophers. But why should this be necessary? Rorty suggests four answers: (i) we need to believe that we are better off by becoming aware of new problems; (ii) the authors of historical and rational reconstructions need to know that they are discussing the major figures; (iii) philosophy has an important honorific use, so we need to know on whom to confer the title of 'philosopher'; (iv) we need heroes. The genre of *Geistesgeschichte* fulfils these needs.

This leaves doxography which, Rorty claims, should be allowed to wither away: it 'inspires boredom and despair'; its existence is 'calamity itself, and not the mere risk of it'; and the works involved 'decorticate' and unintentionally mummify the thinkers they discuss (Rorty, 1984, p. 62). There are two main features of doxography to which he takes such exception. The first is that it is unimaginative. It never alters the canon in the way *Geistesgeschichte* do (ibid., p. 67).[9] It eschews the question of how we are better or worse off than our predecessors (ibid., p. 72). The chapter headings of doxographies, he argues, are known in advance; certain chapters are missing for lack of material; and important thinkers are skipped over because they had nothing to say on the 'central problems' (ibid., p. 65). He suggests that doxography is badly done, perhaps simplistic, history, as when he claims that 'the real trouble with doxography is that it is a *half-hearted* attempt to tell a new story of intellectual progress ... half-hearted because it lacks the courage to readjust the canon to suit the new discoveries' (ibid., p. 63). These are objections that apply to textbooks: to Passmore's doxographical histories.[10] The second is that doxography is based on 'the idea that "philosophy" is the name of a natural kind – the name of a discipline which, in all ages and places, has managed to dig down to the same deep, fundamental questions', implying that anyone identified as a 'great philosopher' has to be described as studying these questions (ibid., p. 63). This is a more fundamental criticism of doxography. Starting from the position that knowledge is the property of specific discourse communities, Rorty is drawing the conclusion that there are no continuing, clearly defined, central philosophical problems: different communities construct different problems.

---

[9]  His comment that experimental alterations of the canon make it possible to avoid doxography suggests that he regards this as a *necessary* characteristic of doxography.

[10]  A good example of the 'histories' to which such objections apply is perhaps the history of the theory of the consumption function found in most macro textbooks.

## The argument so far

Rorty's evaluation of alternative types of history is based on his pragmatist perspective. His approval of historical reconstructions, rational reconstructions and *Geistesgeschichte* is based on his assessment of their usefulness to the philosophical community. Similarly, he rejects doxography on the grounds that it contributes nothing. One response, therefore, is to take issue with his conclusions on pragmatic grounds. One might argue, for example, that he underestimates the importance of 'unimaginative' histories for teaching, or for the process whereby knowledge is consolidated. Alternatively, it is arguable that the category of doxography is too loose to be usable, the boundaries between rational reconstructions, *Geistesgeschichte* and doxographies being very unclear.

The most important aspect of Rorty's critique, however, is his argument that there are no continuing central problems of philosophy. It is the key argument against problematic histories, and rests on the notion that knowledge pertains only to specific communities. This is the argument that Weintraub uses to criticize Whig history. We turn to it in the next section.

## NON-CONSTRUCTIVIST HISTORIOGRAPHY

### The possibility of a non-foundationalist epistemology[11]

In Rorty's writing the reader is presented with a stark choice: either accept that knowledge is socially constructed, and abandon any attempt at epistemology; or adopt a foundationalist approach, according to which people have a secure, completely reliable, privileged source of knowledge that can be used to pass authoritative judgement on the truth or falsity of knowledge-claims. As he has put it, 'no description of how things are from a God's-eye point of view, no skyhook provided by some contemporary or yet-to-be-developed science, is going to free us from the contingency of having been acculturated as we were (Rorty,

[11] A more comprehensive treatment of this question is provided in Backhouse (1992).

1991, p. 13). Though expressed in a different language, many of the critics of economic methodology offer us just this choice. McCloskey invites us to choose between rhetoric and modernism, defining the latter as 'the notion that we know only what we cannot doubt' (1986, p. 5). Similarly, Mirowski attacks the quest for certainty as the 'Cartesian Vice' (Mirowski, 1988, p. 119), whilst Weintraub refers to epistemology being concerned with 'refuting the sceptic' (1991a, p. 150). Faced with such a choice, who could resist Rorty's position?

This is, however, a false choice. Methodology does not have to be based on indubitable foundations. The Popperian approach, for example, is emphatically *not* Cartesian, for it involves accepting that we do not have *any* certain knowledge, and that all knowledge is provisional. For Popper, as much as for Rorty, all knowledge ultimately rests on a conventional foundation:

> there are no uninterpreted '*data*'; there is nothing simply 'given' to us uninterpreted; nothing to be taken as a basis. *All* our knowledge is interpretation in the light of our expectations, our theories, and is therefore *hypothetical* in some way or other.
>
> (Popper, 1983, p. 102)

Another example is the literature on the sociology of science, where, though the emphasis is frequently on how scientists construct theories, it is recognized that there are certain things that scientists cannot do (see, for example, Bazerman, 1989, or Collins, 1985). There are empirical constraints under which scientists are working. Such constraints may not give us a 'God's-eye view', but they may be a sufficient basis on which to construct a methodology. Hacking (1983), for example, uses experimentation as the basis for a form of scientific realism. These examples are enough to make the point that there are alternatives to the anti-epistemological position of Rorty and Fish.

## The need for evaluative histories of economic thought[12]

Rorty argues that it is inappropriate to ask whether a discipline is in good shape:

> those who wish to reduce objectivity to solidarity – call them 'pragmatists' – do not require either a metaphysics or an epistemology. They view truth as ... what is good for *us* to believe. ... Insofar as a person is seeking solidarity, she does not ask about the relation between the practices of the chosen community and something outside that community. ... [Pragmatists do not see] the gap between truth and justification as something to be bridged by isolating a natural and transcultural sort of rationality which can be used to criticize certain cultures and praise others.
>
> (Rorty, 1991, pp. 21; 22–3)

One appraises economic theories only in relation to the standards and aims of the community of economists: one does not introduce 'outside' criteria which might bring those standards into question. It is compatible with McCloskey's view that the 'economy of intellect [is] running just fine' (McCloskey, 1986, p. 28).

If we can do nothing other than assume that contemporary economics is in good shape, we can safely abandon not only methodology, but also the idea of appraising the history of economic thought. Many economists, however, have argued that there are serious problems with contemporary economics – that we cannot assume the discipline to be in good shape.[13] If we accept that there are problems with contemporary economics we can hardly avoid the task of inquiring into the nature of the malady and exploring possible cures. This, almost by definition, involves methodology. It is then a short, and defensible, step from appraising contemporary economics to appraising past economics –

---

[12] The term 'evaluative' is used, not to denote a genre additional to those distinguished by Rorty, but as a shorthand for the approaches to the history of economic thought which evaluate the economics of the past according to criteria the writer believes to be appropriate. It may cover rational reconstructions, *Geistesgeschichte*, and even some types of what Rorty terms doxography.

[13] See, for example, Colander (1990) and Leontief (1971). See also Backhouse (1993b).

indeed, where does the history of thought begin?[14] Though it is important not to treat past ideas anachronistically, it could be argued that we have little choice but to use the history of economic thought as a testing-ground for methodology. If we avoid methodology, we avoid evaluation.

This view of the history of economic thought requires that the subject retain its links with both philosophy and economics. The argument for breaking away clearly has its attractions: historical sensibilities are important, and there would be great freedom to be derived from studying the subject simply for its own sake; and Weintraub and Schabas may even be right when they say that historians of economic thought have paid too much attention to philosophers. However, to jump from this to a position that rules out, virtually *a priori*, any application of ideas from another discipline would seem to be going too far. Physics may not be the only discipline worth taking into account (Schabas is almost certainly right, for example, to reprimand historians of economics for not paying more attention to psychology) but it has undoubtedly had great successes. Any claim that economists have nothing to learn from physics has to be argued on historical grounds: on the basis of detailed arguments about the nature of the two disciplines.

The argument that the history of economic thought should become autonomous, studied for its own sake along lines such as those suggested by Weintraub and Schabas, therefore, pays insufficient attention to the critical role the discipline should play *within* economics.[15] Economists may not wish to listen to methodologists and historians of economic thought. Sometimes this will be for good reasons, but on other occasions, lessons from the history of economic thought may be important. If we turn our backs on evaluative histories, the usefulness of our histories will be severely limited.

**The case for problematic histories of economics**

Of the genres discussed in section 3, the one against which the constructivist criticisms are most clearly aimed is that of problematic

14 See, for example, Walker (1988).
15 This is similar to the conclusion reached by Walker (1992).

history.[16] These are histories concerned with what Schumpeter called 'the filiation of economic ideas' (1954, p. 6). Such accounts may appear to be doxography, for they may discuss what each of a series of writers has to say on a particular problem. It is assumed that there is a particular problem (such as the theory of value), and that each of the writers considered has something to say on this particular problem. To justify such accounts we need to defend the notion that there can be common problems in the history of economics.[17] Once we do this, the distinctions between Rorty's various genres become blurred.[18]

Although some very sweeping claims have been made concerning the implications of the constructivist perspective, Rorty himself is more modest. Firstly, he argues that it may indeed be possible to find common problems over limited periods of time (say a century or two): it may make sense, for example, to write 'a story of the steps which led from Descartes to Kant' (Rorty, 1984, p. 65).[19] Secondly, Rorty claims only that his arguments apply to philosophy, suggesting that they may not apply to 'science'. Specifically, he argues that *Geistesgeschichte* are not needed in science, for four reasons: (i) science does not need the legitimation provided by *Geistesgeschichte*; (ii) canon formation is not a problem in science; (iii) there exist uncontroversial parts of any science, which can be taken as the goal towards which the history of science leads; and (iv) there is no need to ask whether, say, contemporary biochemistry is in good shape (Rorty, 1984, pp. 57–9). This contrast is important not because such a sharp contrast between philosophy and

[16] We leave aside the question of how far this genre overlaps with rational reconstructions and *Geistesgeschichte*.

[17] Insofar as there are common problems, it will be valid to use contemporary concepts in historical reconstructions. See Blaug (1990, pp. 28–9).

[18] To say this is not to say that there will always be common problems. It is to say that the question of whether or not there are common problems can be settled only in particular cases and on the basis of textual and other evidence. Similarly, it is not being claimed that unimaginative, doxographic histories do not exist: of course they do, but this should not be muddled up with historiographic arguments.

[19] Interestingly, this example covers about 175 years, comparable with the period from the *Wealth of Nations* to the 1950s.

science is defensible,[20] but because it makes the important points that disciplines may differ, and that the way in which the history of a subject is told should depend on the nature of the discipline concerned. This brings us back to methodology, for we cannot discuss the nature of a discipline without discussing methodological issues.

Of particular importance is the role of empirical evidence. Where empirical evidence imposes constraints on the economic theories that can be constructed, the existence of perennial 'real world' economic problems may explain the persistence of certain problems in economic theory. For example, one might argue that it is reasonable to write a history of the different ways in which unemployment has been explained: a clear example of 'problematic' history. In such a history one might stress the role of empirical evidence. The fact that the concept of 'unemployment' is constructed and has meant different things in different periods, does not invalidate such an approach. Indeed, the very purpose of such a history may be to show how the meaning of the concept has changed over time.[21]

The importance of methodological questions concerning the role of empirical evidence will clearly vary according to the branch of economics being considered. It would appear to be no accident that the first consistently constructivist history of economic thought is concerned with general equilibrium theory. Weintraub found he was able completely to dispense with methodology in *Stabilizing Dynamics*. In part this reflects the questions to which he wanted to find answers. It is, however, natural to wonder whether it would have been as easy to avoid appraisal had he been investigating a branch of applied economics, or a branch of economics closely tied up with economic policy-making. General equilibrium theory has been criticized for having become little more than a branch of pure mathematics distinguished by its origins, so it is hardly surprising if questions of empirical testing, falsifiability, empirical progress and so on prove to be

[20] There are many people who would take exception to his characterizations of both philosophy and science.
[21] See, for example, Backhouse (1994a, Chapter 5).

irrelevant. It can equally be argued that the 'stability of general equilibrium literature' is irrelevant to most economics.

## CONCLUSIONS

This chapter has been critical of the constructivist approach to the history of economic thought. In making these criticisms it has been taken for granted that the constructivist perspective on the history of economic thought has much to contribute: it forces us to ask new questions and to look at history in a new light. In *Stabilizing Dynamics*, for example, Weintraub has provided a clear example of the insight that can be obtained by adopting such a perspective. What this chapter has taken issue with is the claim that the philosophical arguments underlying this perspective invalidate other ways of writing the history of economic thought. This implies that we need many types of history, including not only cultural histories, or historical reconstructions, such as Weintraub and Ross wish to write, but also the evaluative histories that Walker advocates.[22] Such a pluralist position is compatible with the view expressed by Rorty:

> There is, in our view, nothing general to be said in answer to the question 'How should the history of philosophy be written?' except 'As self-consciously as one can – in as full awareness as possible of the *variety* of contemporary concerns to which a past figure may be relevant.
>
> (Rorty, Schneewind and Skinner, 1984, p. 11)

Such a pluralistic approach, recognizing the many purposes served by histories of economic thought, means we require not only 'thick' histories, rich in detail, but also 'thinner' histories, which seek to see how far certain aspects of the historical record can be explained in terms of a few bold generalizations. McCloskey is certainly right in saying that philosophy of science is thin compared with the history of science, and

---

[22] Blaug (1990) uses Rorty's categories to make this point, stressing the importance of being clear about what type of history we are writing.

it is easy to lampoon the philosophy of science on these grounds.[23] But that is not the point. In the sense that a good theory abstracts from irrelevant detail to focus on important relationships, Friedman was right to say that unrealisticness is a sign of a good theory. The test of a theory is not descriptive accuracy, but whether or not it works according to whatever criteria we are employing. If our theories become too thick, therefore, they will lack power, an issue which has emerged in debates over the merits of analytical versus narrative history (see, for example, Stone, 1979; Dray, 1985).

The question may be raised as to whether it is right to bracket the historians of economics we have discussed with Rorty, and the philosophical position that this implies. Surely, it might be argued, these writers are arguing simply that we take history seriously, opposing simplistic histories such as those written by economists who uncritically accept a few ideas from the philosophy of science in the light of which they fit some episode of economics into a 'reconstruction'. In this light, what we have presented as arguments for cultural history are simply arguments to take the task of writing history seriously: to pay attention to evidence, to alternative sources and so on.

Of the historians discussed in section 2, the only one who completely avoids entanglement in epistemological issues is Schabas: her appeal to historians of economics *can* be seen simply as an appeal to do better history.[24] The suggestion that historians of economics should move out of economics departments, however, implies that they should distance themselves from the concerns of contemporary economists. Their role *vis à vis* the rest of economics would clearly be different. Next comes Ross, whose emphasis is still very much on doing history, her sources of inspiration being other historians of the social sciences rather than philosophers, but who adopts a view, like Rorty's, of discourse as a

23 In just the same way that we can ridicule neoclassical economic theory on the grounds that its models are hopelessly simple compared with real economies.

24 Indeed, *A World Ruled by Number* (Schabas, 1991) shows that it is possible to combine historical sensibility with the willingness to appraise for which Weintraub criticizes Walker.

conversation. At the other extreme is Weintraub.[25] *Stabilizing Dynamics* is not only a history of a branch of economics: it is also a manifesto for a particular way of doing history, grounded explicitly on a particular view of truth.[26] Furthermore, he makes it clear that in criticizing Walker and Samuelson he is criticizing 'the history of economic thought *as usually presented*' (1991a, p. 149, emphasis added). He may not buy Rorty's typology, but the epistemological arguments he uses are the same.

Constructivist historiography has been presented as a radical new departure, subversive of traditional approaches to the history of economic thought. It is important, however, not to exaggerate the extent to which this is required. Many of the issues raised, such as the theory-ladenness of facts, have long been recognized.[27] In addition, constructivist history need not look very different from conventional history. Weintraub (1991b) stresses the constructed nature of priority, and argues that 'We may, of course, reconstruct the past as we wish' (p. 395). This does not preclude him from conducting an investigation into the past record from which he concludes, unambiguously, that it is wrong to award priority to Allais for using a Liapunov function. What Allais used, Weintraub concludes, is not 'that modern proof at all' (ibid., p. 389); 'The issue is, for assessing "priority," whether Allais's argument actually used a Liapunov function. Unambiguously the answer is no' (p. 393). There is no suggestion here that we are free to

---

[25] It is tempting to place Mirowski alongside Weintraub, for he has explicitly endorsed Rorty's critique of doxography, and he is hostile to traditional historiography. However, his publications contain few explicit historiographical statements.

[26] Weintraub does state that he has no interest in recapitulating the arguments for a constructivist point of view, and that he has only a residual interest in philosophy. On the other hand, he argues that there is nothing productive to be said about the connections between theory and reality, about the truth of theoretical propositions (1991a, p. 110); that he cannot 'confidently appreciate' what it would mean to say that one discursive act is 'closer to the Truth than any other construction' (ibid., p. 150); that statements such as 'the economy is not stable' are simply invitations 'to participate in a (Wittgensteinian) language game to be played according to a particular set of rules' (ibid.); that models, theories, stories and data 'do not "describe" except as they create that which is to be described' (ibid., p. 151).

[27] See the essays reprinted in Blaug (1991a).

interpret the historical evidence as we wish, or that different discourse communities might construct these facts differently: there are certain statements that are not allowable.[28]

The claims made in this paper are that the epistemological arguments on which such historiography is based are not compelling, and that if historians of economic thought lose interest in methodology and the appraisal of economic ideas, the importance of their studies will be greatly reduced. Some previous accounts of the principles on which the history of economic thought were constructed may sometimes have been expressed in excessively 'positivist' terms, and it may be that some need to be rewritten. However, to argue that such accounts must be abandoned in favour of a perspective that precludes looking for progress in economics, or investigating the health of contemporary economics, is to throw out the baby with the bath water. Facts may be problematic, but to treat everything *simply* as fiction is to abandon what should be one of the main tasks of the historian of economic thought: to draw conclusions about the merits of different approaches to the study of economic phenomena.

---

[28] It is tempting to argue that constructivist historiography can have no consequences for the writing of history, in the same sense that Weintraub has argued that methodology can have no consequences for economic arguments (Weintraub, 1989). It can, of course, like methodology in Weintraub (1989), have consequences in the sense that anything can have consequences if it makes people change their behaviour.

# Chapter 4

# History's many dimensions

## INTRODUCTION

In 'Fact, fiction or moral tale?' (Chapter 3) I argued against the historiographical position Weintraub put forward in his recent book, *Stabilizing Dynamics* (1991a). In view of his reaction to my paper (Weintraub, 1992), I wish to make it clear that, though I cannot accept his historiographical position, I regard *Stabilizing Dynamics* as a serious contribution to our understanding of general equilibrium analysis. In my view his historical thesis can stand independently of his statements concerning the nature of truth, and independently of his attacks on the history of economic thought as it is usually done. My criticisms concerned only his historiographical arguments.[1]

## EXTENDING THE AREA OF AGREEMENT

Weintraub observes that he and I agree on two things. (1) Histories of economic thought are written for a variety of purposes, and this requires that they be written in a variety of ways. (2) Constructivist historiography has led to new insights. Our agreement, however, extends further than this. (3) Histories are created, and are not

---

[1]    In arguing that *Stabilizing Dynamics* should be viewed as a manifesto for constructivist history, based on a particular conception of truth, I was interpreting a text on the basis of what I found written in it. My evidence for regarding the book as a historiographic manifesto included the following: (1) It is sub-titled 'Constructing economic knowledge'. (2) The final chapter, entitled 'Conclusions', one finds a critique of 'Whig' history – in other words, he presented his critique of 'Whig' history as the book's main conclusion.

'neutrally' found objects waiting to answer methodologists' questions (Weintraub, 1992, p. 4). This is obvious, for histories are not mere collections of facts, but of necessity involve selection and interpretation. Having been trained as a historian, this is something I have never disputed. (4) It is important to be serious about historical evidence.

Weintraub's comment suggests that we might agree on two further points. (5) We both value the work of historians such as Blaug and Walker (Weintraub, 1992, p. 10).[2] In my view this statement will surprise most readers of the 'Conclusion' to *Stabilizing Dynamics*. (6) I agree with Weintraub's statement that 'the division of Facts from Fictions from Moral Tales must be resisted' (Weintraub, 1992, p. 10): indeed, I thought that this was one of the clearly stated points of my paper. The problem with this statement is that it seems inconsistent with Weintraub's clearly stated lack of interest in appraisal. I interpreted him as arguing that we *should* banish moral tales from the history of economic thought.[3]

Beyond this, however, we disagree. In the remaining pages of this reply I identify the point at which Weintraub abandons historical argument for what he terms 'the philosophical ether' (1992, p. 7). Once this is pointed out, it becomes clear exactly where we part company.

## TWO ARGUMENTS FOR THICK HISTORY

Weintraub claims, without qualification, that 'thicker is better'. In discussing this it is vital to define 'thickness', a term Weintraub (1992, p. 9) takes from McCloskey (1988).[4] McCloskey defined thin histories as ones that try to explain history in terms of very simple notions. He

[2] To avoid unnecessary disagreement I cite only those historians cited in both Weintraub (1991a) and (1992).

[3] Perhaps the problem is that the phrase 'moral tale' is ambiguous. I used it in my title as a convenient shorthand to refer to histories from which we can draw normative conclusions concerning economics, precisely the type of history to which I thought Weintraub was taking exception.

[4] As far as I know, *Stabilizing Dynamics* does not use the term 'thickness'. However, in the introduction, Weintraub cites McCloskey's discussion of these issues as marking a turning-point in his thinking.

argued that philosophers' conceptions of how science works had been shown to be too thin, with even people who use philosophy of science complaining about its thinness. Weintraub (1985), for example, had complained about Popper reducing 'the rich conversation of empirical work down to a falsifying "fact" ' (McCloskey, 1988, p. 246). In the same vein, Weintraub claims that histories which can be used to test methodology are 'too often uninteresting historically', and that histories have to be sufficiently 'rich' if they are to satisfy one's 'historical sensibility' (1992, p. 4). This is an argument with which any historian will sympathize: who could possibly argue in favour of 'thin' history, which makes science 'lie down on the bed [of methodology] with suitable trimming at head and foot' (McCloskey, 1988, p. 246).

So far, the argument is consistent with many philosophical positions. McCloskey and Weintraub, however, go beyond this to develop a case for thick history which is based on a very specific epistemological position. Once again, it is helpful to consider McCloskey first. He claims that: (1) Any 'philosophical' criticism of science is necessarily thin. (2) A 'thicker' way of thinking is to be found in the humanities, in particular in literary criticism:

> Happily, there exists alternative thinking about how to do the thinking, thick and rich. It is called the humanities [presumably excluding philosophy?]. ... What historians and methodologists of economic thought mainly do anyway, without knowing it, is literary criticism. Sophisticated criticism is *merely* understanding how the texts of economists produce their effect, as one criticizes poetry.
>
> (McCloskey, 1988, p. 253, emphasis added)

(3) A literary model can lead to a better, because thicker, way of examining conversations amongst economists. (4) Criticism does not involve appraisal.

Weintraub's arguments are similar. (1) He rejects philosophy as a source of interesting questions that philosophers might wish to answer. (2) He argues that it does not mean anything to speak of stability or instability, 'except as that claim is understood as imposing a discursive order on phenomena. It is an invitation ... to participate in a (Wittgensteinian) language game to be played according to a particular set of rules ...' (1991a, p. 150). Lest there be any doubt in the reader's mind that he rejects completely the notion that science might be about discovering the truth, he writes:

> I submit that nothing whatsoever is lost, in economics or in the history of economics, by giving up the notion of representation as 'discovery of the other'. ... We do represent the economy with our accounts, models, theories, stories and data; but *except as a burdensome fiction*, those representations do not 'describe' except as they create that which is to be described. *Except as a confusion*, models of the economy do not 'depict' except as they instantiate a vision to be shared, and profitably discussed.
>
> (1991a, p. 151, emphasis added)[5]

(3) He rejects the notion that historians should be seeking to appraise the economic theories of the past (1992, p. 6).

Weintraub and McCloskey offer two types of argument for thick history. The first is what might be termed the 'historian's' argument, which rests on the observed complexity of history in relation to any theoretical scheme. In this argument, thickness means simply complexity. The second is the philosophical argument, resting on claims about the nature of truth. Here, thickness has a social component, for it involves viewing truth as socially negotiated. These arguments must not be confused.

## THE MERITS OF THICKNESS (IN ITS DIFFERENT SENSES)

The 'historian's' argument is attractive to anyone who has struggled to make sense of a mass of uncooperative historical evidence. As Weintraub puts it, histories must be sufficiently 'rich' if they are to satisfy one's 'historical sensibility' (1992, p. 4). The major weakness of the argument is that the notion of 'historical sensibility' is unanalysed. Though Weintraub clearly does not wish to understand it in this way, it seems dangerously near to Ranke's argument for writing history 'wie es

---

5    Cf. the quotations in Chapter 3, p. 50, footnote 26.

eigentlich gewesen ist' (how it really was).[6] Such a perspective, resting on naive induction, is inconsistent with both Weintraub's views and mine on the nature of history.

A further problem is that the bold claim that 'thicker is better' is hard to reconcile either with the claim that history is socially constructed, or with the claim that histories have to be written in different ways for different purposes. As Weintraub has written, 'We may, of course, reconstruct the past as we wish, read the past in any one of a number of ways. Indeed we are forced to provide such readings' (1991b, p. 395). Our reconstructions may be informed by sociology of science or by literary criticism rather than by philosophy, but they are still reconstructions, imposing order on the material with which we are confronted. To understand we have to generalize. What is required is an appropriate balance between 'thickness' and generalization, the nature of this balance being determined by the particular problem being considered.

This leaves the epistemological argument for thick history. This is important because if, as Weintraub has argued, economics were nothing more than a Wittgensteinian language game, then it would follow that the historian could do nothing more than analyse the way meanings have been negotiated. Thick history, understood as the history of such social negotiation (which is also quite likely to be thick in the sense of complex), would be the only sensible history. Histories which concerned themselves with truth would be completely uninteresting. Weintraub (1992, p. 3) rejects my description of *Stabilizing Dynamics* as a manifesto for a particular way of doing history grounded on a particular view of truth, but this philosophical argument is so powerful, so consistent with Weintraub's attack on 'Whig' history, and so prominent in the book, that it is difficult not to interpret *Stabilizing Dynamics* in this way.

The objection to this argument is that there are several ways in which we can defend the notion of truth (see Backhouse, 1992). Once we recognize this we have an extra dimension to consider. As Mäki (1993) has persuasively argued, there is nothing to prevent us holding to a

6   Weintraub says 'thicker is better', but where would he stop?

coherence theory of justification at the same time as a correspondence theory of truth. Such a perspective allows for a richer set of questions than does a perspective which completely rules out the question of whether economic theories are true or false.[7] Weintraub's history may be 'thick', but it is one-dimensional: there is nothing to explore except persuasion and negotiation. If we reject Weintraub's epistemology, on the other hand, we can explore issues of progress and truth *as well as* the issues Weintraub wishes us to address.

## INTERPRETIVE COMMUNITIES

Weintraub clearly places great emphasis on interpretive communities as determining meaning. This is a valuable insight, the implications of which need to be explored. However, Weintraub repeatedly appears to use the notion of interpretive communities in a way that I cannot accept. In particular, he appears to treat economists, historians of economic thought and philosophers/methodologists as three separate communities which have nothing to say to each other. For example, he argues that our histories

> are poor histories, precisely to the degree and extent that we construct our histories to answer one or another of the current conundrums posed by the community of economists, or the community of methodologists on behalf of those economists.
>
> (Weintraub, 1992, p. 6)

He assumes that the interests of historians and of economists have little in common – otherwise why should attempting to answer economists' conundrums make for poor histories. A sharp separation of the communities of philosophers and historians explains how Weintraub is able to say 'thicker is better' whilst claiming that no philosophical position can 'provide a warrant for believing that one kind of history is

---

7   Mäki (1993) argues that his (realist) conception of rhetoric is, for this reason, thicker than McCloskey's. The same could be said about a realist approach to the history of economic thought. This remark is confined to a footnote so as to avoid the confusion that might be caused by using the term 'thick' in yet another sense.

always, and for all purposes, better than another' (1992, p. 5). Though the philosopher, a member of another community, cannot provide any reason for favouring one type of history over another, the historian can do so. It is as a historian, not as a philosopher or methodologist that Weintraub makes the claim that 'thicker is better'. Similarly, such a distinction explains how it is possible to live with a historiography that precludes appraisal. As an economist Weintraub can, of course, appraise economic theories, even though he cannot do so when speaking as a historian.

This is a position that I have criticized elsewhere (Backhouse, 1992), but it needs to be mentioned here because it explains, at least in part, why Weintraub takes exception to the passage in which he locates my alleged shift 'from fair comment to the philosophical ether' (Weintraub, 1992, p. 7).

(1) He claims my use of 'we' is ambiguous, referring to several communities – those of economists, of methodologists and historians. However, a second theme in my paper, which Weintraub omits to mention – presumably because it was directed not against his work but against the thesis of Schabas (1992) – dealt with just this issue. Schabas's argument was that historians of economics ought to break away from economics. I was arguing that they should not do so. It was thus clear that the community I was addressing was that of *economists studying the history of economic thought*. I simply do not accept that economists, methodologists and historians of economic thought constitute completely separate communities – the overlaps are too great.

(2) Weintraub incorrectly suggests that I regard the task of repairing contemporary economic analysis as a task for philosophers. *Of course* the task of repairing contemporary economics (if that is needed) is a task for economists. My point is that systematic consideration of the principles of reasoning underlying the subject (methodology) may be an invaluable input into this process. 'Philosophical' questions arise *within* economics, not just in a separate discipline called philosophy. 'Outside' perspectives may be valuable, for they may reveal things hidden to

insiders,[8] but to suggest that this is amounts to saying that philosophers should repair economics is nonsense.

(3) Weintraub sees the step from appraising contemporary economics to appraising the history of economic thought as insurmountable because it involves a jump between two different interpretive communities: 'Whig' history, in which people appraise history as economists, not as historians, crosses this boundary. In contrast, the reason why I consider the step a short one is that I do not accept that these two communities can, or should, be so sharply distinguished from each other. Our views as economists, whether we try to conceal it or not, inform our views of history; and, equally important, our perceptions of history influence our perceptions of contemporary economics. Our perceptions of contemporary economics are constructed just as much as are our perceptions of history.

## CONCLUSIONS

Having read Weintraub's comment, I stand by my interpretation of *Stabilizing Dynamics*. I regarded the notion that economics was nothing more than a Wittgensteinian language game as central to the book because in addition to providing one justification for the type of history he wished to write, it was the main argument used in Weintraub's attack on conventional ways of writing the history of economic thought. Weintraub may not like my interpretation, but I believe it is a natural reading of his text.[9] Without the philosophical arguments, it is hard to see what reason he had for mounting such a strong attack on Blaug, Walker and Samuelson. The main purpose of my paper was to attack these philosophical arguments, and, because of its clarity and elegance, *Stabilizing Dynamics* was a natural example to take.

Weintraub emphazises that his purpose in writing history is not to appraise, but to understand. This, however, is a very dangerous line. It

[8]  The classic example is McCloskey's (1986) use of rhetorical analysis to make economists aware of their own rhetoric.

[9]  One thing we have learned from literary criticism is that the author is not the sole custodian of the meaning of a text.

is impossible for anyone to write 'neutral' history. In arguing that economics is nothing more than Wittgensteinian language games, Weintraub is advocating a philosophical position that is perfect for defending general equilibrium theory.[10] Issues concerning empirical evidence and predictive success, on which general equilibrium theory is very vulnerable, are ruled out of court. By the same token, general equilibrium theory is the ideal example with which to make the case for constructivist history. When discussing general equilibrium theory, and notions like stability of equilibrium, it is very easy indeed to dispense with the notion of truth in the sense of correspondence with reality. Had Weintraub's subject been, for example, macroeconomics or labour economics, his task would have been considerably more difficult.

[10] Weintraub's use of constructivist epistemology appears 'Methodological' in the sense defined in Weintraub (1989).

## Part II

# Macroeconomics before Keynes

## Chapter 5

# J. A. Hobson as a macroeconomic theorist*

## INTRODUCTION

J. A. Hobson made some very important contributions to what we now term macroeconomics, the subject which deals with the economy as a whole, including issues such as the determination of the price level (and hence inflation), aggregate output and employment. We start with his theory of money, to which most commentators have paid scant attention,[1] after which we turn to his much better-known theory of underconsumption.[2] Hobson was, of course, concerned with many aspects of economics and his contributions to many of these formed part of a coherent system of thought. His theory of underconsumption, for example, was linked to his theory of distribution and it formed the basis for his views on imperialism and international trade. For reasons of space, however, and in order to focus attention on Hobson's distinctive contributions to macroeconomics, these wider issues are neglected here. In addition, the focus here is on Hobson's contribution to macroeconomic theory, leaving aside his contributions to debates on macroeconomic policy.

\* I am indebted to Peter Cain and Michael Freeden for valuable comments on this paper. Neither bears any responsibility for any remaining inadequacies.

1 Nemmers (1956) gives the subject two pages. Others neglect Hobson's treatment of money altogether, despite the fact that, as we shall see, it is fundamental to any appraisal of his theory of underconsumption.

2 See Nemmers (1956), Coppock (1953), Richmond (1978) and Allett (1981).

## MONETARY ECONOMICS

### Money, spending and prices

The starting point in all Hobson's work on money and prices was the assumption that the prices were determined by supply and demand for the goods in question, not by the quantity of money. This notion was forcefully expressed in *The Physiology of Industry*:

> So long as the sellers of commodities can sell all they have to offer at the current price, prices cannot fall, and this holds good equally, whether gold is scarce or plentiful. Sellers do not trouble to ask any question as to the state of the Bank reserve, or the cost at which gold is being produced. All they care to know is, whether they can sell everything they have to offer at the current price. If they believe they can, neither scarcity of gold, nor anything to do with gold, will induce them to take a lower price. If, on the other hand, they believe that they will not be able to sell all they have to offer at the current price, then prices will fall, no matter how plentiful gold may be, or to what depth its cost of production may have fallen.
>
> (Mummery and Hobson, 1889, pp. 196–7)

Supply and demand was, for Hobson, a general explanation of prices.

This perspective led Hobson to focus exclusively on flows of purchasing power to such an extent that in *Gold, Prices and Wages*, his most comprehensive treatment of money, he defined money to mean what we would nowadays refer to as aggregate income.

> By quantity of money, regarded as a factor in price-change, we signify the amount of purchasing power actually applied in buying goods during a period of time, for example a year.
>
> (Hobson, 1913, p. 9)

Money for Hobson was thus currency plus bank deposits *multiplied by* the velocity of circulation or, in other words, the total flow of expenditure during a year. Given this definition there would undoubtedly be a close relationship between 'money' and prices: if total expenditure increases and the flow of goods does not it is inevitable that the price level will rise. In this sense the quantity theory was true: indeed, it was a truism.[3]

Where Hobson parted company with orthodox economists was in his view of the relationship between money, understood as currency and bank deposits, and the level of spending. He argued that the main source of what he called money was previous receipts. In addition to this, however, there are two other sources of purchasing power: the minting of new gold coins, and new bank credit. New gold coins are not received in payment for goods but 'represent fresh gold dug out of the ground and coined and stamped as legal tender by governments for the miners'.[4] Bank deposits represent new purchasing power provided that they are the result of bankers' making new advances: if bank deposits increase simply because businessmen have paid in a corresponding amount of coins, notes or cheques there will be no change in the level of spending (Hobson, 1913, p. 15). To sum up,

> The supply of money, the aggregate of purchasing power expended upon the supply of goods and services during any given year, consists thus of three contributions. First and chief, the gross receipts from the payments or purchases made during the year. Secondly, the additional gold or notes issued as currency during the year. Thirdly, the additional credit issued as loans, discounts or other advances by banks.
>
> (Hobson, 1913, p. 19)

This view of what determined spending led to some strong conclusions about the price level. The first is that if prior receipts were the only source of income, there could be no change in the price level.

> If all money were thus derived from prior acts of sale ... it would appear as if the quantity of money must vary directly and proportionately with the quantity of goods, and that therefore prices must remain stable.
>
> (Hobson, 1913, p. 13)

---

3  When he wished to refer to what we now define as money he used terms such as 'money-instruments' (p. 62) or 'pieces of money' (p. 152).
4  Hobson (1913, p.14).

Conversely, if new money is created, either by government or by the banks, the volume of spending will rise. If production is unchanged prices must, therefore, rise.[5]

It might be thought that such an approach, stressing the circular flow of income and providing for an exogenous source of spending, would have led Hobson towards a Keynesian multiplier theory.[6] This was not the case. Hobson explicitly denied the existence of any 'second round' effects of bank credit on spending: after an increase in bank credit had been spent once it would, he claimed, have no further effects.

> When the banker first loaned it, placing it to the deposit account of his customer, it operated as a creation of new purchasing power. He who received the credit found himself in possession of so much more 'money', and no one had any less than before. Of course, as soon as this specially created money has once been expended, it begins to appear in the gross receipts of the businesses producing the goods on which it has been expended, and passes into bank accounts on ordinary terms with other cheques. What effect this bank-made credit has upon prices is, of course, exhausted by its first use by the borrower who uses it to supplement *ab extra* his ordinary supply of money got from selling goods. The person who receives it next receives it in payment for goods which the borrower buys, gets it not as an addition, but as an ordinary part of the gross earnings of his business. ... its further 'circulation' produces no further effect on prices.
>
> (Hobson, 1913, pp. 16–17)

Elsewhere Hobson is even more emphatic about there being no multiplier effects.

---

[5]   This process can be described by a simple equation. Using modern terminology define $Y$ as nominal income and $\Delta M$ as the increase in the money supply (which may comprise either new currency or bank deposits). Hobson's theory is then

$$Y_t = Y_{t-1} + \Delta M_t.$$

It is easy to see that the conclusions described in the text follow from this equation.

[6]   The role of new money in this theory is very similar to that of government expenditure in Keynesian theory.

If the increase of £10,000,000 entering our national income were all expended directly in demand for commodities, it is manifest that its effect on prices would not exceed our estimate. The very common notion that it would is based upon a quite illicit line of reasoning to the effect that the trades producing the goods first bought with the £10,000,000 would use this increased income in demanding a corresponding increase of commodities on their part, and so on with other trades supplying these commodities, until the original increased demand and its effect on prices are multiplied many times over. This argument is utterly fallacious; the effect of the £10,000,000 upon the aggregate demand and so on prices is completely exhausted on the first application, all that is added to the total income and so to the total purchasing-power of the community for the year is £10,000,000.

(Hobson, 1910, pp. 272–3)[7]

Hobson's rejection of the multiplier could hardly be more explicit or more emphatic. In this respect he was even further from Keynesian ideas than were more orthodox economists such as Bagehot (1896) and Walker (1889).[8]

### The quantity theory of money

This theory of how money was linked to spending and hence prices formed the basis for a critique of the quantity theory.[9] His first argument, used in both *The Physiology of Industry* and *Gold, Prices and Wages*, was an empirical one: he took estimates of gold production and of national income and worked out the changes in the price level predicted by his theory. In 1889 the issue was falling prices, which many economists blamed on a shortage of gold.[10] It was widely

---

[7]    See also Hobson (1913, pp. 25–9).

[8]    See Chapter 5. For further discussion of the history of the multiplier theory see Wright (1956).

[9]    Hobson (1913) was clearly a response to Irving Fisher's *The Purchasing Power of Money* (1911).

[10]    Bimetallism (basing the currency on silver as well as gold) was being proposed as a remedy. For a concise introduction to the main monetary controversies of this period see Backhouse (1994a, pp. 132–43).

believed amongst those who blamed falling prices on a shortage of gold that there was a shortfall in gold production amounting to about £2m. per annum. Total expenditure in the UK was estimated at £1,270m. Hobson used his theory to put these figures together and to argue that the shortage of gold could account for a fall in demand of only 2/1270 or 0.16% per annum.[11] The alleged shortage of gold could thus explain only a small fraction of the 30% fall in prices which took place between 1872 and 1885. Twenty-four years later he used the same argument to show that the rise in gold production between 1895 and 1910 was insufficient to cause any significant rise in the price level. The world stock of gold was believed to have increased by £67m. during this period. The gross British national income was estimated at £10,000m. and on the assumption that this comprised no more than 10% of world income Hobson conjectured that world income must be at least £100,000m. Gold production could account for a rise in the price level of at most 0.1% (the actual increase in prices was about 20%). This led him to conclude that even if 'the entire output of gold was directly expended by those who get it from the mines in purchasing goods, the effect in raising prices would be very trifling' (Hobson, 1913, p. 25).

In *The Physiology of Industry* this was the main argument against the quantity theory, but in *Gold, Prices and Wages* it was supplemented by a number of arguments, all based on the role of credit in an industrial economy. The first of these arguments was that increases in the volume of credit had been far larger than increases in the quantity of gold and that this was the main monetary factor behind the rise in prices: 'so far as an increased quantity of money is responsible for the rise of prices, it consists mainly in expansion of credit'.[12]

[11]   Mummery and Hobson (1889, pp. 200–1). For reasons that we will not go into here, Hobson argued that this represented the maximum effect of the shortfall in gold production.

[12]   Hobson (1913, p. 71). The statistics on which this conclusion is based are on pp. 50–1. It is worth noting that these statistics are also used to provide support for some of the arguments discussed below: for example the argument that credit has expanded in response to demand and that the rise in holdings of gold is a response to this (see the summary on pp. 51–2).

The second argument was that credit was created in response to demand. Credit, Hobson argued, was created not out of gold but out of goods.

> The main staple out of which credit is made is vendible goods, and the extension of credit must be attributed mainly to a growth of the vendible goods which can be used for making it. ... Credit is based on goods and expands with the quantity of goods available as valid security.
>
> (ibid., pp. 72–3 and 88)

Credit is based on the ability of borrowers to repay, with all credit being backed by some sort of collateral. Provided that suitable borrowers are available bankers will lend the maximum they can safely lend (cf. ibid., p. 35).

It might be objected that if credit rests on goods in this way, every expansion of credit would be matched by an expansion of goods, with the result that credit could never be responsible for a rise in prices.[13] Hobson's answer to this was that credit could be increased by reorganizing production.

> Large masses of new credit are due, not to the production of more goods, but to the reorganization of businesses in forms rendering these goods available as securities for credit issues. So long as this change is proceeding, increased quantities of credit will come into being without any necessarily corresponding increase of goods. That goods in general are expanding along with, and partly as a result of, the new organization of businesses may be taken for granted, but there is no reason to presume that this increase of goods will be commensurate with the increase of credit.
>
> (Hobson, 1913, pp. 88–9)

Hobson also argues that saving can increase credit: when saved income has performed its 'real task' of purchasing capital goods, the share

---

13  Though Hobson does not refer to it by name, this is the so-called 'real bills doctrine', used by Adam Smith and widely held in the early nineteenth century.

certificates created can be used as the basis for a further expansion of credit, unaccompanied by any expansion of goods.

In this process of credit-creation gold is important only because bankers have to hold reserves in order to retain the public's confidence. Gold, however, and this is Hobson's third argument, was of declining importance. As confidence in banks had grown, he argued, so reserve ratios had fallen (Hobson, 1913, p. 63). This was a process which could proceed even further, for gold was not 'economically' necessary: its value was dependent on confidence just as much as was the value of paper currency. Even the Bank of England's reserve contained a large quantity of securities. Hobson thus concluded that 'the credit system of this country is based, in its final economic analysis, not on gold but on the real wealth of the country' (Hobson, 1913, p. 81). A further consequence of increasing confidence in paper money was that not only was a smaller gold reserve required, but 'money-instruments' would change hands more frequently: the velocity of circulation would increase (Hobson, 1913, pp. 62, 151).

The implications of this for the quantity theory can best be seen by considering Fisher's equation of exchange,

$$MV + M'V' = PT.[14]$$

In this equation $M$ denotes the quantity of notes and coin and $M'$ the quantity of bank deposits, with $V$ and $V'$ their respective velocities of circulation. $P$ is the price level and $T$ the volume of transactions. Quantity theorists such as Fisher argued that changes in $M$ led to changes in the level of income, $PT$.[15] To do this they argued that (1) $M'$ was related to $M$, and (2) that $V$ and $V'$ were stable. Hobson's arguments, discussed above, sought to show that neither of these assumptions was justified.

In his discussion of the quantity theory Hobson also addressed the problem of the observed behaviour of gold supplies, prices and interest

[14]   Hobson discusses this equation, though he did not write it down explicitly, in (1913, pp. 143–6). The equation is of course a generalization of Fisher's more well-known $MV = PT$.

[15]   They also argued that it would be $P$ rather than $T$ which changed in response to $M$. Hobson, however, was not concerned with this stage in the argument.

rates. This is interesting because this was a problem which also concerned orthodox quantity theorists such as Fisher and Wicksell. If changes in the money supply were the cause of changes in prices and interest rates we would expect falling prices to be associated with high interest rates, and rising prices with low interest rates. If the supply of gold increases bankers will find themselves with increased reserves and will try to increase their lending. To do this they will have to reduce the rates of interest charged on loans: bank rate will fall. The resulting credit expansion will raise spending and hence prices. An equilibrium will be reached when prices have risen enough to absorb the additional quantity of credit. If there is a shortage of gold the process is reversed.[16]

The problem was that the opposite was observed. Hobson focused on gold reserves and interest rates in England from 1890 to 1911, whereas others (such as Wicksell) considered the relationship between prices and interest rates over a longer period, but both sorts of evidence led to the conclusion that monetary expansion and rising prices were associated with high, not low, interest rates.[17] Hobson's explanation was that the motive force was profitability. If opportunities for profitable investment increase then demand for credit will rise, raising interest rates. As credit increases so demand for reserves will increase and gold will be attracted.[18] This explanation of why rising gold reserves were associated with high interest rates, which Hobson saw as undermining the quantity theory, was very similar to the explanations offered by quantity theorists, such as Fisher and Wicksell, of which he was so critical.[19] Hobson also noted that this expansion of credit might be cumulative: rising credit leads to rising prices, which in turn lead to a larger borrowing power (collateral securities will be worth more) and

16  See Hobson (1913, pp. 36–7). Hobson is here presenting the orthodox argument.
17  Wicksell's evidence is discussed in Backhouse (1994a, pp. 139–42).
18  This theory explained why the greatest credit expansions should have been in North and South America, countries where enormous investment opportunities were available Hobson (1913, pp. 49–53).
19  Wicksell's argument was expressed in terms of the natural rate of interest. Increased opportunities for investment would raise the natural rate relative to the market rate of interest, causing inflation. Though expressed in a different way Fisher's explanation of the paradox was substantially the same.

to a further rise in credit, and so on. This is Wicksell's cumulative process.[20]

## The interest rate and the price of money

At the end of his critique of the quantity theory Hobson puts forward ideas on what constitutes the real 'price of money'. The puzzle he is concerned to resolve is the fact that the hire-price of money (the interest rate) frequently moves in the opposite direction to the purchase-price of money (the reciprocal of the price level). With other goods, he claims, such behaviour is impossible: if the purchase-price of cars rises, for example, the hire-price must also rise. Hobson's explanation is that, with the exception of governments and financial institutions, people never purchase money: they merely hire it. A sovereign, for example, should be regarded as 'a vehicle of transport, an instrument in the process of exchange, which passes through the temporary possession of a series of persons, each of whom receives it and uses it for this single act of service' (Hobson, 1913, p. 153). It is thus not the purchase-price but merely the hire-price which matters, the real 'price of money' being the interest rate. Recognition of this principle, he claimed, 'will clear up a good many obscurities in the movements of money and prices' (Hobson, 1913, p. 178).

## Hobson as a monetary theorist

Hobson clearly had some very important insights into monetary economics. He was right in insisting that prices must be explained in terms of supply and demand, and that monetary factors could affect prices only through affecting supply and demand. His observations that the velocity of circulation varied and that credit was the main feature of the monetary system were very important. There were, however, a number of crucial flaws in his monetary theory.

Hobson's analysis of the way in which flows of new money effected the economy stood in a long tradition, going back to Cantillon in the

[20] The same theory, including the cumulative process, had also been worked out by Thornton (1802). There is no evidence as to whether Hobson had read either Thornton or Wicksell.

eighteenth century.[21] It was an approach to monetary economics that was capable of development, but Hobson's theory suffered from two notable shortcomings. First, he completely failed to see the multiplier effects that would ensue. Other writers may not have worked out these effects completely satisfactorily but there was no justification for Hobson's wholesale rejection of the idea. Second, Hobson failed to allow for the possibility of hoarding. The level of spending is equal to income plus new money *minus* hoarding.[22] Hoarding offsets the effects of new money, and explains why income may fall if insufficient new money is created.

This failure to see the significance of hoarding is linked to the major defect in Hobson's monetary theory: his complete failure to see the need for an analysis of supply and demand for stocks. This failure is made clear by a passage from *The Physiology of Industry*.

> We have seen that the only demand which the community can exert is a demand for consumable articles by consumers, all other so called demands being resolvable, when regarded from the community's point of view, into mere changes of ownership. Currency, therefore, cannot be demanded; the community possesses exactly the same number of sovereigns whether any given sovereign is in the pocket of A. or B., or C., or in the cellars of the Bank of England.
>
> (Mummery and Hobson, 1889, p. 189)

In this passage Hobson and Mummery argue that it does not make sense to talk of demand for currency or any other asset. Their argument here is fallacious. Although it may be impossible for buying and selling to alter the stock of an asset, it is still possible to examine the conditions under which the community will be satisfied with the stock that it

---

[21] *Essai sur la Nature du Commerce en Générale* (1755).

[22] Using the terminology of a previous footnote,

$$Y_t = Y_{t-1} + \Delta M - \Delta H,$$

where $\Delta H$ is the increase in hoards of money. $Y$ will rise or fall according to whether $\Delta M$ is greater or less than $\Delta H$. Hobson's reasons for neglecting hoarding are discussed below.

holds: in other words to examine the conditions under which demand will equal this given stock.[23]

This failure to see even the possibility of analysing the demand for a stock, let alone the necessity of doing so, had several implications. Firstly, there is the failure to allow for hoarding, discussed above. Secondly, the quantity theory is essentially a proposition about the relationship between the stock of money and the flow of income. Thus although Hobson was able to understand many of the arguments used by quantity theorists, he never understood the theory properly. Thirdly, his arguments about the rate of interest are faulty because of his inability to see the significance of stocks and stock/flow relationships. The purchase-price of an asset is the price of a stock, and the hire-price is the price of the flow of services yielded by the asset. The two are linked by the rate of interest. If the interest rate changes, the hire-price and the purchase-price of an asset may diverge. For example, if the purchase-price of a car is fixed and the rate of interest rises, the hire-price will rise (if the car is financed by a bank loan the hirer will have higher costs to recoup).[24] There is thus no paradox to explain.

When he claimed to have undermined the quantity theory Hobson interpreted it as involving a very strict relationship between gold and prices: he viewed the quantity theory as a theory of gold control. He thus ridiculed Fisher for proclaiming the quantity theory at the same time as conceding that neither the ratio of currency to deposits nor the velocity of circulation was constant (Hobson, 1913, pp. 145–6). Hobson's arguments were, however, much less effective against more flexible versions of the quantity theory. Indeed, there is a remarkable similarity between some of Hobson's arguments and Wicksell's: a major part of Wicksell's argument was conducted in terms of a 'pure credit' economy, where gold played no role whatsoever. Whereas Hobson saw himself as

[23]   In terms of a supply and demand diagram, Hobson and Mummery's argument is that the supply curve for money is vertical. This does not mean we cannot draw a demand curve.

[24]   If we had a small fall in the price of a car together with a large rise in the interest rate it would be possible for the purchase-price to fall and the hire-price to rise.

This aspect of the stock/flow relationship is not merely a modern theoretical construction. It was clearly stated by Walras (1874).

destroying the quantity theory, however, Wicksell saw himself as developing and extending it.

Hobson may have been right in claiming that there had been, over the preceding decades, a progressive rise in both the velocity of circulation and the ratio of credit to gold, but given the banking system's need for reserves (which he accepted) it was quite feasible for the supply of credit to be constrained by the stock of gold in the short run. He never followed up the implications of this. It is thus fair to conclude that whilst Hobson had no problem in disposing of the simplest, popular versions of the quantity theory, his arguments contained many flaws, and were weaker than those of more sophisticated quantity theorists such as Wicksell.[25] Because of his complete neglect of the problem of stock/flow equilibrium he simply by-passed some of the central issues of monetary economics.[26]

## THE THEORY OF UNDERCONSUMPTION

### Saving and investment

As is well known, Hobson explained unemployment in terms of under-consumption or over-saving. In any attempt to understand this theory the most important thing to note at the outset is the way in which he thought of saving and its relationship to investment. He made the assumption, strange to economists brought up on Keynesian theory, that savings were, by and large, invested: that a high rate of saving implied a high rate of capital accumulation.

> Saving means something more than this ['not consuming']. It signifies not only abstention from consumption, but application as a means of further production.
>
> (Mummery and Hobson, 1889, p. 47)

---

[25] Fisher's quantity theory was certainly far from being such a simple theory. He presented it, however, using a series of extremely simplistic, mechanical analogies, playing down the complications, in such a way as to leave himself open to misinterpretation.

[26] His writing touches on such issues in several places, such as where he refers to the need for additional credit to be absorbed, but he does not follow them up.

> Every act of saving in a complex industrial society signifies making,
> or causing to be made, forms of capital which are essentially
> incapable of present consumption – *i.e.*, future of productive goods.
>
> (Hobson, 1906, p. 292)

> A person who, instead of spending, saves, invests his savings.
>
> (Hobson, 1910, p. 50)

There were two reasons for this. The first is that Hobson attempts to
view the problem from the point of view of society as a whole.[27] Thus
'saving' that merely transfers income from one individual to another
(for example, a thrifty individual lending money either to a spendthrift
or to a fraudulent promoter of companies) is, from a social point of
view, not saving at all. In addition, 'saving' which simply results in the
creation of excess capacity, though it may increase the capital owned by
the individual concerned, does not increase the community's 'real'
capital and should not be considered as saving.[28] The second reason for
Hobson's conflation of saving and investment is his refusal to attach
much significance to hoarding.[29] He acknowledged the possibility of
hoarding, but argued that in modern industrial societies this was
abnormal (Hobson, 1910, p. 50). As a result he attached little
significance to hoarding and adopted a position close to Say's law.

> In modern industrial society there is no wish to keep more money
> idle, in men's pockets or in their bank accounts, than is required for
> the normal conveniences of economic life. It might, therefore, be
> assumed that all incomes when received would without much delay
> be employed either in buying consumables (spending) or in buying
> capital goods (saving).
>
> (Hobson, 1930, p. 33)

Despite this view of saving, however, Hobson took issue with John
Stuart Mill's dictum that 'everything which is produced is consumed;

---

[27] Coppock (1953, p. 3) refers to this as a concern with the normative aspects of saving.

[28] He defined real capital as capital that is 'animated by the productive force in
economical work' (Mummery and Hobson, 1889, p. 51). In other words, it is the capital
stock adjusted to remove any excess capacity.

[29] This was discussed in a different, though related, context in section 2 above.

both what is saved and what is to be spent; and the former quite as rapidly as the latter' (Hobson, 1906, p. 295). Mill's argument is essentially that when individuals save they lend the money to investors who employ workers to create capital goods. What happens, therefore, is that savings are used to pay for consumption by workers in the investment goods sector. Hobson's criticism was that Mill failed to see that the person who saves 'necessarily produces something which neither he nor anyone else consumes at once' (for example, steam engines). He is thus looking a stage further ahead than Mill.[30]

## Saving and consumption

Hobson's main argument about unemployment was that it was necessary to have the right balance between saving and consumption, and that underconsumption would emerge if savings were too high relative to consumption. The reasoning is that because all savings are invested, high saving will lead to high investment which increases the flow of future output. If there is to be a market for this output it is necessary that there is a sufficiently high level of future consumption. Problems arise because building a factory, for example, though it may create an immediate demand for consumption goods, does not create any future demand to match this increased supply. If this future demand is not forthcoming the result will be excess capacity and unemployment once the factory comes into operation. Excessive saving, therefore, creates a problem not whilst the investment is being undertaken, but once it is in place and is beginning to produce output.[31]

The need for future consumption to provide a market for the output produced by new capital goods means that it is necessary to have the right balance between investment and consumption. There is, however, an asymmetry. If there is excessive saving the result is unemployed

---

[30] That Hobson's view is, terminology aside, substantially the same as Mill's is shown by a passage where Hobson writes, 'So long as the "saving" is actually in progress – *i.e. so long as the factory and machinery are being made* [note the identification of saving and investment] – the net employment of the community is just as large as if the money were spent to demand commodities' (Mummery and Hobson, 1889, p. 79).

[31] See, for example, Mummery and Hobson (1889, p. 75); Hobson (1930, pp. 74ff.); Hobson (1910, pp. 305–6).

resources; whereas if there is insufficient saving the fact that incomes will be constrained by full employment output means that excess demand will not emerge.

Hobson's view of the need for a balance between saving and consumption is clearly summed up in the following passage.

> In a stable society ... all the income is spent: there is no place for saving. But in a progressive society where the future rate of consumption is to exceed the present, for a larger population with a higher standard of comfort saving is essential. A little saving will only make provision for a slight rise in the volume of consumption; more saving is needed for a larger rise. The right amount of saving out of a given income, i.e. the right proportion of saving, will be determined by the amount of new capital economically needed to furnish a given increase of consumption goods. Over a period of years there will be a rate of saving which will assist to produce the maximum quantity of consumption goods.
>
> (Hobson, 1910, p. 54)

He implicitly takes the growth rate as given, arguing that a certain level of saving is required if capital is to be accumulated at the right rate.[32] If capital is accumulated too fast, consumption will not keep pace with demand. This is the same as the problem that underlies the Harrod–Domar growth model: the difference is that Hobson takes the

---

[32]  Define

$$g = \frac{\Delta Y}{Y}$$

as the growth rate of income,

$$v = \frac{I}{\Delta Y}$$

as the incremental capital–output ratio (the accelerator) and

$$s = \frac{I}{Y}$$

(savings are equal to investment). It is then easy to show that

$$s = \frac{I}{Y} = \frac{\Delta Y}{Y} \frac{I}{\Delta Y} = gv.$$

Given $v$, therefore, we can calculate the value of $s$ needed to sustain any given growth rate.

growth rate as given, calculating the appropriate saving rate, whereas Harrod and Domar took the savings ratio as given, calculating the 'warranted' growth rate.[33] It is worth noting that Hobson clearly understood what we now refer to as the accelerator, the relationship between investment and the growth of output that is necessary to derive an optimal savings ratio. As the following passage makes clear, he believed the accelerator (or capital–output ratio) to be at least 4.

> The plant required to produce any individual commodity by modern standards vastly exceeds in value the individual commodity itself, and we certainly do not over-estimate this difference if we assume that an increase of ten per cent. in the annual consumption of any community would require an increase of fifty per cent. in the production of that commodity during the year of increase. ... Thus if a community increases its consumption from $10x$ wealth to $11x$ wealth a year, production must during the year in which this increase takes place exceed consumption by $4x$ wealth in order to accumulate the additional forms of capital required; that is to say, production must during this year amount to $15x$ wealth. So soon, however, as consumption, having reached $11x$ annually, no longer increases, a production of $11x$ wealth annually alone is required.
>
> (Mummery and Hobson, 1889, pp. 85–6)

This is a remarkably precise statement of the acceleration principle.[34]

The orthodox position on Say's law was that although there could not be general underconsumption, it was possible for there to be insufficient demand in one sector and excess demand in another: that there could be an imbalance between the level of demand in two sectors. Hobson claimed that a similar argument could be used to explain 'general' underconsumption. In a situation of under-consumption what was happening was that people were trying to postpone too much consumption to the future. There was thus an imbalance between

---

[33] Harrod (1939); Domar (1946). See Coppock (1953, pp. 9–10); Nemmers (1956, p. 86).

[34] Because this idea is found only in *The Physiology of Industry* it is impossible to know how far it should be associated with Hobson: it is possible (though there is no evidence for this) that it was an idea of Mummery's to which Hobson never paid any attention.

present and future consumption caused by the fact that whilst there were no limits to the extent to which individuals might wish to postpone consumption, there were strict limits as to the amount of consumption that the community as a whole could postpone to the future. Not only were limits imposed by depreciation, obsolescence and limited knowledge of the future,[35] but there was also the limitation imposed by the need to ensure that current consumption was high enough for existing productive capacity to be fully utilized. The problem of underconsumption was thus one of inter-temporal disequilibrium. This is summed up in the following quotation.

> It is universally admitted that from ignorance or miscalculation too much new capital often flows into certain industries or groups of industry, and too little into others; some are congested, others starved. ... But if this waste from misdirection in the application of capital at a given time is admitted as a natural occurrence, why is it unreasonable to expect that a general misdirection of capital, not as between one set of industries and another, but as between one period of time and another, may occur?
>
> (Hobson, 1906, pp. 306–7)

### The causes of underconsumption

Hobson's views on why underconsumption was likely to be a perennial problem changed significantly during the 1890s. In *The Physiology of Industry* (1889) he and Mummery emphasized the difference between the interests of the individual and the interests of the community. Individuals are in competition with each other and may invest what, from a social point of view, is an excessive amount in the hope of gaining a competitive advantage over their rivals.[36] As one commentator has put it, 'the economic taproot of oversaving ... was to be found in the independent nature of corporate decision-making in a market economy' (Allett, 1981, p. 105).

---

[35] See, for example, Hobson (1906, pp. 306); Hobson (1933, pp. 407–8).
[36] Mummery and Hobson (1889, pp. 114–16). He likens the sitution to that of a competitive examination.

During the 1890s Hobson started to see the cause of under-consumption as resting in a maldistribution of income, relating this to his theory of surplus. In *The Problem of the Unemployed* (1896) he attributed high savings to the high level of 'unearned' incomes.

> The reason why attempts are made by individuals to establish more forms of capital than are socially required, is that they possess certain elements of income which are not earned by effort, and which are therefore not required to satisfy any present legitimate wants. ... a man who draws a large income without working for it cannot and does not spend it.
>
> (Hobson, 1904, pp. 88–9)

The simplest illustration of this was that one cannot enjoy a good dinner without having performed some physical exercise. He quotes J. J. Astor as saying that he has all the necessaries of life and that as a result he can do nothing with his income but invest it. Given that a large proportion of the nation's capital was owned by wealthy individuals, the result was that savings were very high.

> The failure to fully utilise consuming-power is due to the fact that much of it is owned by those who, having already satisfied all their strong present desires, have no adequate motive for utilising it in the present, and therefore allow it to accumulate.
>
> (Hobson, 1904, p. 92)

The final stage in the evolution of Hobson's theory was to explain the origins of 'unearned' income using the theory of the surplus which he developed during the 1890s.[37] The surplus was the amount by which output exceeded the amount needed to maintain the factors of production (workers' subsistence plus depreciation of capital). Part of this surplus was 'productive', in that it provided the incentives necessary for growth to take place: it included the interest payments necessary to induce savers to supply the required amount of capital, and the wages necessary to stimulate growth in the quantity and quality of labour. The remainder was the 'unproductive surplus', which

---

[37] This theory is discussed in *The Economics of Distribution* (1900).

comprised all economic rent plus all factor payments beyond those necessary either to maintain factor supplies or to stimulate growth (Hobson, 1910, Chapter 4, especially p. 80). This 'unproductive surplus', he argued, was the cause of underconsumption, for the right level of saving will occur only if the ratio of saving to consumption is determined by 'a close comparison between present and future pleasures and pains'.

> The rightness of such calculations would be based upon the fact that all saving required a proportionate effort on the part of the individual or the community that made it. If in a society that was not communistic but individualistic this prime condition were present, and all saving involved a corresponding effort or sacrifice, the right adjustment between saving and spending would be equally secure. But if, as regards any large proportion of the saving, this condition is not present, there is no automatic guarantee for the maintenance of the right proportion between spending and saving. Now that 'saving' which is made out of unproductive surplus income is not amenable to this calculus; unearned in origin, such 'surplus' is not allocated to the supply of any particular human needs, as is the case with that income required to maintain or stimulate human efficiency of production. It may, indeed, be said that human craving for expenditure on luxuries is insatiable, and that wealthy owners of 'surplus' income must be conceived as balancing present against future satisfactions, and so making painful sacrifices when they save. But such balancing will be far looser and will yield very different results from the balancing of working men who are called upon to save.
>
> (Hobson, 1910, pp. 284–5)

Hobson is thus going much further than merely assuming, as was the case in his earlier works, that the rich save more than the poor.

There are two main problems with this theory. The first is that Hobson does not make it clear why consumption should be linked to the effort involved in earning the income (Coppock, 1953, p. 4). It may be that the rich take less care in working out the optimal balance between consumption and saving than do the poor (they have less need and less incentive to do so), but there seems to be no good reason why this should be linked to effort. The second problem is that in this passage Hobson appears to be suggesting that if everyone were deciding their saving behaviour in an optimal way, the resulting level of savings would be socially optimal. But the point of Hobson's other arguments is that there is a divergence between the private and social benefits from saving: that it is in the interests of individuals, when considering their own position, to save more than is socially optimal. The argument about the surplus thus seems irrelevant to Hobson's main theory. This is not, of course, to say that the distribution of income may not be an important cause of high saving.

## Hobson and 'Keynesian' unemployment

Hobson's main explanation of unemployment was clearly the one outlined above. There are, however, some passages which suggest an explanation of unemployment that is much closer to Keynes's. Consider the following passage from *The Physiology of Industry*.

> The community considered as the recipient of money incomes produces consumable articles; the community considered as the spender of money incomes buys and consumes these articles. If, owing to its desire to save, it refrains from spending the whole of its money income, the whole of the consumable articles produced cannot be sold. Over-supply is, in consequence, caused, and prices and incomes fall until the production of consumable articles is reduced to the total actually consumed.
>
> (Mummery and Hobson, 1889, pp. 98–9)

The significant feature of this passage is that it distinguishes saving from investment: contrary to what is claimed elsewhere, this passage analyses saving independently of investment. Such saving is, furthermore, related explicitly to hoarding, for his argument is that people save up for the future either through investing their savings or through hoarding money (Mummery and Hobson refer to storing up money in a stocking).[38] Interestingly, Mummery and Hobson quote Alfred Marshall as saying that 'though men have the power to purchase, they may choose not to use it', describing him as being 'alone amongst economists' in holding this view (Mummery and Hobson, 1889, p. 102). They fail to note that such a remark could just as easily have been taken from John Stuart Mill (1844, p. 70).

The final point to note is that it is because Hobson neglects the possibility of hoarding that his monetary theory remains separate from his theory of saving and investment.[39] If we take his theory whereby expenditure comprises income and newly created money and introduce hoarding we can very easily show that this is the same as assuming that demand equals income plus the difference between investment and saving.[40] This is very close to the theory Keynes put forward in his *Treatise on Money* and it has much in common with Wicksell's theory.

---

[38]  Mummery and Hobson (1889, pp. 107–8). Once again we have the problem of not knowing how far this passage reflects Hobson's thinking.

[39]  Keynes (1930, volume I, p. 161), referring to 'Mr J. A. Hobson and others', commented that 'I do not think they have succeeded in linking up their conclusions with the theory of money or with the part played by the rate of interest.'

[40]  Define savings as

$$S = \Delta H + I^S,$$

where $I^S$ is the amount of investment directly financed by savers. Similarly, assume that new money is created by banks lending money to investors, so that

$$I = I^S + \Delta M.$$

Our earlier equation becomes

$$Y_t = Y_{t-1} + \Delta M - \Delta H$$
$$= Y_{t-1} + I - S.$$

The explanation of why $I$ and $S$ can be unequal is that we have postulated an income–expenditure lag: this year's income equals last year's spending. Saving is thus the difference between this year's consumption and last year's expenditure, whereas investment is the difference between this year's consumption and this year's expenditure. In his *Treatise on Money* Keynes achieved a similar result through defining saving as the difference between consumption and 'normal earnings'. We have simply used last year's earnings instead of 'normal' earnings.

## CONCLUSIONS

Hobson was, despite his many failings, a remarkable macroeconomic theorist. Firstly, his theory of money and output, with its stress on the role of expenditure flows in determining the price level, contained important insights. Had Hobson allowed for the possibility of hoarding, he might easily have produced a theory very similar to that found in Wicksell's *Interest and Prices* or Keynes's *Treatise on Money*. Allowing for the possibility of hoarding would also have provided a link between his monetary economics and his underconsumption theory. Secondly, his statement (jointly with Mummery) of what we now call the acceleration principle over a decade before other economists took up the idea, could hardly be bettered. The only doubt here is whether it was Hobson or Mummery who was responsible for it. Finally, in perceiving the connection between the accelerator, the savings ratio and the growth rate he was anticipating a problem not tackled until Harrod's work many years later. Like his predecessor, Malthus, even though he never managed to express his ideas in a form that convinced his orthodox colleagues, he was right in persisting with his theory of underconsumption.

Hobson's main limitation was his failure properly to understand the arguments of his orthodox contemporaries. As things were, not only were there serious weaknesses in some of his arguments, but he expressed his ideas in such a way as to make it easy for economists to dismiss them. For example, although *Gold, Prices and Wages* was a *much* better book than Keynes claimed,[41] Keynes was to a great extent justified in claiming that,

> One comes to a new book by Mr. Hobson with mixed feelings, in hope of stimulating ideas and of some fruitful criticisms of orthodoxy from an independent and individual standpoint, but expectant also of much sophistry, misunderstanding, and perverse thought.
>
> (Keynes, 1913, p. 388)

---

[41]  Keynes (1913) described the book as 'very bad' and 'much worse than a stupid book could be.'

Hobson's complete dismissal of the ideas underlying the multiplier represented not just a failure to anticipate later Keynesian theory, but rather a rejection, apparently for no good reason, of generally accepted ideas. More important, his failure to analyse demand for stocks and the consequent neglect of hoarding resulted on the one hand in his misunderstanding of the quantity theory and on the other hand caused him to produce a theory of money and income which had some very strange implications. His definition of money as income, and of saving as investment in order to derive paradoxical results could be seen as examples of sophistry.[42]

Of course, Keynes did later make amends when he described Hobson and Mummery as members of 'a brave army of heretics' who preferred to see the truth obscurely and imperfectly rather than to maintain error, reached indeed with clearness and consistency and by easy logic but on hypotheses inappropriate to the facts (Keynes, 1930, pp. 364, 366, 371). However, although there are places where Hobson, in his work with Mummery, seems to have approached a 'Keynesian' theory of deficient demand, these were no more coherent and were given no more prominence than the equivalent passages of J. S. Mill, whose work we have to take as representing the classical orthodoxy. Though it may have led him to similar policy conclusions, Hobson's real break with orthodoxy did not run on Keynesian lines, but involved his argument for long-term stagnation, where he has to be seen as a precursor, not of Keynes, but of Harrod and Domar.[43]

[42] We should perhaps be charitable towards the latter in view of the problems Keynes and his colleagues had, during the 1920s and 1930s, in working out appropriate definitions of saving and investment.

[43] See Keynes (1930, volume I, p. 161), and also Clarke (1990).

## Chapter 6

# F. A. Walker's theory of 'hard times'*

## INTRODUCTION

Francis Amasa Walker (1840–97) is widely recognized as an important figure in the history of American economics, having been the first president of the American Economic Association. His most well-known economic writings (he was also a notable statistician) are those concerned with wages and bimetallism. *The Wages Question* (1876) sparked off the controversy over the wages fund which led to the establishment of marginal productivity theories of distribution (see Gordon, 1973), whilst Walker's writings on bimetallism (e.g. Walker, 1896b), though no longer of great interest, concerned one of the most contentious political issues of his day.

On his own admission Walker was not a great economic theorist, his strength lying rather in his keeping firmly in touch with practical life (see, for example, Dorfman, 1949, p. 109). His writings contain, however, a remarkable exposition of how an equilibrium with substantial unemployment might emerge. The passage which contains these ideas, included both in his *Political Economy* (1885, 1896a) and in his *Money, Trade and Industry* (1879/1889), has been neglected by most historians of the business cycle (e.g. Haberler, 1943; Hansen, 1964). An exception to this neglect is Hutchison (1953). Even Hutchison, however, fails to do justice to Walker's arguments. The aim of this chapter,

* I am indebted to Denis O'Brien, Warren J. Samuels, and an anonymous referee for helpful comments on an earlier draft of this article. Responsibility for any remaining errors or inadequacies is mine alone.

therefore, is to remedy this situation, and in doing so to say something
about the nature of Keynes's later work on the subject.

## WALKER'S THEORY OF PERSISTENT UNEMPLOYMENT

### Bagehot's theory of fluctuations

To understand Walker's theory of hard times we need to consider the
theory on which it appears to have been based, namely the theory of
fluctuations contained in Bagehot's *Lombard Street* (1896).[1] Bagehot, in
seeking to explain fluctuations in credit ('why Lombard Street is often
dull and sometimes excited'), provided an account of the interdependence that exists between industries:

> No single large industry can be depressed without injury to other
> industries; still less can any great group of industries. Each industry
> when prosperous buys and consumes the produce probably of most
> (certainly of very many) other industries, and if industry A fails and
> is in difficulty, industries B, and C, and D, which used to sell to it will
> not be able to sell that which they had produced in reliance on A's
> demand, and in future they will stand idle till industry A recovers,
> because in default of A there is no one to buy the commodities which
> they create. Then as industry B buys of C, D, &c., the adversity of B
> tells on C, D, &c., and as these buy of E, F, &c., the effect is
> propagated through the whole alphabet. And in a certain sense it
> rebounds. Z feels the want caused by the diminished custom of A, B,
> and C, and so these do not earn as much either.
>
> (Bagehot, 1896, p. 128)

He developed this idea further when he considered the effect of a rise in
the price of corn, such as could result from a bad harvest:

[1]    Walker does not cite Bagehot in this context, but given his familiarity with Bagehot's
*Lombard Street*, which he described as 'his standard work' (1896a, p. 174), together with the
similarity in their arguments, it seems reasonable to assume that Bagehot's well-known
account of the cycle (it was used by Marshall) was the basis for Walker's work. Bagehot's
theory is discussed in the context of other writings on the multiplier in Wright (1956).
Wright, however, neglects Walker.

When the agriculture of the world is ill off, food is dear. And as the amount of absolute necessaries which a people consumes cannot be much diminished, the additional amount which has to be spent on them is so much subtracted from what used to be spent on other things. All the industries, A, B, C, D, up to Z, are somewhat affected by an augmentation in the price of corn, and the most affected are the large ones, which produce the objects in ordinary times most con-sumed by the working classes. The clothing trades feel the difference at once, and in this country the liquor trade ... feels it equally soon. Especially when for two or three years harvests have been bad, and corn has long been dear, every industry is impoverished, and almost every one, by becoming poorer, makes every other poorer too.

(Bagehot, 1896, pp. 129–30)

There are, in these passages, a number of key ideas. The main one is that of interdependence between industries, expressed in a manner reminiscent of input–output analysis. Bagehot does not specify whether this interdependence arises through one sector using other sectors' products as inputs, or through capitalists and workers in one sector consuming the other sectors' products. Another important idea is the notion that when income falls, consumers cut their consumption of non-essential goods. When making use of this idea Bagehot distinguishes simply between agricultural and industrial products, seeing the former as essentials, the latter as non-essentials. He uses the notion that demand for agricultural produce is very inelastic to argue that a rise in agricultural prices will reduce demand for industrial products, but after this it plays no role in his analysis.

## The propagation of economic shocks[2]

Walker takes over and develops Bagehot's argument in a number of important ways. His starting point is that of 'a disaster' befalling a highly organized economy. This disaster, which may be 'financial or industrial' in origin, 'temporarily diminishes the productive power of the community as a whole' (Walker, 1889, p. 126). This reduction in

[2]   This and the following sub-heading are taken from the exposition of Walker's theory in Walker (1896a).

productive power leads to a fall in consumption, the effects of which Walker analyses in the following way:

> Immediately the consumption of the articles least essential to comfort and decency is in a degree checked. If we suppose the thousands of articles known to the market to form twenty-six groups, A to Z, the importance to human welfare diminishing from the head of the alphabet to the foot, we may assume that the first effect of the calamity we have supposed to take place will fall upon the consumption of articles in groups X, Y and Z. The demand for the products of the trades furnishing these articles falls off rapidly. No matter, as we said, where the blow first fell, the labourers affected produce less for the time, and must limit their consumption, which they do by cutting off entirely, or greatly restricting, their use of articles below group W.
>
> (Walker, 1889, pp. 126–7)

Capital and labour are not easily transferred from one industry to another, so workers in X, Y and Z are employed on short time or at reduced wages:

> in their distress they cut their consumption of all articles except those of prime importance, say from A to M. This involves a reduced demand for the products N to W.
>
> (Walker, 1889, p. 127)

Workers in groups N to W now find themselves having to reduce their consumption, and they start by buying less from groups X, Y and Z. This forces workers in groups X, Y and Z to reduce their consumption still further, cutting the use of their products from H downwards. Workers in groups H to M will now be affected and will reduce their consumption, starting with the least essential goods, which means that workers in X, Y and Z will see yet another fall in their income. 'This very complicated process will continue', Walker argues,

> until even the favoured producers A to D experience some reduction in the demand for their products, and producing less in consequence, have less to exchange for the products of others, just as a stone

thrown anywhere into a lake produces a wave which extends out-wards in every direction till it reaches the bank even in the most retiring nook along the shore.

(Walker, 1889, p. 128)

In this process the feedback effects, whereby a fall in one industry's production makes workers in other industries worse off, thus reducing the demand for its own product, are crucial. Particularly important are those industries producing the least essential articles, for it is the workers in these industries who have their income reduced the most and who have to cut back their consumption furthest. It is thus the extent to which these workers, in X, Y and Z, have to cut back their consumption which determines how far up the alphabet the effects of the initial shock extend.

In these passages Walker has modified Bagehot's theory in a number of ways. The first is that whereas Bagehot merely assumed some sort of input–output interdependence between industries, Walker focuses on the interdependence that arises through workers spending their income on the products of other sectors. Consumption behaviour is thus much more important to Walker's theory than to Bagehot's. The second modification is that Walker has generalized Bagehot's argument about essentials and non-essentials. Thus whereas Bagehot used the distinction between essentials and non-essentials merely to produce the initial shock, Walker uses it to explain how the shock is propagated through the economy. Finally, the feedback effects of one sector's production on demand for its own product play an important role in Walker's argument. Though Bagehot was aware of such effects, he did not make much use of them.

It can be argued that there is a multiplier implicit in Walker's theory, for in addition to the initial reduction income there is a series of further income reductions. As all these reductions in income are in the same direction, the final reduction in aggregate income must exceed the initial fall. Walker, however, writes:

the ultimate result of all this would be the distribution of the whole initial shock over the entire producing body. *No addition would be made to the force of that shock as the movement proceeded,* and the effect upon each successive trade or group of producers would be less as it was found further removed from the part suffering the original impact.

(Walker, 1889, p. 128, emphasis added)

This passage, especially when read in the context of the passages discussed below, suggests a multiplier of unity. The problem here is, of course, that Walker's argument is much too loose for it to be possible to say exactly what he is going on. In particular we do not know enough about the nature of the original shock and how its size compares with the initial fall in production in groups X to Z.

## The aggravation of economic shocks

Though Walker does, as we have just seen, argue that a shock may be distributed throughout the economy without being amplified by what we would now call multiplier effects, this view is only the preliminary to the following argument:

Let but the shock be sharp and severe, and let it fall in with an anxious, apprehensive mood of the public mind, or find the producing body a little unstrung by reason for political or industrial disturbance, and we shall see the impulse propagated with ever-increasing force from subject to subject till the movement acquires great violence. The commercial panic we are all familiar with, by experience or report. ...

A manufacturer feels the demand for his goods fall off somewhat. In ordinary times he receives the fact as an intimation to reduce his production, but only to a corresponding extent. Indeed, in good times he would receive the intimation in a somewhat skeptical spirit. He would not be disposed to believe that any serious check was to be experienced. He would look to see trade start up again at the opening of the next season, and in this mood he would reduce his production somewhat less than correspondingly. ...

But let the shock be at first severe, and let it come upon the public mind in a suspicious mood, and the consequences may be indefinitely more serious. The merchant feels the demand for goods fall sharply off. He fears that there is more to come. He is determined not to be caught with a large stock on his hands, and in his orders to the manufacturer he exaggerates the natural and proper effect of the change in the market. He orders even less than the present condition of things might justify. The manufacturer, on his part, knows nothing of the actual falling off in demand ..., exaggerates the evil and reduces his production more than proportionately. His concern now is, not so much to make profits, as to save his capital.

(Walker, 1889, p. 130)

Walker is thus arguing, very much in the tradition of J. S. Mill, Bagehot, Marshall and, later, Pigou, that though there are no multiplier effects inherent in the normal process of income and spending, such effects can arise through producers overreacting to changes in demand (see, for example, Pigou, 1927). Such errors are attributed to the general 'mood' of industry, which may be one of optimism or pessimism.

## Unemployment equilibrium

Walker then proceeds to the most interesting part of his argument, going beyond his predecessors to ask whether, if contractions can be amplified in this way, output could be reduced to zero:

May the movement to check production proceed till all industry is locked fast in a vicious circle, no one producing because others will not consume, and no one being able to consume the products of others because he himself produces nothing with which to buy them?

(Walker, 1889, p. 131)

Walker's answer to this question is 'No', his reason being that demand for some products (the most essential ones) is so constant that panic can never affect them.[3] On the other hand, contraction might fall a long way before any equilibrium was reached:

---

[3]    Hutchison (1953, pp. 369–70), claims that Walker uses this argument about consumption of essentials as an explanation of why revival will eventually take place. Such an interpretation does not seem justified. Indeed, in the absence of any accelerator (and there is no suggestion that this was available to Walker) there is no theoretical reason why a floor to output should be enough to stimulate recovery.

there could, I think, be no question that the causes we have been considering might result, after the series of actions and reactions should be completed, in bringing the aggregate production down to two thirds of its former amount. It ... might even proceed till one half the labor power and capital power of the community were for the time neutralized.

(Walker, 1889, pp. 132–3)

Such a state might, he continued, last indefinitely, at least in theory. It would end only when something happened to 'revive courage and enterprise', the one essential condition for recovery being that 'speculation be initiated – that is, that men begin to look ahead, to anticipate demand, and to discount the future'. The result of this is:

One man begins to produce no longer on orders, no longer cautiously and fearfully as if it were too much to believe that his goods will be taken off his hands, but in a more sanguine spirit, assuming the initiative in production, and boldly encountering its risks.

(Walker, 1889, p. 133)

Walker is arguing that what is required is for an entrepreneur to produce more than current demand conditions justify, for in the same way that producing less would cause depression, so producing more will lead to a level of demand sufficient to justify the higher level of production. The speed with which recovery emerges thus depends crucially on business attitudes.

It is worth pointing out that Walker believed that the initiative had to come from entrepreneurs ('men of business', or 'the employing class'), for only they had the power to revive business in this way. Elsewhere in *Money, Trade and Industry* he wrote:

I asked, what have the laborers of this country done during the five weary years of industrial prostration to secure their own employment? and we saw that they have done nothing, because there was nothing which they could do but await the returning power and disposition of the employing class to revive their activity.

Now I ask, what have the capitalists of this country done, as capitalists, in the same period, to initiate production? What could they have done? The answer is the same; absolutely nothing beyond awaiting ... the revival of productive enterprise on the part of the employing class.

(Walker, 1889, p. 90)

This emphasis on the need for businessmen to be willing to take risks, explore unknown fields, and undertake costly experiments in order to search out new channels for productive energy (cf. Walker, 1889, pp. 86–7) is reminiscent of Keynes's 'animal spirits' or Schumpeter's view of the entrepreneur.

## THE SIGNIFICANCE OF WALKER'S THEORY

To see the significance of Walker's account we need to see the context in which it occurs. Consider first its use in *Political Economy* (1885). The chapter concerned is Chapter 7, 'The Reaction of Exchange upon Production', in which Walker develops his argument in three stages: (i) the evil possibilities involved in the division of labour; (ii) fluctuations in production; and (iii) 'hard times' (the chapter's fourth sub-heading is simply an extension of this). In the first of these sections Walker explains how speculation and division of labour 'increase enormously the liability of misunderstanding between producers and consumers' (Walker, 1896a, p. 183), and how the organization of production by entrepreneurs leads to caution, the reason for this being that even small fractions of stock remaining unsold can be enough to eliminate an entrepreneur's profit altogether. In the second section he goes on to discuss fluctuations, quoting Marshall's 1879 account of the cycle (a similar account is provided in Marshall, 1920, pp. 710–12). Such cycles, Walker concludes, involve 'great and permanent loss of productive force' (Walker, 1896a, p. 187), there being waste in periods of both high and low activity.

It is after this that Walker moves on to the subject of 'hard times':

Nothing needs to be added, of clearness or of force, to Prof. Marshall's statement of the course which trade and industry run from the time they first cross the line of reviving prosperity to the moment they plunge into the abyss of broken credit, falling markets, commercial panic, failing banks and commercial distress. But there is one industrial phenomenon of very great significance in respect to our question, why the actual production of a community comes so far short of its productive capability, which economists have not been accustomed to explain; and that is, the long continuance of the periods of industrial depression and restricted production.

(Walker, 1896a, p. 188)

Walker is thus not concerned with the cycle, but with prolonged periods of unemployment, for he assumes that underproduction will result in a mixture of wage cuts, short-time working and unemployment (see, for example, Walker, 1889, p. 127; 1896a, pp. 188–9). It is here, not in his discussion of the cycle, that we find his discussion of a multiplier process.

As an example of hard times, Walker cites the prolonged depression from 1873 to 1878–9, when 'at least one fourth of the mechanical power of the United States' was paralysed, 'vast amounts of labour power and capital power remain[ing] unproductive' (1896a, p. 189). This unemployment of both capital and labour, he argued, occurred despite workmen being willing to work and owners of capital being willing to lend it if they could but find opportunities to invest it. It is thus a crucial aspect of Walker's argument that recovery from such a depression is not automatic: that it may last indefinitely. Though continued demand for necessities will prevent output from falling to zero, this will not be enough to ensure a recovery, and production will stagnate until there is a revival 'of courage and enterprise among men of affairs, or a stimulus to production administered from ... some unexpected quarter' (1896a, p. 194).

Hutchison (1953, p. 369) has described Walker as seeing the main problem as one of disproportionate production. Evidence for this is Walker's discussion of 'over-production' and 'under-consumption':

> Over-production, as alleged by those who would explain hard times, *is partial over-production*, production, that is, which has gone on in certain lines ... until it has exceeded the normal demand. This excess supply in certain lines leads to the accumulation of vast stocks of unsaleable goods, which is *partial under-consumption*.
>
> (Walker, 1896a, p. 323)

It was possible to have overproduction only in certain lines, not general overproduction. Walker saw the real problem as one of general underproduction, something which might arise as a consequence of partial overproduction, for excess stocks in one line of activity would lead to unemployment in the sector concerned, spending by employees in this sector would decline, and production in other sectors would have to fall.

It might be thought that Walker would have greater sympathy with underconsumption theories, for it is increased spending that he sees as the key to revival. This was, however, not the case, for two reasons. The first reason was that he saw depression as characterized by an unusually high average propensity to consume: 'never in our history has consumption followed so closely upon production ... never has the margin of possible saving been so small as in these five years past' (Walker, 1889, p. 120). Walker considered underconsumption a strange term with which to describe such a situation. The second reason, to which he attached more importance, was that he saw underconsumption as implying that wealth 'cannot be produced unless the existing stock be eaten, worn out, or burned up, or by some means gotten rid of' (ibid., pp. 120–1). Consumption, he argued, would 'generally look after itself' (ibid., p. 121). The main task, therefore, was not to raise consumption, but to raise production.

Though Walker recognized that it was possible to make sense of terms such as overproduction and underconsumption, he distrusted them. Underproduction was a term he accepted more readily as being an accurate description of the state of affairs in a depression. His attitude is made clear in his treatment of the problem in *Money, Trade and Industry*, where, following a discussion of overproduction and underconsumption, he writes:

> Setting aside these terms in which, as we have seen, lurks so much deceit, let us analyze the processes of industry to find out how it can be that, with natural agents unexhausted, capital and labor power may be absolutely precluded from remunerative employment, while

yet capitalists and laborers are eagerly and anxiously desirous to take part in production.

(Walker, 1889, pp. 122–3)

He thus tries to go back to first principles (to 'analyze the processes of industry') in order to explain hard times, thus avoiding what he saw as useless disputes over terminology.[4]

In analysing the processes of industry Walker, following Bagehot, used a simple process analysis, showing how an initial disturbance would filter through the economy. This was the method of the great eighteenth-century writers on monetary economics – Law, Cantillon and Hume. To see this, it is only necessary to turn to Walker's discussion of hard times in *Money, Trade and Industry*, where the context is a discussion of the effects of a monetary contraction. In the preceding chapter, Chapter 4, Walker had analysed the opposite case of a monetary expansion, basing his argument explicitly on Hume's account of a monetary inflation. Although his assumptions are not the same, and although he is concerned with new problems, Walker's method is that of Hume.

Walker, as was noted above, did not consider himself a great theorist. He once wrote to J. B. Clark:

I have not an analytical mind [having a] great weakness in the matter of abstract reasoning. … I have often said that I was like a navigator before the discovery of the compass and other instruments. I cannot

---

4    His attitude is made beautifully clear in this passage: 'In the absence of any attempt by professional economists to account for the phenomenon, public speakers and the newspapers are driven to answer for themselves the question with which we started. This they generally do by the use of one of two phrases, which seem to be regarded as mutually exclusive. "Over-production" says one party, "under-consumption" retorts another; and those who say over-production ridicule those who allege under-consumption, while the latter retort with equal scorn.

'Let us examine the process by which wealth is produced and brought to market. Perchance we shall find that, like all condensed phrases, over-production and under-consumption signify more than one thing each; that, in certain senses, each phrase embodies a great deal of arrant nonsense; that, taken otherwise, each embodies a vital truth; and that, so far as either means any thing at all, that meaning is exactly identical with what is expressed in the other' (Walker, 1889, p. 118).

put thought out to sea and sail a course for weeks knowing that after just so many miles, I shall sail straight into a harbour. I have to *coast* along and run from point to point that I can see.

(Walker, quoted in Dorfman, 1949, p. 109)

This going from point to point along the coast seems an apt description of Walker's method in analysing hard times: the very concrete process analysis of Hume, and, before him, Cantillon and Law. The resulting analysis had great limitations, notably imprecision at several crucial points, but it was nonetheless capable to being used to tackle problems that were more difficult to tackle with more refined equilibrium analysis.

## WALKER AND KEYNESIAN ECONOMICS

It is now well established that pre-Keynesian economics did not fit into the mould of Keynes's 'classical economics'. Walker's work provides one more piece of evidence for this, particularly interesting because his concern was with long-term unemployment, rather than with the business cycle itself, or with monetary economics – in *Money, Trade and Industry* he describes his discussion of hard times as a 'long excursion into general economics' (Walker, 1889, p. 135). His failing was that, though he saw that it would be possible to have an equilibrium with high unemployment, he did not develop his ideas sufficiently systematically. He lacked the techniques (these including both simplifying assumptions and methods of working with those assumptions) necessary to analyse the problem properly. The difference between Walker's *Political Economy* and Keynes's *General Theory* is that, whilst both dealt with the same problem, of persistent unemployment, Keynes was able to use the aggregative approach developed by Marshall and Pigou, and the techniques of savings–investment analysis developed by a number of economists in the 1920s, whereas Walker used much more primitive techniques.

To make this point clearer, consider what is possibly the best attempt to define the crucial theoretical innovations contained in the *General*

*Theory*, that of Patinkin (1982). For Patinkin there were three essential components to Keynes's argument: (i) an increase in expenditure will produce multiplier effects; (ii) there may be equality of savings and investment at a variety of levels of income; and (iii) changes in output provide a mechanism through which, independently of changes in profitability, savings and investment can be brought into equilibrium. On each of these three points it is limitations in his technique which prevent Walker from achieving Keynes's insights.

(i) Walker clearly understood, as had Law, Cantillon and Hume before him, the income–consumption–income mechanism, but he went astray in tracing the change in income resulting from an initial shock. There were a number of reasons for this. The main one is probably that Walker did not manage to separate expenditure from production and income. There is no notion of autonomous expenditure in Walker's work, which means that whenever he wished to speak of a change in expenditure he had to argue in terms of a prior change in production or income. Thus where Keynes would have argued that a rise in autonomous expenditure was needed to lift an economy out of an unemployment equilibrium, Walker saw a rise in production as the key factor. This separation of expenditure from income, a prerequisite for Keynesian economics, involves a step analogous to that involved in separating investment and savings. The experience of the economists such as Keynes and Robertson who worked on this problem in the 1920s shows that it was far from being a straightforward task.

A further reason why Walker went astray in trying to analyse the propagation of an economic shock through the economy was that leakages from the circular flow of income are very important in this process, something that Walker failed to appreciate. In this he was not helped by the excessive complexity of the model he was trying to work with: analysing the interdependence of twenty-six sectors of the economy, using a comparatively complicated theory of consumption, was an extremely difficult task. It defeated even Pigou (1927, pp. 54–62), who had much better analytical tools available.[5]

---

[5]    In some ways Walker's treatment of multiplier processes is superior to that of Pigou, who, using very peculiar assumptions, manages to obtain multipliers of 25 and 320 in two

(ii) The idea that there might be an equilibrium with production equal to demand, and with firms holding no unwanted inventories, at more than one level of income, is clearly implied by Walker's writing. As with his analysis of multiplier effects, it is the technical device of savings–investment analysis, together with the conceptualization of income and expenditure that go with it, that is missing from Walker's theory, together with the simplifications concerning consumption and investment behaviour needed to render such analysis tractable.

(iii) Walker has quantity adjustments as a means by which the economy moves into an unemployment equilibrium.

Keynes's innovation was thus not so much to gain a new insight into the nature of capitalism, as to show how the problem of persistent unemployment might, through the making of certain important simplifying assumptions, be analysed using the newly developed apparatus of savings–investment analysis. In the words of J. M. Clark, Keynes's great achievement was to construct 'a coherent logical system or formula having the quality of a mechanism' (see Keynes, 1971–83, XXIII, p. 191) that could be used to analyse contemporary economic problems. It is these mechanical, and potentially quantitative, aspects of the *General Theory* which, for all the dangers attached to their too-indiscriminate application, are its vital feature. Quantitative analysis was something that Walker's more concrete methods could never achieve.

(Continued from previous page)
of his numerical examples. It should be noted that elsewhere (e.g. 1929, pp. 188–91) Pigou provides much more plausible numerical examples.

## Chapter 7

# Keynes, American institutionalism and uncertainty

## INTRODUCTION

When defending the *General Theory* (1936) against critics, Keynes ignored most of the technical criticisms levelled against the book and instead focused on one issue: the pervasiveness of uncertainty. In a much-quoted passage, he argued,

> I accuse the classical economic theory of being itself one of those pretty, polite techniques which tries to deal with the present by abstracting from the fact that we know very little about the future.
>
> (Keynes, 1937, p. 218)

Such passages, together with Chapter 12 of the *General Theory* and certain passages in the *Treatise on Money* (1930), have formed the basis for an important strand in post-Keynesian macroeconomics.[1] They are often discussed as though Keynes were the first to write about uncertainty in such terms. If we turn, however, to American institutionalists writing before the *General Theory*, we find views on uncertainty and the operation of the market mechanism that, superficially at least, resemble those of Keynes, and which would be congenial to many post-Keynesians. In view of recent attempts to find common ground between post-Keynesians, institutionalists and other heterodox economists, it is of some interest to look at these seemingly

---

[1]    Harcourt and Hamouda (1988) call this 'Strand 1', the other strands being neo-Ricardianism and the Kalecki/Robinson theory of investment and growth.

similar passages, to ask how far these similarities were real, and to explore where the differences between Keynes and American institutionalists lay. This chapter, therefore, points out and comments on the implications of some passages in which two prominent American institutionalists, W. C. Mitchell and J. M. Clark, discuss uncertainty in terms that are reminiscent of Keynes.

## WESLEY CLAIR MITCHELL

Of the many economists to write on the problem of the business cycle, the context in which unemployment was most frequently discussed prior to the *General Theory*, one of the most important was Wesley Clair Mitchell. Though he is sometimes presented as an advocate of pure empiricism, he worked within a definite, if loose-knit, theoretical framework. For Mitchell the business cycle was characteristic of a particular form of economic organization: the 'business' economy or 'profit' economy.

> We do not say that a business economy has developed in any community until most of its economic activities have taken the form of making and spending money. That way of organizing production, distribution and consumption is the matter of importance – not the use of money as a medium of exchange.
>
> (Mitchell, 1927, p. 63)

This point of view was taken from Veblen, who had distinguished sharply between business and industry – between making money and making goods. For Mitchell, as for Veblen, 'industry is subordinated to business, the making of goods to the making of money' (Mitchell, 1927, p. 183). The existence of money was thus fundamental to Mitchell's conception of the economy.

Mitchell stressed the complexity of the economy, this arising for several reasons.

1 There is an enormous degree of interdependence within the economic system. Production and distribution are, in a business economy, regulated by prices, all of which 'are continually

influencing one another. To account for any one item in the system, one must invoke the whole' (Mitchell, 1927, p. 115).

2   The economy is conceived as always being in motion. Though Mitchell described the interdependence of prices in Walrasian terms, explicitly citing Walras, he did not accept the notion of static equilibrium, preferring instead to 'trace the main channels through which price fluctuations propagate themselves' using statistical rather than theoretical methods.

3   The business economy itself makes for complexity.

> An economic system which distributes incomes in money, and lets recipients spend the money in any way they like, makes extremely difficult the task of adjusting the supply of each kind of good to the profit-paying demand for it. To cope with this task of directing production in detail, the business economy has evolved an elaborate system. Business managements play the most active role in guiding production; but they must have the assistance of technical experts of various sorts, and they must submit most of their important projects to review by lenders of credit or investment funds.
>
> (Mitchell, 1927, pp. 184-5)

Mitchell, therefore, rejected the notion that the mechanical analogy of equilibrium could fruitfully be applied to problems of the business cycle.

> the problems of business cycles are the opposite of 'static'. If we are to conceive of them in terms of mechanical forces we must conceive of an equilibrium among numerous forces which are constantly changing, changing at different rates, and influencing one another as they change.
>
> (Mitchell, 1927, p. 186)

If a 'mechanical contrivance' were to be designed so as to represent business cycles it would, Mitchell claimed, be too hard to understand, too uncertain in its application to interest anyone except its inventor. Thus when Mitchell used the concept of equilibrium, he used it solely in the sense of a balance sheet equilibrium – referring to the relationship between two sums of money which might, or might not, balance (Mitchell, 1927, p. 187).

A concomitant of this complexity was uncertainty, this being understood in Knight's sense as involving more than simply risk.

> 'Uncertainty' … is thus an all-pervading phase of every business undertaking. Its tap root is uncertainty concerning what people will buy at what price. Its lateral roots are uncertainty concerning what competitors, direct and indirect, will sell at what prices; uncertainty what supplies of all needed kinds can be bought at what prices, and uncertainty what will happen within the enterprise, or within its business connection, to affect its profits. The fruits of uncertainty appear in the emotional aberrations of business judgements and competitive illusions.
>
> (Mitchell, 1927, pp. 156–7)

This uncertainty increased with the size of the market and with the scale of business enterprise.

A further important characteristic of Mitchell's theory is his emphasis on income flows. There is in his work the circular flow of income which is implicit in any general equilibrium system where factor incomes are used to purchase goods, in turn generating further factor incomes. Mitchell, however, went further than this. Using empirical data for the United States, he analysed expenditure flows, coming to the conclusion that the flow of payments between enterprises was far larger than that between enterprises and consumers. In addition, he found saving to be highly variable, businessmen and property owners, whose incomes were the most variable, accounting for most saving (Mitchell, 1927, p. 153). A major aspect of the problem of the business cycle, he claimed, was the aggregate level of savings.

## JOHN MAURICE CLARK

J. M. Clark provided, in *Strategic Factors in Business Cycles* (1934), a clear account of a 'Keynesian' model. Towards the end of the book he turns away from the question, 'How does business operate?' to the narrower question of 'Why does it *not* operate according to the picture of ideal equilibrium?' (Clark, 1934, p. 124). The main reason he gives in answer to this question is that the requirements for balance (equality of supply and demand) in different markets have not been harmonized.

> Supply and demand for *goods* may reach momentary balance at very different levels of price and of volume of production and of levels of employment.
>
> (Clark, 1934, p. 129)

Equality of supply and demand for goods, however, is balance only in a superficial sense. Balance in a more fundamental sense requires not only this but also equality of supply and demand for labour. He went on to argue,

> The fact that supply and demand for goods can be balanced at present only at volumes of production that mean an intolerable amount of unemployment ... is evidence that the requirements of balance in the superficial and in the fundamental senses have not been harmonized, in our present system.
>
> (Clark, 1934, p. 130)

A major reason for this lack of balance is that the credit system allows expenditures to diverge from incomes.

> Expansion of credit makes it possible for expenditure to increase beyond income already realized, and to lead to an increase of production, leading in turn to a subsequent increase of incomes.
>
> (Clark, 1934, p. 87)

On the one hand, consumers' expenditure is not constrained to equal their income, whilst on the other hand, 'immediate expenditures on capital equipment depend more on the businessman's demand for capital than on the supply of original savings' (Clark, 1934, p. 141). In such a credit economy, cumulative impulses will be common, an increase in spending on one thing often meaning more spending on other things too. This cumulative process was explained in terms of both the multiplier (an increase in consumption leading to further increases in consumption) and the accelerator (increases in consumption leading to increased investment).

It was possible, Clark argued, for balance to be achieved, with demand sufficient to absorb the total supply of labour and capital, for 'effective demand is the reflection of the volume of production; and is potentially capable of absorbing more goods than we have yet produced' (Clark, 1934, p. 135). Price and wage cutting, however, though it would make sense from an individualistic point of view, would not work for the economy as a whole: 'If prices, wages and profits all fell in harmony, nothing might be accomplished' (Clark, 1934, p. 136). Neither would wage cuts that lowered real wages.

> And if wages fell more than the other shares, might there not be a cutting-off of markets for consumers' goods which would defeat the purpose of the whole process? There is need of a balance between the portion of income saved, and this will be disturbed by any sudden shifting of incomes from wage and salaried workers, who spend most of their incomes, to profit-takers, from whom the bulk of the savings comes.
>
> (Clark, 1934, p. 136)

Easy money would not raise expenditure unless there were other factors creating an impulse to spend (Clark, 1934, p. 87).

As was the case with Mitchell's remarks on uncertainty and the cycle, Clark's approach to the problem of unemployment followed naturally from his general approach to economics. His theoretical framework stemmed not only from Veblen, but also from his father, John Bates Clark. An important feature of J. B. Clark's economics was his stress on dynamics: he considered the economy always to be in motion, with the result that static theory could do no more than suggest the direction in which dynamic forces were moving the economy. In J. M. Clark's work these dynamic forces received even more attention because of his work on overhead costs. In *The Economics of Overhead Costs* (1923) he argued that the presence of large overhead costs ruled out the possibility of a stable competitive equilibrium. Because costs fell continually with output, most markets would be characterized either by price discrimination or by cut-throat competition in which prices were driven below cost. The problem of overhead costs, he argued, was inherently dynamic.

Most of the special significance of overhead costs is due to dynamic changes in industry. But for this, size of plants and output would be so adjusted that constant costs would practically disappear, including even the costs of knowledge, for it is chiefly the knowledge of new things that is costly. Dynamic and organic – such are the dominant qualities of our modern economy of science, machines and elastic credit systems. Its intricacies are baffling, especially to one whose previous notions of economic law have been largely confined to the static economics of more or less mechanical addition and division which we often imagine ourselves to have received from our ancestors – with what injustice to our ancestors we cannot now pause to inquire.

(Clark, 1923, p. 479)

For Clark, dynamic economics had to be built around overhead costs, 'for they are part of its essential framework' (ibid.).

## MITCHELL, CLARK AND KEYNESIAN ECONOMICS

Clark and Mitchell shared with Keynes two important beliefs: they considered uncertainty to be endemic to a capitalist economy; and they viewed unemployment as arising from the normal working of a market economy. To this extent, they can be regarded as adopting what is nowadays considered a post-Keynesian perspective. This, however, does not justify jumping to the conclusion that Clark and Mitchell anticipated Keynes's system. The reasons for this need to be considered carefully.

Clark himself saw what he called 'income-flow analysis' as marking a major advance over all previous work.

It has seemed to me that what I call the 'income-flow analysis', of which yours is the most noted presentation, has done something which has not been done in comparable degree since Ricardo and Marx: namely constructed a coherent logical theoretical system or formula having the quality of a mechanism, growing directly out of current conditions and problems which are of paramount importance and furnishing a key for working out definite answers in terms of policy.

(Clark in Keynes, 1971–83, XXIII, p. 191)

The contribution he emphasizes here is the provision of a tight, logical system or formula – presumably we would now say mathematical model – relevant to the problem in hand. However, he went on to point to dangers in such an approach.

> On this [the coherent logical theoretical system] a 'school' has grown up. All that has tremendous power; and is also exposed to the dangers of too-undiscriminating application, from which 'classical' economics suffered.

(ibid.)

He saw Keynes as belonging to a school which placed greater emphasis on logical formulae than himself. He related this difference to his institutionalist position.

> I am myself enough of an 'institutionalist' (whatever that may mean) to have more than a lurking distrust of formulas and equations! But not enough of an institutionalist to ignore their importance: merely to want to think all round them and reckon with the imponderables that modify their action.

(Clark in Keynes, 1971–83, XXIII, pp. 191–2).

There was thus a methodological gap between Clark and Keynes.

Davis has made the point that one of the main differences between Clark and Keynes was that though Clark 'built a theory of aggregates' using 'building blocks not dissimilar to those Keynes later used in his own theory', he was exhibited an 'unwillingness to synthesize the various elements' (Davis, 1971, pp. 83–4). This unwillingness to synthesize was even more marked in Mitchell's work. After surveying theories of the business cycle he argued for a form of theoretical pluralism.

> One seeking to understand the recurrent ebb and flow of economic activity characteristic of the present day finds these numerous explanations both suggestive and perplexing. All are plausible, but

which is valid? None necessarily excludes the others, but which is the most important? Each may account for certain phenomena,; does any one account for all the phenomena? Or can these rival explanations be combined in such a fashion as to make a consistent theory which is wholly adequate?

There is slight hope of getting answers to these questions by a logical process of proving and criticizing these the theories. For whatever merits of ingenuity and consistency they may possess, these theories have slight value except as they give keener insight into the phenomenon of business cycles. It is by study of the facts which they purport to interpret that the theories must be tested.

(Mitchell, 1913, p. 19)

He claimed that 'neglecting phenomena which do not fit neatly into preconceived schemes' was 'the besetting sin' of business cycle theorists (Mitchell, 1927, pp. 48–9). Though Mitchell was not the naive empiricist he is sometimes claimed to be, and though Clark was significantly less pluralistic than Mitchell, there was a significant methodological gap between both of them and Keynes.

The institutionalists also thought of uncertainty and the market mechanism in a different way from Keynes. Clark and Mitchell both came to the conclusion that the pervasiveness of uncertainty and the tendency of markets to malfunction using a theoretical framework that was very different from Keynes's. For Mitchell the framework was based on Veblen's distinction between business and industry. Given the way modern economies were organized, uncertainty was endemic and there could be no presumption that production would be organized efficiently. Though he was prepared to use neoclassical ideas, he never started from a neoclassical view of markets and human behaviour. Interdependence and complexity were the sources of uncertainty. Similarly Clark, despite his leanings towards neoclassical economics, did not accept the neoclassical competitive framework. Overhead costs imply increasing returns to scale, ruling out any stable competitive equilibrium, and render economic problems inescapably dynamic. Like Mitchell, he also considered the complexity of modern economies a feature that could not be neglected.

# Part III

# Methodology and macroeconomics

# Chapter 8

# Macroeconomics since Keynes: two interpretations*

## INTRODUCTION

The purpose of this chapter is to provide a general perspective on macroeconomics has evolved since Keynes's *General Theory*,[1] focusing on how the subject has developed over the past fifty years. Although this might seem of only academic interest it is important for economists, or anyone else (including policy-makers), using economic ideas, to understand where the ideas they use have come from and how they have developed over time. Without this we are unlikely to understand either the significance or the limitations of present-day economic ideas.[2]

Given our interest in economic policy it is tempting to start an account of this period with a discussion of Keynesianism, monetarism and macroeconomic policy. This would, however, be inappropriate, for arguments about macroeconomic policy are based on macroeconomic

* This is a substantially revised version of part of a paper presented to a seminar on 'Post War Economic Thinking and its Relevance for Policy' at the Katholieke Universiteit, Leuven, in May 1988. I am grateful to participants in the seminar and also to Tony Brewer, Mark Blaug and Roy Weintraub for helpful comments on the original draft. Needless to say, none of them can be held responsible for the use I have made of their ideas.

1   In view of the way Keynesian ideas dominated macroeconomics in the immediate post-war period, Keynes's *General Theory* is the only sensible starting point.

2   This belief was the reason why, several years ago, I took the unusual step of including a brief chapter on the history of macroeconomics in an otherwise fairly conventional, elementary textbook on macroeconomics (Backhouse, 1983). This theme is discussed in a broader setting in Backhouse (1994a), especially Chapter 7.

theories. Macroeconomic theories evolve in response to pressures which have nothing to do with policy-making. We start, therefore, with a discussion of the evolution of macroeconomic theory since Keynes. Only after doing this do we turn to matters more directly relevant to policy.

## THE EVOLUTION OF MACROECONOMIC THEORY

### Rational behaviour

In the post-war period economic theory has been dominated by the attempt to explain economic phenomena in terms of rational behaviour. In macroeconomics this has taken the form of providing a microeconomic foundation for macroeconomic theories: deriving macroeconomic relationships as the outcome of individuals' optimizing subject to the constraints imposed by their endowments, markets and technology. There has been an aversion to what Lucas has termed 'free parameters': parameters describing individual or market behaviour that are not derived from the assumption of utility or profit maximization.

Such an attitude towards the construction of macroeconomic theories could be justified in a number of ways. The justification which probably reflects the views of most economic theorists[3] is described in the following quotation. In it Bliss is criticizing the use in economic models of constants (for example the propensity to save or the mark-up of prices over costs) that are not derived from any formal economic theory.

> The trouble with this method [called 'Ricardian' by Schumpeter and 'implicit theorizing' by Leontief] is not merely that things are assumed to be constant which are certainly not constant ... but also that factors which ought to be analysed and made the subject of economic theories remain unanalysed, or are analysed only crudely.
>
> (Bliss, 1975a, p. 125)[4]

---

3    This is, of course, a wild conjecture for which I have no firm evidence!
4    The words in square brackets are from earlier in Bliss's paragraph.

The account which follows runs in terms of a continuing attempt to remove 'free parameters' from macroeconomic theories.[5] A prerequisite for this is, of course, that macroeconomic theories be expressed formally. This is the first stage.

**Stage I: Formal modelling of the macro economy**

Economists who read Keynes's *General Theory* today find that the book contains many informal arguments and that it is full of 'unorthodox' ideas that have not made their way into mainstream macroeconomics. At the time, however, it struck many economists as a relatively mathematical work in which macroeconomic relationships were simplified in order to permit the construction of what was, by the standards of the time, a fairly formal mathematical model. It is thus possible to see the major contribution of the *General Theory* as providing the basis for a simplified model that could provide the basis for a new type of relatively mathematical macroeconomic theorizing. J. M. Clark, one of the leading US authorities on the business cycle, expressed this beautifully when, in a letter to Keynes, he wrote,

> It has seemed to me that what I call the 'income-flow analysis', of which yours is the most noted presentation, has done something which has not been done in comparable degree since Ricardo and Marx: namely, constructed a coherent logical theoretical system or formula having the quality of a mechanism, growing directly out of current conditions and problems which are of paramount importance and furnishing a key to working out definite answers in terms of policy.
>
> (Keynes, 1971–83, XXIII, p. 191)

Others, though perceiving Keynes's contribution in essentially the same way, were more hostile. Schumpeter claimed that Keynes's method of simplifying the economy was dangerous and misleading:

5    This account has much in common with the one in Gerrard (1988). The main difference is that he deals simply with Keynesian economics, whereas the account here applies to the whole of mainstream economics. Other contrasts with Gerrard's account are noted below.

his work is a striking example of ... the Ricardian Vice, namely, the habit of piling a heavy load of practical conclusions upon a tenuous groundwork, which was unequal to it yet seemed in its simplicity not only attractive but also convincing.

(Schumpeter, 1954, p. 1171)

The marginal propensity to consume, the investment function and the liquidity-preference function were for Schumpeter the 'three great simplifiers' in the Keynesian system (Schumpeter, 1954, p. 1176). Similarly Leontief (1937) criticized Keynes for what he called 'implicit theorizing': of assuming theoretical relationships without specifying them sufficiently precisely for it to be possible to say exactly what they implied.[6]

The process of constructing a simple, formal model capable of being used to tackle issues of macroeconomic policy was completed by Hicks (1937) with his IS–LM apparatus.[7] This takes as its starting point the consumption function, the marginal efficiency of investment and the liquidity preference schedule, no attempt being made to derive these from optimizing behaviour. The wage rate was taken as a parameter of the model. When Hicks came to justify the use of such a model in *Value and Capital* (1939)[8] he argued that it described a 'temporary equilibrium' of supply and demand given expectations about the future, a defence consistent with Keynes's approach of taking the state of long-term expectations as given. We thus have a macroeconomic theory in which: (a) behavioural relations are frequently adopted on the basis of informal arguments rather than being derived from models of maximizing

---

[6]   This view is in contrast to that of Gerrard (1988) who places Patinkin's model alongside the rationing models of Barro and Grossman *et al.* Gerrard is right to point out the parallels between Clower's arguments about the consumption function and Patinkin's theory of labour demand. In addition, both are 'disequilibrium' models in the Walrasian sense. Beyond this, however, the two types of model are, for reasons explained below, very different.

[7]   The reduction of Keynes's *General Theory* to the IS–LM apparatus was not the work of Hicks alone but of a group of economists (see Young, 1987). It was Hicks's interpretation, however, which caught on.

[8]   The phrase 'such a model' is important, for Hicks did not mention his IS–LM paper in *Value and Capital*.

behaviour; (b) prices and expectations are frequently taken as given or changed parametrically. The main difference from macroeconomics prior to the *General Theory* is that simple formal models are being used. It was because economists could make such assumptions that the work of extending the *General Theory* into new areas could progress so fast, the best examples of this being work on the business cycle (notably Samuelson, 1939) and growth (Harrod, 1939; Domar, 1946).

So far the story has been entirely about Keynesian economics, but there are many important 'monetarist' examples of this type of theorizing. When they were discussing 'classical' economics, economists were working within the framework established by Hicks, and indirectly by Keynes. Friedman's famous restatement of the quantity theory rests on a theoretical foundation that is just as informal as Keynes's. There was less of a problem for 'monetarists' in that, even if they did not spell it out in detail every time, there was a well-established theory of what determined output, whereas Keynesians had no formal theory to explain why the price level should be at whatever level it was.

The most striking example of a 'monetarist' theorizing in this way, however, came very late, in Friedman's theoretical framework, first published in 1970 (Friedman, 1970a, 1974). His theory was essentially an IS–LM model with two equations, $M / P = L(y,r)$ and $I(y,r) = S(y,r)$ to determine three unknowns, $y$, $r$ and $P$ (using standard notation). Friedman argued that Keynesians took $P$ as given whilst monetarists assumed $y$ to be given. $P$ and $y$ were thus taken to be parameters determined outside the main model.

## Stage II: The piecemeal removal of 'free parameters'

The next stage in the evolution of macroeconomics involved the piecemeal removal of 'free parameters': parameters not grounded on optimizing behaviour. The first step was to produce optimizing models to explain the behavioural functions that Keynes had simply postulated. The stories of the theory of the consumption, investment and demand for money functions are well known. The models of macroeconomic equilibrium were unaffected, the equations used in them being seen as simplified versions of those implied by formal optimizing models. This is the approach to macroeconomics that is characteristic of most contemporary textbooks.

A different approach was taken in the literature on 'disequilibrium' models which developed in the late 1960s and 1970s. Here the concern was still with applying theories of optimizing behaviour but the emphasis was on market interdependence and the constraints imposed when markets failed to clear. Clower (1965) pointed out that if households could not sell as much labour as they wished, their consumption spending would be constrained by the amount of labour they managed to sell; and Patinkin (1965) argued that firms' demand for labour would depend on the quantity of output they managed to sell. These and similar insights were incorporated into a so-called 'general disequilibrium' model by Barro and Grossman (1971). During the 1970s numerous economists developed similar models.

The final example of this stage in the development of macroeconomics is Friedman's presidential address to the American Economic Association (published as Friedman, 1968) together with the literature stemming from this. Though his address contains no explicit mathematics his theory is firmly based on utility and profit maximization, his criticism of the by then orthodox Phillips curve being that it failed to apply neoclassical price theory consistently. His theory contained, however, a vital free parameter, for he assumed that inflationary expectations adjusted to actual inflation with a lag. There was no optimizing theory to explain the speed with which expectations adjusted, a vital parameter in his theory. Even Friedman's theory, therefore, applied the notion of maximizing behaviour only in a piecemeal fashion.[9]

### Stage III: The systematic application of optimizing behaviour

Since the 1970s economists have become very wary of models which rely on either inflexible prices or inflexible adjustment of expectations. This could loosely be described as the 'rational expectations revolution'.

---

[9]    I am not sure whether I would place Friedman's earlier work on the 'long and variable lags' in monetary policy (papers reprinted in Friedman, 1969) here or in stage I.

If we use such a term, however, we must be careful not to regard rational expectations as synonymous with the new classical macroeconomics, for the rational expectations revolution has had effects on Keynesian economics as well.

The notion that optimizing behaviour should be applied systematically to all aspects of macroeconomic models, including the formation of expectations, was first put forward by Lucas in the early 1970s. Since then many economists have taken up his ideas, seeking to explain macroeconomic phenomena without abandoning the axiom that markets are continuously in equilibrium, with supply equal to demand. This is the new classical macroeconomics. In new classical models individuals maximize utility subject to the constraints imposed by competitive markets which are continually in equilibrium. Expectations are assumed to be based on all the information that agents could possibly have at their disposal. To derive their conclusions concerning economic policy, however, Lucas and his followers have to assume not only rational expectations but also that markets are always in equilibrium. It is claimed that this too follows from utility maximization, for if markets were not in equilibrium this would imply that mutually beneficial trades were not taking place: in other words, that utility was not being maximized. It can thus be argued that because they use optimizing models to derive not only demands and supplies, but also expectations and market equilibrium conditions, optimizing behaviour is being applied systematically in these models in a way that was not true of earlier work in macroeconomics.

The attempt systematically to get rid of 'free parameters' is also characteristic of much recent work on the foundations of 'Keynesian' economics. The most well-known example is the now extensive literature on wage contracts and bargaining which tries to explain why wage rates may be inflexible. Similarly it has been shown that uncertainty about workers' productivity and asymmetric information may lead to wage rates above the market-clearing rate. Hart (1982) has shown how imperfect competition in both product and labour markets can result in models which have Keynesian features. In all these theories it is assumed that price and wage stickiness must be explained. In addition, most of these models are consistent with rational expectations. Optimizing behaviour is thus being applied systematically in Keynesian as well as new classical models.

## MONETARISM AND KEYNESIANISM

### Keynesianism

Keynes tried to establish his ideas as not only an explanation of mass unemployment but also an alternative to 'classical' ways of thinking about the economy. The central theme of his challenge to the orthodox theory of unemployment was his claim that an economy might get stuck in an equilibrium at less than full employment. Because 'classical' theory allowed for the possibility of periods of 'disequilibrium' unemployment, his claim that a situation of unemployment might represent a genuine equilibrium was very important: without it his ideas would mark a much less radical break with orthodox theory. Early discussions of the *General Theory*, therefore, focused on the circumstances under which an unemployment *equilibrium* might exist. This was the first phase in the evolution of Keynesianism: the use of the IS–LM framework to explore this issue.

As the debate went on it became clear that when all the implications of price changes (including in particular the real balance effect) were taken into account a situation of unemployment could not be an equilibrium unless wages were completely unresponsive to unemployment. Wages might, however, be slow to fall and the real balance effect might be very weak with the result that unemployment might persist for long periods of time. We thus find Patinkin explaining Keynesian unemployment as unemployment which market forces are too weak to eliminate within a 'socially acceptable' period of time. Keynesian unemployment ceased to be understood as an equilibrium phenomenon, being understood instead as the result of persistent disequilibrium.

Keynesian economics was also understood as the economics of disequilibrium in the literature on rationing models which developed in the 1970s. There was, however, a profound change in the way disequilibrium was conceived.[10] In these models disequilibrium means simply that markets do not clear: that supply and demand are unequal. In other respects these are models of unemployment equilibrium: a vicious circle of low employment and low spending may emerge. Demand for labour is low because firms cannot sell all the goods they wish to sell, and demand for goods is low because workers cannot sell all the labour they wish to sell. The economy can get stuck in a vicious circle in which 'effective' excess demands (that is the excess demands which emerge when rationing constraints are taken into account) are negative, or maybe even zero, everywhere. In contrast to Patinkin's model, there can be no presumption that the economy is moving, even very slowly, towards a full, Walrasian equilibrium. The 'general disequilibrium' literature, therefore, revived the notion that Keynes might have provided a radical alternative to 'classical' ways of thinking about the economy: he had provided the basis for a new way of characterizing equilibrium in economies where Walras's auctioneer was absent.

During the 1970s, however, most economists concluded that it was unacceptable to take prices as given when constructing models of macroeconomic equilibrium. 'Fix-price models', as 'general disequilibrium' models are sometimes called, are defended on the grounds that they show how, if an economy somehow lands up with an inappropriate set of prices, the resulting rationing constraints may cause the resulting equilibrium to be stable. Although prices are initially fixed outside the model, therefore, they may become equilibrium prices. Even if this is a justifiable procedure, however, there is still the problem that the models assume that prices are less responsive than quantities to excess demands. In a world where inflation was the major problem confronting policy-makers, such an assumption was unacceptable. In addition, taking prices as given was hard to reconcile with individuals' optimizing behaviour. In response to the new-classical challenge, therefore, it was necessary to develop new models of unemployment. We find implicit contract models, models of imperfect competition and

10   Compare with the quotation from Bliss on page 118 above.

models of imperfect and sometimes asymmetric information emerging. This is another new conception of Keynesian equilibrium.

At the same time as these attempts to find new ways of explaining unemployment equilibria there have been new other attempts to explain it in terms of disequilibrium. This time, instead of the price-adjustment mechanisms of the IS–LM model the argument is in terms of inflation and the dynamics of the Phillips curve. Layard, Nickell and Jackman (1991), for example, think of demand-deficient (i.e. Keynesian) unemployment as the difference between the actual unemployment rate and the NAIRU, a disequilibrium phenomenon.[11]

## Monetarism[12]

In the late 1940s and for much of the 1950s the quantity theory of money was neglected. The velocity of circulation was clearly not stable and the quantity theory had little to offer by way of competition to Keynesian ideas. The starting point for post-war discussions of the quantity theory is Friedman's attempt to revive it in 1956. The main claim made in this paper and in his work in the early 1960s was that the demand for money function was stable. He inferred from this that there was a close link between the money supply and the level of nominal income. Given that there were important factors that affected the supply of money but not the demand for money, something he established not with theoretical arguments but with his *A Monetary History of the United States* (1963) the conclusion had to be drawn that it was changes in the

[11] It has recently been argued (Gerrard, 1988) that the succession of attempts to reinterpret Keynesian economics has led nowhere. In order to respond to this we need to note that, as mentioned at the start of this section, there are two themes to the *General Theory*. If we see the overthrow of classical theory, root and branch, as Keynes's main task, then Gerrard's conclusion has some force. If on the other hand we see Keynes's main task as being to establish, once and for all, that aggregate demand might be deficient and that we need a theory of aggregate demand if we are to explain unemployment, then we can see enormous progress. Successive attempts to reinterpret the *General Theory* may not have destroyed classical theories, but they have provided numerous new insights into why market failures of the type Keynes was concerned with may occur.

[12] Satisfactory definitions of this term have proved hard to find. For our purposes it is enough to define it very loosely, so as to include opponents of Keynesian demand management policies.

money supply which were the cause of changes in nominal income. Friedman's emphasis on an empirical approach to the quantity theory is shown by his failure to provide a clear statement of his theoretical framework and how it related to that of mainstream economics. When he did provide such a framework (see Gordon, 1974) he produced something substantially similar to the Hicksian IS–LM model. He did this, however, only very belatedly: during the 1950s and early 1960s, when the IS–LM model provided the main framework within which macroeconomic issues were being discussed, he did not use it, preferring instead a more empirical approach.

These arguments about the quantity theory, however, were not enough to establish the case for what is now termed 'monetarist' policies. Here Friedman argued that the lags between the implementation of policy (whether monetary or fiscal) and its effects on the economy were long and variable. This meant that policy could not be used to stabilize the economy. The best policy was to minimize disturbances to the economy by ensuring that monetary policy did not itself become a source of disturbance. A constant growth rate of the money supply would do this.

The emphasis changed completely with the advent of the expectations-augmented Phillips curve and the 'natural rate' hypothesis. This had two implications. The first was that the Phillips curve could no longer be used to determine the inflation rate: any inflation rate is compatible with the natural rate of unemployment. The obvious course was to bring in the quantity theory to determine the inflation rate. The second implication was that the natural rate hypothesis provided, for the first time, a powerful argument against using Keynesian demand management policy to alter the level of employment and output. Attempts to lower unemployment below the natural rate, for example, would produce not merely a higher rate of inflation but accelerating inflation. They would thus eventually be self-defeating. The advent of the natural rate hypothesis, therefore, produced an important change in the way monetarist policies were defended. The nature of the Phillips curve and the formation of expectations became the central issues.

A further change took place with the 'rational expectations revolution'. The new classical macroeconomics provided the basis for a much more thoroughgoing critique of Keynesian policies than had earlier monetarist theories, for the new classical economists were able to show that, given rational expectations and continuous market clearing, effective stabilization policies were not just very difficult to implement:[13] they were impossible. Whatever measures the government might take to stabilize the economy would be undone by the resulting changes in the behaviour of the private sector. The radical nature of the new classical arguments is shown by the fact that some 'monetarists' have moved beyond the quantity theory. New classical theories have been used to argue the case for free banking and even competition in central banking. Some economists have drawn the conclusion that the quantity theory is merely an artefact of a particular system of financial regulation (see, for example, Hall, 1982). Interest in the real bills doctrine has been revived (Sargent and Wallace, 1982). Such theories, which are 'monetarist' in that they imply the absence of any role for stabilization policies, are very different from the monetarism of economists such as Friedman.

### The Keynesian–monetarist controversy

In discussing Keynesianism and monetarism we have implicitly covered some of the main aspects of this controversy. Many of the theories discussed above were developed in order to justify either Keynesian or monetarist policy prescriptions. Consider three of the main examples. (1) The debate over 'Keynes and the classics', which concerned the validity of the Keynesian claim that an unemployment equilibrium might emerge, concerned the central issue in the Keynesian–monetarist controversy: whether or not deviations from full employment were self-correcting. When they found ways of making sense of Keynes's general theory economists were at the same time providing arguments against the quantity theory. (2) Friedman developed the expectations-augmented Phillips curve as an argument against Keynesian demand management policies. Keynesian policies had been based on the

13   This is the 'Lucas' critique of stabilization policy (Lucas, 1976).

presumption that there was a trade-off between unemployment and inflation, the task of policy-makers being to reach the optimal point on the Phillips curve. By showing that there was no usable trade-off Friedman was demonstrating the futility of such policies and the necessity for targeting the growth rate of the money supply. (3) Recent attempts to provide a microeconomic rationale for wage stickiness and to reach Keynesian conclusions through working out the implications of imperfect competition are an attempt to defend a Keynesian position against the arguments used by the new classical school.

Economists have, however, tried to do more than merely develop opposing theoretical positions. There have been several attempts to test the rival theories. Three such attempts will be considered here: the attempts made in the early 1960s to test the Keynesian multiplier theory against the quantity theory; tests of the natural rate hypothesis made around 1970; and some recent attempts to test the new classical theory.[14]

The first important attempt to test Keynesian theory against the quantity theory came in the early 1960s.[15] Friedman and Meiselman tackled the question by comparing the stability of the Keynesian multiplier (the relationship between income and investment) with the stability of the velocity of circulation (the ratio of income to the money supply). They discovered that the velocity of circulation was more stable, a result which they interpreted as justifying the monetarist position. This was, of course, challenged. Ando and Modigliani argued, for example, that all autonomous spending, not simply investment, used to be used in estimating the Keynesian multiplier. Making this and other modifications to Friedman and Meiselman's test they were able to produce the opposite result. Many economists contributed to this

[14] These examples comprise only a tiny fraction of the empirical work that could be discussed here, for virtually all macroeconometric modelling has, at least indirectly, some relevance.

[15] Developments in econometrics and the availability and price of computing resources have clearly had a major impact on the use of econometric techniques to test economic theories. The enormous reduction in the cost of computing power which has taken place since the 1960s goes a long way towards explaining the differences between applied economics then and now.

debate the outcome of which was that the simple reduced-form models economists were using could not possibly discriminate properly between the two theories (see Brainard and Cooper, 1975).[16]

During the 1960s there were many attempts to estimate the Phillips curve. This was important because Friedman's natural rate hypothesis was justified only if wages responded fully to price changes. If they did not (i.e. if there was money illusion) there would still be a long-run trade-off between inflation and unemployment (albeit a much steeper one) and the Keynesian view of policy-making would be vindicated. Thus when Friedman put forward the natural rate hypothesis it was inevitable that econometric methods would be applied to the problem. There was a problem in that inflationary expectations, which played a crucial role in Friedman's theory, were unobservable, but once this was overcome by postulating that expected inflation was a lagged function of actual inflation, tests of his theory became easy to perform. At first a considerable number of studies suggested that wages did not fully adjust to price changes, with the result that the long-run Phillips curve, though steeper than the short-run one, was not vertical. As the 1970s progressed, however, more and more economists came to the conclusion that the Phillips curve was vertical in the long run.

There were a number of reasons why this conclusion was reached. One is that as the 1970s progressed more and more econometricians found vertical long-run Phillips curves. A likely reason for this is that the world was changing in that when inflation rates rose from the late 1960s people became more conscious of it and wages began to respond more fully to price changes. The other main reason is that economists began to accept the theoretical arguments about why the long-run Phillips curve must be vertical. Money illusion was rejected inconsistent with rational, optimizing behaviour. Though econometric evidence played a part this was not a simple case of econometrics settling a theoretical dispute.

Resolving the controversy over the slope of the long-run Phillips curve did not resolve the controversy over the role of stabilization policy, for even if the long-run Phillips curve is vertical, demand

[16] In 1965 an entire issue of the *American Economic Review* was devoted to it.

management can be used to prevent unemployment rising too far above the natural rate.

During the 1970s interest shifted towards testing the hypothesis of rational expectations.[17] This is a hypothesis that can be tested only indirectly, through testing the implications of theories that contain it. For example Lucas (1973) tried to test the prediction that output would be less responsive to unanticipated monetary shocks in countries where the growth rate of the money supply was very erratic.[18] He found evidence to support this prediction. In another study Barro (1977) showed that only unanticipated monetary growth (the residual obtained from a regression of monetary growth on various lagged variables) affected unemployment. He soon extended this result to show that (a) there was 'a one-to-one, contemporaneous link between anticipated money and the price level', and (b) unanticipated money movements affected output faster than prices (1978, p. 549). His evidence supported the new classical theory.

These results were the subject of much research. Some economists managed to produce similar results using different sets of data whilst others produced results which were inconsistent with the new classical theory. These debates covered both technical issues concerning how the tests had been set up and the economic issues involved. It was claimed, for example, that Lucas's results could be explained by either errors in the measurement of income or variables he had omitted from his equations. Barro was criticized for using inappropriate statistical tests: it was argued that although his model fitted the data quite well, it was possible to construct a Keynesian model that fitted the data even better. Another study found that anticipated changes in nominal income had

[17]  A good account of the literature discussed here is Attfield, Demery and Duck (1985, Chapters 7–9).

[18]  The reason for this is that in the new classical model output responds to monetary shocks only because agents cannot distinguish changes in aggregate demand (which should affect only the price level) from changes in demand for their own product (which should affect their production). Loosely, the argument is that if aggregate demand is very variable firms will assume that a higher proportion of observed demand shocks are due to changes in aggregate demand, and they will thus alter their output by a smaller amount than if aggregate demand fluctuates little.

strong effects on output, claiming that Barro's results arose because changes in the money supply had little effect on aggregate demand. Barro's results could thus be given a very 'Keynesian' explanation.

The evidence provided by Lucas and Barro was striking enough to persuade economists to take their models seriously, but subsequent research has thus shown that the evidence for rational expectations is much more mixed. This conclusion is reinforced by evidence from tests of the rational expectations hypothesis in other contexts. The foreign-exchange markets, for example, are markets where one might reasonably expect many of the assumptions made in new classical models to hold. Here, too, tests have proved inconclusive. The main reason why definite results are hard to obtain is that it is impossible to test one hypothesis at a time: tests are always of rational expectations plus a number of other assumptions.[19] Thus even when tests produce clear-cut statistical results it is rarely possible to be sure about exactly what conclusions should be drawn from them.

In discussing tests of Keynesian and monetarist theories we have concentrated on tests of the main assumptions: the multiplier, the quantity theory, the natural rate hypothesis and rational expectations. There have also been extensive discussions of specific historical events. For example, many economists would see the 'monetarist experiment' in Britain after 1979 as demonstrating fairly conclusively that even fully anticipated changes in the money supply can produce large real effects. Because of the large number of factors involved, however, even events as dramatic as this are open to different interpretations.

## CONCLUSIONS

The first lesson to be learned from this survey of macroeconomics since the war is that to tell the story simply in terms of an endless controversy between two firmly entrenched schools of thought, with both sides continually adjusting their theories as soon as their previous positions

---

[19]    In Barro's model, for example, rational expectations was tested jointly with structural neutrality: the assumption that anticipated changes in the money supply affect prices but not output or unemployment.

became untenable, is very misleading. Focusing instead, as we have done here, on the common themes underlying the development of both Keynesian and monetarist ideas shows that this adjustment and re-adjustment of theories has been far from *ad hoc*. The desire to explain macroeconomic phenomena in terms of rational, optimizing behaviour has opened up a large research agenda. This common agenda provides one reason why the controversy between monetarists and Keynesians has, despite popular impressions to the contrary, been far from sterile, new issues being raised at each stage of the debate. As was pointed out in section 3, Keynesianism and monetarism have both changed in response to similar pressures and as the self-understanding of each has changed, so too has the nature of the issues debated.

The second lesson is that we cannot expect empirical evidence ever to provide us with definitive, simple solutions to macroeconomic problems. It has not done so in the past and there is no reason to suppose that it will do so in future. Part of the problem is that policy prescriptions depend not only on beliefs about how the world works, but also on value judgements. Our choice between inflation and unemployment, for example, will depend not only on the constraints imposed by how the economy works, but also on the importance we attach to inflation relative to unemployment. An equally important reason is that macroeconomic phenomena are very complicated: not only do all macroeconomic models ignore certain factors (that is inevitable) but behaviour may change in response to developments in economic theory. Completely general macroeconomic models may simply not be available, the best that is possible being a series of provisional models,[20] each appropriate to specific circumstances.

The third lesson is that, even though it has not been able to resolve disputes completely, attempts to test competing theories have produced a sharpening of the issues.[21] A good example is the recent literature seeking to establish whether unemployment is demand deficient or the result of supply-side factors.[22] Layard, Nickell and Jackman (1991) may

---

[20]   See Hutchison (1981), Chapter 8.
[21]   See Blaug (1980), Chapter 12.
[22]   See also the other papers in the same issue of *Economica*.

not have settled the issue, but their work has made it possible to debate certain issues in a way that purely theoretical arguments would never have done. In addition, empirical evidence has rendered certain simple theories untenable: the Keynesian 'certainties' of the 1950s have been ruled out, as have the crudest monetarist theories; it has been firmly established that supply and demand factors have to be considered and that forward-looking behaviour (not necessarily rational expectations) has to be taken into account, especially in markets such as the foreign exchange market.

# Chapter 9

# A methodological appraisal of Keynesian economics

## INTRODUCTION

### Why is Keynesian economics so interesting from a methodological point of view?

Keynesian economics raises many questions that are of interest to students of economic methodology.

1 The rise of Keynesian economics in the late 1930s and 1940s provides what is frequently argued to be the best available example of a scientific revolution in economics. Why was Keynesian economics so successful in attracting supporters so quickly?

2 Keynesian theories have changed very substantially in the fifty years since *The General Theory*. Why have these theories changed in the way that they have?

3 During the 1970s and early 1980s Keynesian economics was eclipsed first by monetarism and later by the new classical macroeconomics, but it then experienced a renaissance in the late 1980s. What explains first the decline and later the resurgence of Keynesianism?

Answering these questions is a good way to find out about how economic theories change, about the criteria that are used to choose between theories. Although the questions posed above are historical ones, being concerned with the criteria that economists used, either implicitly or explicitly, during the past half-century, they are closely related to methodological questions such as: According to what criteria should we judge macroeconomic theories? In what senses, if any, has there been progress in macroeconomics since Keynes? Whilst an examination of the historical record may not answer these questions, it provides valuable evidence which economists concerned with such issues cannot afford to neglect.

## Why should economists be interested in methodology?

These arguments suggest that Keynesian economics may be a rich area for methodologists, but it does not follow that economists whose concerns are simply to learn about the economy, or to be able to offer solutions to practical problems of economic policy, should think explicitly about methodological issues. Surely, it could be argued, economists should concentrate on doing economics, and not waste valuable resources in thinking about abstract philosophical issues.

Such a view might be thought to have been reinforced by recent developments in the philosophy and sociology of science. Since Thomas Kuhn's *The Structure of Scientific Revolutions* (1962; 1970) there has been a move away from general theories about the nature of science towards analysing the history and sociology of science. In much of this literature it is emphasized that knowledge is constructed, not found: knowledge is the property of specific communities, each having a shared set of presuppositions and understandings, without which knowledge would not be possible. The notion that scientific theories can be evaluated in terms of whether or not they are approaching the truth is held not to be a meaningful question. Applying such arguments to economics, it has been argued that the 'traditional' approach to the history of economic thought, in which we look for progress, criticizing economists for being wrong, and praising them for being right, is worthless, for there is no way we can know whether an economic theory is closer to the truth than any other theory.[1]

For students of macroeconomics, however, such a view is entirely inappropriate. Methodological questions may be difficult, abstract and incapable of being answered definitively but they are unavoidable. If methodological issues are not faced directly, all that happens is that

---

1    For a general critique of this view, see Chapter 3.

methodological decisions are made implicitly, without being discussed. Macroeconomics is a field where it is particularly important to consider methodology explicitly, for without doing so it is impossible to make sense of the many conflicting types of argument that have been used during the half-century since the *General Theory*.

This is not to say that we can simply turn to the philosophy of science and obtain a reliable, 'off-the-shelf' methodological prescription. Far from it. Though economic methodologists may once have talked in such terms, such a position is now hard to defend. Whatever the excesses of the anti-methodological post-modernism of recent years, the point has been made that studies of methodology cannot be divorced from the study of economics itself.

## Appraising economic theories

How might economic theories be appraised? Simply to argue that good economic theories must correspond closely to reality is inadequate. We cannot observe the real world independently of our theories, so it is not an operational criterion. In addition, economic theories are, as Friedman emphasized forty years ago (Friedman, 1953), always inaccurate representations of reality. This is particularly obvious in macro-economics, which deals only with aggregates. We need more specific criteria. In this paper focus on two: the criterion that theories should correspond with our *a priori* beliefs; and the criterion that theories should survive attempts to test them.

The *a priori* approach has a long history in economics, the classic statement being Robbins's *An Essay on the Nature and Significance of Economic Science* (1932), a work which he saw as making precise the nature of propositions in economic theory which had already been established, not as putting forward any new approach to economics. Robbins argued that the fundamental aspect of economic problems was scarcity, defining economics as 'the science which studies human behaviour as a relationship between ends and scarce means which have alternative uses' (Robbins, 1932, p. 16). A fundamental assumption was that individuals have preferences which they can, and do, arrange in order. He argued that though people might dispute the precise logical status of this assumption, no one would question its universal applicability: it is a generalization 'known to us by immediate acquaintance' (1932, p. 105) for which we do not need empirical evidence.

The simplest version of falsificationism is usually termed naive falsificationism. This involves the notion that theories should be tested by comparing their predictions with empirical evidence, with theories being rejected when they fail such a test. This approach was introduced into economics by Hutchison (1937). Taking up the logical positivists' distinction between analytical statements (tautologies, true by definition) and empirical statements (which could be falsified by empirical evidence), Hutchison criticized virtually the whole of economic theory for being tautological. Though Samuelson drew very different conclusions concerning its implications for economic theory, this was similar to what Samuelson (1947) termed 'operationalism', where operational theories were defined as theories which might conceivably be refuted.

Though it stemmed from very different philosophical roots,[2] Friedman's 'methodology of positive economics' (1953), with its emphasis on the importance of testing predictions and on the unimportance of unrealistic assumptions, provided an enormous stimulus to falsificationist ideas.[3] Such ideas were also boosted when economists turned, somewhat belatedly, to Popper (see de Marchi, 1988). For Lipsey and his colleagues at LSE in the 1960s, Popper's methodology of falsificationism provided new ideas about how to do economics that were not provided by earlier writers.

More important than naive falsificationism is sophisticated falsificationism, associated with some of Popper's later writing, and above all with Lakatos (1970). This involves appraising theories not simply according to whether they have survived attempts to falsify

[2]   Hirsch and de Marchi (1990) have argued that Friedman's starting point is emphatically that of a working economist, not someone familiar with the philosophical ideas. Insofar as his position can be tied to a specific philosophical position, it is the pragmatism of Dewey, not the falsificationism of Popper.

[3]   The story has been deliberately told in this way to make the point that falsificationism is, in economics at least, not synonymous with a Popperian approach.

them, but according to their ability to generate novel facts: to predict facts that were not used in constructing the theory.[4] Lakatos's approach also involves switching attention away from individual theories, to 'research programmes'. A research programme comprises a 'hard core' of provisionally accepted assumptions (not open to empirical testing for as long as the programme continues), a 'protective belt' of assumptions that supporters of the programme are free to change, and sets of 'positive' and 'negative heuristics' – rules governing the way theories are to be developed. This methodology recognizes that there is an important conventional element in theories, and that if there is an inconsistency between theory and evidence, theories will often be modified so as to fit the evidence: they will not be abandoned. The key question is whether modifications to a programme result in the generation of novel facts which are then corroborated (what Lakatos terms a 'progressive' programme) or whether modifications merely succeed in patching up a theory so as to deal with known anomalies, not predicting anything new (a 'degenerating' programme).[5]

## THE RISE OF KEYNESIAN ECONOMICS

### The Keynesian revolution

Keynes's *General Theory* was spectacularly and unprecedentedly successful. As Blaug has put it,

certainly never before and perhaps never since has the economics profession been won over so rapidly and so massively to a new economic theory. Those who lived through it felt themselves

---

[4]    Novel facts have been defined in a variety of ways, this definition being the Worrall–Zahar one. The exact definition is not important for the present argument.

[5]    Lakatos also developed what is usually called the methodology of *historical* research programmes. According to this, methodologies should be appraised according to their ability to explain actual scientific practice. If scientists repeatedly moved out of degenerating research programmes into progressive ones, that would be evidence for the methodology of scientific research programmes. If they did the opposite, it would be evidence against it.

impelled to repudiate virtually the whole of received economic doctrine, and many took up the Keynesian system with an ardor that is more commonly associated with religious conversions.

(Blaug, 1991b, p. 171)

It is hard to avoid the conclusion that Keynesian economics is an outstanding example of successful economics. It is, however, much more difficult to agree on exactly what that success comprised.

An opinion which would command widespread support is that of J. M. Clark. In a letter to Keynes, he wrote:

It seems to me that what I call the 'income-flow analysis', of which yours is the most noted presentation, has done something which has not been done in comparable degree since Ricardo and Marx: namely, constructed a coherent logical theoretical system or formula having the quality of a mechanism, growing directly out of current conditions and problems which are of paramount importance and furnishing a key to working out definite answers in terms of policy.

(Keynes, 1971–83, XXIII, p. 191)

For Clark, Keynes's theory provided a device that could be used for solving important problems. One could further argue that Keynes's explanation of unemployment was deeper, simpler, more general and explained known facts (unemployment) better than the classical theories it displaced.[6] One could also argue that Keynesian economics opened up vast areas of research, presenting new concepts that cried out for theoretical and empirical analysis; that it came at the right time in relation to developments in national income accounting and econometrics.

These are powerful arguments for which much evidence can be found, and they tell us much about the nature of Keynes's success. They do not, however, get to the heart of the matter, for they do not establish that there was any empirical progress: that Keynesian economics was in any sense nearer the truth than was classical economics. New mathematical theories may be deeper, simpler and more general than

6    Cf. Hands (1990, p. 78).

their predecessors, but say nothing about the world. To appraise Keynesian economics we need to evaluate it according to methodological criteria.

If we were to adopt an *a priorist* methodology, we would wish to ask whether Keynesian economics were based on more satisfactory axioms than classical theory. One might, for example, argue that the 'fundamental psychological law' underlying Keynes's consumption function was self-evidently superior to the classical theory whereby savings depended on the rate of interest; that liquidity preference was clearly an important phenomenon; or that it was natural to assume inelastic expectations. Keynesian economics could then be defended on the grounds that its premises reflected reality better than did those of classical economics. Such an approach, however, begs the question of how we can know such premises are better than alternative ones. There is the danger that we end up simply claiming that everything makes better sense: a purely subjective criterion.

Can Keynesian economics, therefore, be defended on naive falsificationist grounds? Can we, for example, argue that classical economics was falsified by the experience of mass unemployment and the failure of deflation to restore full employment? Unfortunately, we cannot. It is clear that mass unemployment did create a problem for pre-Keynesian economists, for classical economics placed great emphasis on the self-adjusting properties of the market. It is completely wrong, however, to suggest that classical economics could not explain unemployment. There was a plethora of explanations: from Hayekian over-investment theory to theories of structural unemployment.

## A Lakatosian perspective

To appraise Keynesian economics we should instead turn to sophisticated falsificationism, asking whether or not Keynesian economics was progressive in the sense of predicting novel facts which were subsequently corroborated. The answer is that it did. Blaug (1991b) argues persuasively that the central prediction contained in the *General Theory* was that the multiplier was greater than one, and that as a consequence deficit-financed fiscal policy could be used to restore full employment. Whatever may be the current opinion on the truth of this prediction, economists believed it at the time. The fall in unemployment during the war was read as corroborating evidence, as was the period of, by pre-war standards, unbelievably high unemployment during the 1950s. One of the clearest illustrations of the progressive nature of Keynesian economics was provided when Keynes applied his income–expenditure framework to the problem of wartime inflation. The concept of the inflation gap was successfully used to design policies to finance the war without the inflationary consequences that were experienced in the First World War. The success of such policies could be seen as providing corroborating evidence for Keynesian theories: as evidence that the programme was empirically, as well as theoretically, progressive.

## THE EVOLUTION OF KEYNESIAN ECONOMICS

### The neoclassical synthesis

One feature of the Keynesian revolution is that the *General Theory* was immediately subject to an explicit process of reinterpretation. There were a several reasons for this. (1) The book contained many loose ends, and many different lines of argument. It was not immediately clear which were the ones that mattered. (2) Keynes attacked a target labelled 'classical' economics, but people were not clear about what this was, or about just how Keynes's theory differed from it. Keynes's main example of classical economics, Pigou's *Theory of Unemployment* (1933) was a modern, mathematical work which was itself not widely understood. (3) Keynes had introduced new and unfamiliar concepts, such as liquidity preference, which were not understood. (4) The work of Hicks (1939) and Samuelson (1947) was reviving interest in general equilibrium theory. It was thus natural to interpret Keynesian economics in terms of general equilibrium theory by isolating from the *General Theory* a central core of equations that could be interpreted as market equilibrium conditions. Though his treatment was but one of many (see Young, 1987), the one that became most widely accepted was that of Hicks (1937), with its simple diagrammatic apparatus of what have, following Hansen (1953), come to be called 'IS' and 'LM' curves.[7]

Whilst the IS–LM model can be seen as involving an interpretation of Keynes in terms of general equilibrium theory, it did not require such an interpretation.[8] By the 1950s, however, Keynesian economics was explicitly being interpreted in a general equilibrium framework.[9] Perhaps most significantly, economists were paying much more attention to the microeconomic foundations of Keynesian phenomena. The classic example of this phase in the interpretation of Keynesian economics is Don Patinkin's *Money, Interest and Prices* (1956; second edition, 1965), in which explicit models of household and firm behaviour, based on maximizing behaviour, underlay all macroeconomic relationships. Patinkin argued that Keynesian economics was the economics of disequilibrium, in which firms' demand for labour depends on the output they are able to sell, and becomes relevant when the equilibrating forces are too weak to restore full employment 'within a socially acceptable period of time' (Patinkin, 1965, p. 343).

At the same time, economists were seeking to develop the microeconomic foundations of the individual components of the Keynesian system: in particular the consumption and demand for money functions.[10] The need for this arose, at least in part, because Keynes's almost Marshallian methodology was very different from the methodology of his mainstream interpreters. Increasingly, during the post-war period, economists sought to interpret behaviour in terms of utility-maximizing consumers and profit-maximizing firms. Keynes's informal justification of the consumption function as 'a fundamental psychological law' came to be regarded as inadequate.

---

7   Hicks labelled the curves 'SI' and 'LL'.

8   Hicks (1974) has argued that it is a very different formulation of Keynesian economics from that contained in *Value and Capital*.

9   Modigliani has argued that his mid-1950s model was distinguished from the one in his 1944 paper by being explictly based on general equilibrium. See Young (1987, p. 124).

10   The other components of Keynes's system were taken from 'classical' theory. The marginal efficiency of investment was similar to Irving Fisher's rate of return on capital; the labour demand curve was based on marginal productivity.

To a great extent these developments can be explained in terms of an *a priori* view that behaviour must be seen in terms of maximizing behaviour. Some developments, however, were related to attempts to understand data. The theory of the consumption function being the classic example. When Kuznets constructed data on aggregate consumption over long periods of time, it became clear that the ratio of consumption to income was approximately constant in the long run, a result inconsistent with the consumption function Keynes had postulated in the *General Theory*. Applying standard microeconomic theory of choice over time produced the life-cycle and permanent income theories, which correctly predicted the relationship between the long- and short-run consumption functions. Friedman (1957) also used the theory to predict a wide range of other facts about consumption, showing that they corroborated the theory. It could thus be argued that the neoclassical synthesis was a progressive research programme in the sense of Lakatos. The long period of what, for many countries, was unparalleled growth and prosperity also provided evidence that Keynesian economic policies worked. Many economists, for example, believed that Kennedy's expansion of aggregate demand in the early 1960s provided clear evidence for Keynesian theory: that predictions made with the theory concerning the impact of fiscal expansion were correct.

## Reinterpretations of Keynesian economics

During the late 1960s and the 1970s many economists became dissatisfied with the interpretation of Keynes offered by the neo-classical synthesis. The reason was that such an interpretation did not seem compatible with Keynes's claim to be providing a theory that was more general than the classical theory. Keynesian economics might deal with the case that was relevant for policy-making but, from a theoretical point of view, it simply covered the special case where money wages were sticky. If this were a correct interpretation of Keynes, it was hard to see why Keynes or his followers had made such a fuss about the *General Theory*.

Though Patinkin had moved towards an interpretation of Keynesian economics as concerning the economics of disequilibrium, the seminal contribution to the reappraisal of Keynesian economics in the 1960s and early 1970s was by Clower (1965). Clower argued that the conventional theory of household demand was inappropriate in a situation where households could not sell as much labour as they wanted to sell. If there was unemployment, households would face an additional constraint: that purchases of consumption goods must not exceed *realized* sales of labour. This was Clower's 'dual-decision hypothesis' – that having failed to sell as much labour as they hoped, households had a further decision to make. Either Keynes had a dual-decision hypothesis at the back of his mind, Clower argued, or the *General Theory* was theoretical nonsense.

This idea of Clower's was taken up by Leijonhufvud in *On Keynesian Economics and the Economics of Keynes* (1968). In this book he argued for a new interpretation of the *General Theory* ('the economics of Keynes') that was very different from the neoclassical synthesis ('Keynesian economics'). Keynesian economics, he argued, was more general than classical economics because it was about what happened when there was no Walrasian auctioneer to coordinate transactions. If there were no auctioneer, transactions would inevitably take place at disequilibrium prices, and quantity constraints such as those analysed by Clower would come into effect. Such constraints would be reinforced, Leijonhufvud argued, by inelastic expectations, notably concerning interest rates. If expectations were inelastic, interest rates would change very slowly, and together with the effects of quantity rationing this would impede or even eliminate any forces working to restore full employment.

At the same time as Leijonhufvud was exploring an alternative way of thinking about Keynesian economics, other economists were constructing models which incorporated Clower's dual-decision hypothesis and similar quantity constraints. The earliest was Solow and Stiglitz (1968), but the most well known were probably Barro and Grossman (1971) and Malinvaud (1977). These models made the assumption that quantities reacted to changes in market conditions faster than did prices, with the result that the short-run equilibrium was one in which prices could be taken as parameters, with the level of output and employment being determined in a Keynesian manner.

The impetus underlying these 'fix-price', 'rationing' or 'disequilibrium' models was primarily theoretical. It was the idea that economists ought to be analysing what happened when markets were not in equilibrium. Beyond that, the literature shared with the neoclassical synthesis the notion that agents ought to be modelled as maximizing utility or profits. This is not to say that there was no interest in prediction: disequilibrium models provided enormous scope for predicting the effects of policy changes. By the late 1970s, however, this approach to macroeconomics was generally viewed unfavourably. The main reason is that in the 1970s, with the world economy experiencing high inflation, the assumption that prices adjusted to disequilibrium more slowly than quantities seemed hard to defend. Even though disequilibrium models predicted some novel facts, and were not completely unsuccessful, they were perceived as being irrelevant to the problem of stagflation.

### The monetarist–Keynesian controversy

During the 1960s, Keynesian economics was challenged by monetarism. This challenge was not primarily theoretical, but empirical. Milton Friedman (1956) had reinterpreted the quantity theory, previously considered discredited by evidence on the extreme instability of the velocity of circulation, by arguing that it should be viewed as a theory of the demand for money. He argued that the demand function for money was a stable function of a limited number of variables (mainly nominal income) and that the length and variability of the lags involved meant that stabilization policy was unworkable, more likely to destabilize than to stabilize the economy. In a series of papers during the late 1950s and 1960s he and his associates presented evidence to reinforce this claim (see Friedman, 1969). One of the most dramatic papers was in 1959 when he managed to explain fluctuations in velocity by assuming demand for money was a function not of current income, but of permanent income. Not only did this provide a link with his theory of consumption, but by doing this he provided evidence for his claim that the link between money and income was stable only in the long run.

At the same time, Keynesians started using the Phillips curve to tackle problems of inflation and unemployment. The origin of the Phillips curve was not theoretical but empirical: it described an empirical relationship between inflation and unemployment that Phillips (1958) had discovered, which seemed, in the UK, to have remained stable for a century. Samuelson and Solow (1960) soon interpreted it in such a way as it could be used as a tool for designing macroeconomic policy, and Lipsey (1960) provided a theoretical rationale for the curve, in which unemployment was seen as a measure of excess demand for labour. In their hands, the Phillips curve seemed a natural extension to the Keynesianism of the neoclassical synthesis.

During this period monetarism and Keynesianism were hotly debated. It was taken for granted that empirical evidence *ought* to be decisive. There were thus many attempts to test Keynesianism against monetarism, and to obtain reliable estimates of the key macroeconomic parameters on which the theoretical arguments were believed to rely, particularly the interest elasticity of demand for money and the multiplier. The Keynesian response to the monetarist critique was, therefore, substantially an empirical one. The monetarist challenge did not, therefore, result in any fundamental change in the Keynesian theoretical position. Perhaps the best, and most widely cited, example of the controversy was the debate initiated by Friedman and Meiselman (1963) when they argued that quantity theory of money could be tested against the Keynesian theory by comparing the stability of the Keynesian (expenditure) multiplier with the stability of the money multiplier (the velocity of circulation). Friedman and Meiselman argued that the Keynesian multiplier was less stable than the money multiplier, implying that the quantity theory could predict changes in income more reliably than the Keynesian theory. In response, Ando and Modigliani (1965) argued that when the variables involved were defined in a more appropriate manner, the reverse conclusion could be obtained. Similarly, monetarist arguments such as Friedman's claim that the lag involved in monetary policy was too long and variable for monetary policy to be usable to stabilize the economy, were not seen as raising any fundamental theoretical issues for Keynesian theory. Indeed, when Friedman eventually chose to respond to the challenge of describing his theoretical framework, he used the IS–LM model.

## THE DECLINE AND RESURGENCE OF KEYNESIAN ECONOMICS

### The demise of Keynesianism, 1967 to the mid-1980s

The nature of the debate changed after 1967. Friedman's presidential address to the American Economic Association (Friedman, 1968), and Phelps (1967) introduced the profession to the expectations-augmented Phillips curve and the natural rate of unemployment. This provided a new theoretical argument against Keynesian theory: that when proper account was taken of expectations, and the fact that wage bargainers were concerned with real, not nominal wages, policy-makers could achieve lasting reductions in unemployment or interest rates only if they were prepared to tolerate accelerating inflation.

At first the reaction to this challenge was empirical. Attempts were made to estimate the expectations-augmenting Phillips curve on the assumption that it was of the form

$$\pi = \alpha\pi^e + f(U),$$

where $\pi$ is the inflation rate, $\pi^e$ is the expected inflation rate and $U$ is the unemployment rate. At first, empirical evidence suggested that $\alpha$ was less than 1, which meant that there was a trade-off between inflation and unemployment, even in the long run. Over time, however, estimates of $\alpha$ increased. It is plausible that with increased awareness of inflation, the responsiveness of inflation to inflationary expectations did actually increase, though other explanations are possible (improved econometric techniques or economists looking for a coefficient of unity). More important than this, however, was the change which took place in economists' attitudes. Increasingly it came to be argued that the value of $\alpha$ *must*, on purely theoretical grounds, be unity: it would be irrational for it to be anything different. Less importance was attached to empirical evidence on its value.

During the 1970s macroeconomics came to be dominated by the new classical macroeconomics. The proponents of the new classical macroeconomics made some bold predictions, and produced empirical evidence which appeared to corroborate them. Two of the main ones were Lucas's prediction that the responsiveness of output to unanticipated changes in aggregate demand would be lower in countries where aggregate demand was more volatile (Lucas, 1973), and Barro's prediction that only unanticipated monetary growth would affect the level of unemployment (Barro, 1977). The programme was undoubtedly viewed as being empirically progressive in Lakatos's sense. The main impetus, however, was theoretical, for the assumption that all opportunities for profitable trade were realized was taken as axiomatic. Lucas argued that he could conceive of no other way of making sense of behaviour. From this perspective, Keynesian economics was dismissed not because it could not explain observed behaviour, but because it did not make sense: it was rejected on *a priori* grounds. When coupled with the crisis produced as policy-makers tried to grapple with rising inflation and unemployment after 1973, the result was an almost complete discrediting of Keynesian economics.

**The Keynesian recovery**

The late 1980s, however, saw a revival of interest in Keynesian economics, one of the main stimuli being the persistence of high unemployment rates in Europe. This took the form of a proliferation of theories, based on maximizing behaviour, which could explain the failure of wages to adjust to clear the labour market. The earliest attempts to defend Keynesian economics against the new classical assault had centred on union bargaining and long-term contracts. Long-term contracts, however, were not regarded as a satisfactory solution, partly because they are not much in evidence outside the USA, but mainly because they raise the question of why, if long-term contracts are inefficient, different contracts (whether short term, or involving index-linking) would not be negotiated instead. Keynesian economists have instead turned to efficiency wage theories and models of hysteresis, transactions costs and imperfect competition.

The reason why these new theories have re-awakened interest in Keynesian economics is that they provide an alternative conception of how markets work. In Weiss's model (1980), for example, cutting wage rates will cause the best workers to quit, the result being that firms may have an incentive to keep wages high, even if there is unemployment. The literature on transactions costs shows how transactions costs arise from the way markets are organized. For example, if markets are thin, it will be costly to contact a potential trading partner. When the employment rate falls, it becomes more costly for workers to contact a potential employer – there are fewer around (see Diamond, 1984; Howitt, 1986). In such models, as in imperfect-competition models (Hart, 1982; Marris, 1991), there are frequently multiplier effects and multiple equilibria.

## Keynesianism versus the new classical macroeconomics

Though they claimed that Keynesian predictions of the effects of monetary and fiscal expansion had been shown, by the experience of the 1970s, to be 'wildly incorrect', the new classical attack on Keynesian economics had a much higher theoretical component than did the earlier monetarist attack: Keynesian theory was, it was claimed, 'fundamentally flawed' (Lucas and Sargent, 1979, p. 295).   The assumption of individual optimizing behaviour and, derived from this, the assumptions of market-clearing and rational expectations, are taken as necessary components of any adequate theory. The Keynesian response, in contrast, is primarily empirical: that the new classical macroeconomics cannot explain observed facts. Blinder, for example, argues that the success of the new classical macroeconomics 'is testimony to Lucas's keen intellect and profound influence, not to economists' respect for facts' (Blinder, 1987, p. 132). Empirical evidence, he argues, 'is overwhelmingly against the RE [rational expectations] hypothesis'; simple facts about the labour market (such as the fact that it is layoffs, not quits that rise in a recession) facts suggest that unemployment is overwhelmingly involuntary and unlikely to be alleviated by deflation; persistent high unemployment (especially in Europe during the 1980s) renders the natural rate hypothesis implausible; the Phillips curve is surprisingly stable; and anticipated monetary changes do affect output. In addition, many Keynesians question the need for rigorous microfoundations of the type the new classicals insist upon: they argue that rigour can be achieved only at the cost of making arbitrary assumptions which are inconsistent with empirical evidence, and for which there is no justification (Tobin, 1987).

## KEYNESIAN ECONOMICS AND EMPIRICAL EVIDENCE

Post-war macroeconomics can readily be portrayed as having been dominated by the drive to explain macroeconomic phenomena in terms of individual, optimizing behaviour. Such an imperative explains many aspects of the history of Keynesian economics: the creation of the neoclassical synthesis in the 1950s; the emergence of fix-price models in the 1960s; the abandonment of Keynesian ideas in the fact of the new classical onslaught in the 1970s; and the resurgence of Keynesianism in the 1980s. Keynesian economics appears as having been caught up in the post-war fashion for Walrasian, or neo-Walrasian, formal general equilibrium modelling. Yet even if we accept that this aspect of the history of Keynesian economics is the dominant one, we do not have to opt for an *a priorist* interpretation. We can view the assumption of rational behaviour as part of the hard core of a neo-Walrasian research programme, of which the most important positive heuristic is to explain economic phenomena in terms of rational, maximizing behaviour. The point of such a Lakatosian interpretation is that the programme is judged not according to the acceptability of its hard-core postulates, but according to its ability to generate novel facts which are then corroborated. It is possible to argue, as is done in Chapter 10, that, at least since the 1950s, Keynesianism and the new classical macro-economics both formed part of the same research programme, and that the programme has been progressive. For much of the period, it has been the Keynesian element of the programme that has been progressive, but for a brief period in the late 1970s the progressive element was the new classical macroeconomics. Such an interpretation, explored more fully in Chapter 10, explains much of what happened.

Such an interpretation, however, ignores the fact that much Keynesian economics does not fit into this mould. Keynes himself was not a Walrasian, and his work did not conform to either the hard core or the heuristics of the neo-Walrasian programme. Furthermore, though many of them undertake some work that can be classified as neo-Walrasian, many leading Keynesians (such as Blinder and Tobin) openly dispute the necessity of adhering to the hard core of rational maximizing behaviour. Their attitudes and assumptions seem much closer to Keynes than to Lucas. It thus seems natural to appraise Keynesian economics as a programme in its own right, rather than as a part of an overlapping neo-Walrasian programme. We have already argued that Keynesian economics was progressive in its early years. From the 1960s, and especially in the 1970s, it could be argued that Keynesian economics had begun to degenerate. There were new predictions, but Keynesian economics was on the defensive, relying on what seemed *ad hoc* assumptions to deal with anomalous empirical evidence, such as the breakdown of the Phillips curve. In contrast, the novel facts predicted by Phelps and Friedman were dramatically corroborated by the events of the early 1970s. For several years the new classical macroeconomics, which grew out of this work, was believed by many to be empirically as well as theoretically progressive. Interest in Keynesian economics fell. During the 1980s, however, the situation changed. Accumulating econometric evidence cast doubt on many of the predictions generated by the new classical theory, whilst the experience of persistent, high unemployment, especially in Europe, presented the new classical macroeconomics with the problems as serious as those faced by Keynesian economics in the 1970s.

## CONCLUSIONS

Underconsumptionist theories, which sought to explain the occurrence of long periods of low business activity and high unemployment, have a long history. For much of the past two centuries, however, they have led an uneasy existence on the fringes of economics. Whilst many important economists were prepared to entertain such ideas, they minimized their significance, the classic example being John Stuart Mill. In contrast, spending one's way out of a depression is, intuitively, such a powerful and plausible idea that it has inspired what Keynes called a brave army of heretics, prepared to defend it. Keynes's achievement was to bring such ideas firmly into the mainstream of economic thinking, a place where they remained until the monetarists and the new classicals sought to eradicate them in the 1970s. Keynesian ideas are, however, irrepressible, the obituaries written by Lucas, Sargent and others having proved premature.[11]

Tobin sums up very clearly the case for Keynesian economics:

> Keynesian economics has a future because it is essential to the explanation and understanding of a host of observations and experiences, past and present, that alternative macroeconomic approaches do not illuminate. That includes the bearing of uncertainties and expectations on economic activity. It definitely includes business fluctuations, and fiscal and monetary policies.
>
> (Tobin, 1987, p. 23)

Thus although purely theoretical considerations, in particular the imperative to explain macroeconomic phenomena in terms of individuals' optimizing behaviour, have had a profound impact on the evolution of Keynesian economics, the main argument for Keynesian economics has always been its ability to explain certain macroeconomic phenomena that other approaches to macroeconomics have not been able to explain.

---

[11]   Lucas and Sargent, writing at a time when, in their own words, 'the halcyon days of Keynesian economics' were difficult to recall without conscious effort, were unequivocal in their claims: 'That these predictions were wildly incorrect and that the doctrine on which they were based [Keynesian economics] is fundamentally flawed are not simple matters of fact. ... The task now facing contemporary students of the business cycle is to sort through the wreckage, determining which features of that remarkable event called the Keynesian revolution can be salvaged and put to good use, and which others must be discarded' (1979, pp. 295–6).

# Chapter 10

# The neo-Walrasian research programme in macroeconomics*

## THE PROBLEM

The notion that contemporary macroeconomics can be viewed as part of a 'neo-Walrasian' research programme or something very similar is hardly novel or, perhaps, very controversial. The desire of contemporary macroeconomists to ground their theories in individual optimizing behaviour and to have a coherent microeconomic foundation for what they do, the main characteristic of neo-Walrasian economics, is almost too obvious to require comment. The issue of how far contemporary macroeconomics can legitimately be viewed as part of such a Lakatosian scientific research programme and the process whereby this came about have, however, never been properly investigated. The purpose of this paper is to make a first attempt at filling this gap.[1]

---

* This paper is a greatly revised version of part of a paper presented to a seminar on 'Post War Economic Thinking and its Relevance for Policy' at the Katholieke Universiteit, Leuven, in May 1988. I am indebted to the participants in this seminar, and to Mark Blaug, Tony Brewer and Neil de Marchi for helpful comments on various drafts of this chapter. Special thanks are due to Roy Weintraub whose extensive criticisms and invaluable advice led me to modify the original draft very substantially. Needless to say, none of them should be held responsible for the use I have made of their ideas.

[1] Most accounts of macroeconomics since Keynes either discuss only a part of the story (e.g. Leijonhufvud, 1976; Weintraub, 1979; Gerrard, 1988) or discuss it in terms of monetarism and Keynesianism (e.g. Blaug, 1980, 1985; Backhouse, 1985). As I argue in

The thesis put forward in this paper is that mainstream macroeconomics since Keynes[2] can be viewed in terms of the extension of the neo-Walrasian research programme to encompass theories which previously lay outside its domain and to explain an increasing range of macroeconomic phenomena.[3] The starting point (in section 2) is the definition of the hard-core and heuristics of the neo-Walrasian research programme, together with an explanation of what it means to talk about a research programme's being extended to encompass theories developed outside the programme.[4] We then go on (in section 3) to provide a rational reconstruction of the history of macroeconomics since Keynes. After considering, in section 4, some of the issues involved, we discuss, in section 5, some of the novel facts predicted by the neo-Walrasian research programme. Section 6 tackles the all-important issue of whether or not the research programme is progressive. Conclusions are drawn in the final section.

## THE NEO-WALRASIAN RESEARCH PROGRAMME

The best starting point is Weintraub's definition of the neo-Walrasian research programme (Weintraub, 1985, p. 109). He defines six hard-core propositions.

HC1    There exist economic agents.

HC2    Agents have preferences over outcomes.

(Continued from previous page)

Chapter 8, such approaches are legitimate but they play down important aspects of the way macroeconomic theory, both Keynesian and monetarist, has evolved.

[2]    Both post-Keynesian and 'Austrian' economics, for example, fall outside the scope of this paper.

[3]    In addition to the particular research programmes with which he was concerned, Lakatos recognized that science as a whole could be seen as one huge research programme (1970, p. 47). The neo-Walrasian programme proposed here clearly comes in between these two levels.

[4]    The conventional way to view such issues is to see them in terms of the 'victory' of one scientific research programme over another. Though it might be possible to adopt such an approach it is not followed here: the difficult task of defining a 'Marshallian' research programme (or whatever research programme Keynes was working within) would, even if it were successfully pursued, distract us from the main task.

HC3    Agents independently optimize subject to constraints.

HC4    Choices are made in inter-related markets.

HC5    Agents have full relevant knowledge.

HC6    Observable economic outcomes are coordinated, so they must be discussed with reference to equilibrium states.

There are also positive and negative heuristics such as the following.

PH1    Go forth and construct theories in which agents optimize.

PH2    Construct theories that make predictions about equilibrium states.

NH1    Do not construct theories in which irrational behaviour plays any role.

NH2    Do not construct theories in which equilibrium has no meaning.

NH3    Do not test hard-core propositions.

This definition of a neo-Walrasian research programme was designed for analysing the evolution of general equilibrium theory, something Weintraub manages to do very successfully. If we are to analyse the progress of macroeconomics since Keynes in terms of the neo-Walrasian research programme, however, we need to define the programme a little more broadly. In particular, propositions HC5 and HC6 need to be changed. In addition, certain other heuristics, not stated by Weintraub, need to be made explicit.

The need to drop the assumption of 'full relevant knowledge' is obvious, for limited knowledge is a key factor in many present-day macroeconomic models.[5] Even models which assume rational expectations are not assuming perfect foresight. We could replace HC5

---

[5]    It can be retained, but only at the cost of reinterpreting 'relevant' in such a way as to deprive it of any meaning. Such a strategy fails to capture the two crucial characteristics concerning assumptions about knowledge in neo-Walrasian models: that agents must be in a position to be able to act rationally; and that assumptions must be such as to render formal mathematical analysis possible.

with a weaker hard-core proposition, but it seems better to replace it with an additional positive heuristic:

> PH3    Construct theories in which agents have a well-defined set of information about relevant phenomena.[6]

Proposition HC6 is more difficult, for a number of reasons. In the literature Weintraub was concerned with, equilibrium was a clearly defined concept. In macroeconomics, on the other hand, there are two problems with the concept of equilibrium. One is that the term equilibrium is used in a number of different ways. The other is that much macroeconomics has been concerned with disequilibrium, and with the failure of the market to coordinate economic activities. It would, of course, be possible to define the terms 'equilibrium' and 'co-ordination' in such a way as to render HC6 a hard-core proposition for mainstream macroeconomics, but it seems preferable to replace it with something less misleading. Finding an acceptable alternative is difficult, for proposition HC6 covers two aspects of neo-Walrasian economics: the notion that markets coordinate the actions of different individuals and the idea that we should, in our theories, allow for the effects of market interactions working themselves through. The best solution is simply to drop HC6. The first aspect of HC6 is already covered by HC4. The second aspect can be picked up by modifying PH2 (which has to be modified anyway for the same reasons as we have to drop HC6). A suitable modification is to replace HC6 with the following:

> PH2*    Specify the model-specific meanings of equilibrium and disequilibrium and analyse the model in terms of these.

One of the characteristics of neo-Walrasian economics, which distinguishes it from much earlier economic writing, is that formal models are used. In his appraisal of general equilibrium theory it was not necessary for Weintraub to make this explicit: the whole literature took this for granted. In macroeconomics, however, this is not the case,

---

[6]    It could be argued that HC5 used to belong to the hard core of the neo-Walrasian research programme, but that it was dropped, being replaced with PH3. This change represented a progressive problemshift. It is discussed further below.

many economists having worked with much more rough and ready methods. To define the neo-Walrasian research programme properly, therefore, we need to add to the above list of positive heuristics.

> PH4    Construct    fully-specified,    consistent    models, simplifying where necessary in order to be able to do this, and draw only those conclusions which can be proved to be implied by the models.
>
> PH5    Specify the rules governing the interaction of agents (in terms of game theory, make the game explicit).

In many cases PH5 implies competition, but it is obviously more general. Some equilibrium element is of course implied by the assumption that agents optimize: in this limited sense, therefore, equilibrium is implied by HC2 and PH1.

If we accept these modifications to Weintraub's definition of the neo-Walrasian research programme we have a programme with the following hard core and positive heuristics (the negative heuristics are exactly the same as for Weintraub). Note that the positive heuristics have been placed in a more sensible order and have been renumbered (subsequent references all refer to this new list).

> HC1    There exist economic agents.
>
> HC2    Agents have preferences over outcomes.
>
> HC3    Agents independently optimize subject to constraints.
>
> HC4    Choices are made in inter-related markets.
>
> PH1'    (PH4) Construct fully specified, consistent models, simplifying where necessary in order to be able to do this, and draw only those conclusions which can be proved to be implied by the models.
>
> PH2'    (PH2*) Specify the model-specific meanings of equilibrium and disequilibrium and analyse the model in terms of these.
>
> PH3'    (PH1) Construct theories in which agents optimize subject to constraints.

PH4'    (PH5) Specify the rules governing the interaction of
        agents (in terms of game theory, make the game
        explicit).

PH5'    (PH3) Construct theories in which agents have a well-
        defined set of information about relevant phenomena.

This is slightly, but significantly, broader than the research programme
suggested by Weintraub and it can be used to make sense of the main
developments in mainstream macroeconomics since Keynes. General
equilibrium theory, as analysed by Weintraub, can easily be seen as a
part of this research programme. Overall the research programme
presented here has a smaller hard core and a longer list of positive
heuristics than Weintraub's: in other words, we are placing a greater
emphasis on the neo-Walrasian research programme as a research
strategy rather than a set of assumptions about the world. It has to be
said, however, that the differences are very slight. Whether we use the
term neo-Walrasian to denote the broader programme suggested here,
or the 'sub-programme' described by Weintraub, is essentially arbitrary
and is of no importance.

Finally, before going on to consider the history of macroeconomics we
need to consider the notion that a scientific research programme may be
extended to encompass *theories* that previously lay outside its domain,
for this is not the same as that of a research programme dealing with
anomalies. The idea is that, possibly quite apart from any anomalies,
theories may have been developed outside the research programme
(they may have been developed within another programme) which can
be used and developed in accordance with the programme's positive
heuristics. If this happens it is quite possible that theories may be taken
over before economists have been able to establish whether they are or
are not consistent with the programme's hard core.[7] The theories
concerned may contain anomalies, the hard core being protected from
these in the usual way, or it may be that the question of consistency
with the hard core has, temporarily, been left open. The work needed to
do this may be postponed for several reasons: (a) a desire to tackle

---

7    The question of whether the same thing happens in other disciplines is left open.

problems one at a time; (b) an absence of suitable techniques for tackling certain problems; (c) a desire to try out theories before being convinced that it is worth finding out whether or not they can be integrated into the research programme.

## A RATIONAL RECONSTRUCTION OF MACROECONOMICS SINCE KEYNES

### Phase I: The establishment of the neo-Walrasian research programme

Keynes's *General Theory* was certainly not part of any neo-Walrasian research programme. In particular his theory was based on certain 'psychological laws' which had no grounding in optimizing behaviour. Assumptions HC2 and HC3 were not a part of Keynesian economics. Similarly Keynes did not follow the heuristics detailed above. On the other hand, although Keynes himself was reluctant to use his theory in this way, it was only a short step from the *General Theory* to constructing a formal model of the economy as a whole, for it contained all the necessary simplifications. In addition he defined a new concept of equilibrium appropriate to his model. This achievement was succinctly summed up by J. M. Clark who wrote, in a letter to Keynes,

> It has seemed to me that what I call the 'income-flow analysis', of which yours is the most noted presentation, has done something which has not been done in comparable degree since Ricardo and Marx: namely, constructed a coherent logical theoretical system or formula having the quality of a mechanism, growing directly out of current conditions and problems which are of paramount importance and furnishing a key to working out definite answers in terms of policy.
>
> (Keynes, 1971–83, XXIII, p. 191)

The first stage in the extension of the neo-Walrasian research programme to cover macroeconomics was to take Keynes's simplifications and, following PH1' and PH2', to construct from them a coherent, formal model of the economy. This was the achievement of Champernowne (1936), Harrod (1937), Meade (1937) and Hicks (1937).

In the process of doing this they redefined the notion of equilibrium, expressing it in terms of simultaneous equations (absent from the *General Theory*).[8] The remaining positive heuristics were, at this stage, ignored. The main reason for this was that the most important task was to show that, assuming it could eventually be reconciled with the programme's hard core, the new theory could be used to solve interesting problems: that it constituted a progressive problemshift. This is one of the reasons why Hicks's contribution was so important: although all four worked with what was essentially the same set of equations, it was he who showed, in a way that Champernowne, Meade and Harrod did not, how the new mathematical apparatus could be used to solve the riddle of how Keynes's theory related to that of the classics.

The next stage in establishing the neo-Walrasian research programme was to follow up PH3' and to replace Keynes's somewhat arbitrary (by neo-Walrasian standards) behavioural functions with ones securely based on optimizing behaviour. This took place in the 1940s and 1950s. The main work involved the two most novel aspects of the *General Theory* – the consumption function and the demand for money – and includes the well-known contributions of Friedman, Modigliani, Baumol, Tobin *et al*.[9] The third major component of Keynes's theory, his marginal efficiency of capital, also received attention, though this presented less of a problem as it was believed to correspond fairly closely to traditional concepts thought quite consistent with optimizing behaviour.

At the same time as detailed work was being carried out on the component parts of the Keynesian system, work was also being undertaken on the explicit integration of such optimizing models into a formal model of the economy as a whole, the most important work here being Patinkin's *Money, Interest and Prices* (1956).[10] Earlier writers (e.g.

---

[8]   This process is discussed in detail in Young (1987).

[9]   These are too well-known for exact references to be required.

[10]   There is a problem in knowing how to fit *Value and Capital* (1939) into this story. On the one hand Hicks has claimed that his IS–LM paper and *Value and Capital* grew out of the same earlier work (for references see Young, 1987, p. 46). On the other hand, *Value and*

Modigliani, 1944) had contributed to this process by putting Keynesian/Hicksian equation systems forward as aggregative versions of Walrasian models, but the link between micro- and macro-systems was far clearer and more explicit in Patinkin's work than in previous contributions. In addition the major technical problems concerning the compatibility of Keynesian theory, the quantity theory and Walrasian excess demand functions had by then been solved (or were thought to have been solved).[11] The theory, popularized by Samuelson (1955) as 'the neoclassical synthesis' and of which *Money, Interest and Prices* is the outstanding example,[12] was consistent with the neo-Walrasian hard core and in addition all the positive heuristics bar one had been followed.[13] By the mid-1950s, therefore, the neo-Walrasian research programme in macroeconomics had been securely established.[14] There was still much work to do, but subsequent work can be seen as developing and extending the programme rather than as establishing it.

### Phase II: The development of the neo-Walrasian research programme

The first major challenge to the neoclassical synthesis, as it is reasonable to call the macroeconomic theory that had emerged by the end of the

(Continued from previous page)
*Capital*, surprisingly, contains no reference to the IS–LM paper. It is worth noting the observation made by Maes (1988) that Hicks, although he had developed a portfolio theory of money in the 1930s, failed to use it as the foundation for his macroeconomic writing on money; instead, like most of his contemporaries, he adopted the cruder characterization of the monetary sector derived from Keynes's *General Theory*. This suggests that when telling the story of macroeconomics in the 1940s it may be right to leave *Value and Capital* out. Patinkin acknowledges the influence of *Value and Capital* only on the microeconomic part of *Money, Interest and Prices*: the macroeconomic section refers to IS-LM but not *Value and Capital*.

[11]  I have in mind the literature associated with the real balance effect and the determinacy of the price level, and the question of whether wage rigidity was necessary or sufficient for an unemployment equilibrium to emerge.

[12]  The third edition of his textbook, published in 1955, was the first to use this term.

[13]  HC5' will be considered later.

[14]  Samuelson (1955) claimed that the neoclassical synthesis had the support of 90% of American economists.

1950s, was posed by Clower (1965).[15] The neoclassical synthesis explained unemployment in terms of wage rigidity: the labour market was not in equilibrium. Clower's argument was that if the labour market were not in equilibrium the conventional model of consumer decisions would be mis-specified. It was necessary to re-write the consumer's maximization problem such that demands for goods depended not only on endowments and prices but also on realized sales of labour (or any other good the consumer is trying to sell). More generally, if an agent faces a constraint in one market his or her demands or supplies in all other markets will typically be affected. Clower presented these arguments as a challenge to the prevailing theory, but it is important to note that, though Clower saw them as presenting a fundamental challenge to orthodox ideas, they did not constitute any challenge to the neo-Walrasian research programme *as it is defined here*: indeed, his work could be construed as following its heuristics very closely. He observed an inconsistency in the existing theories and modified the theory in such a way as to protect the hard core.

Clower's ideas were soon taken up by several economists (e.g. Solow and Stiglitz, 1968; Barro and Grossman, 1971; Malinvaud, 1977)[16] who used them as the basis for new models of macroeconomic equilibrium. The assumption of wage inflexibility made in the neoclassical synthesis models was generalized to the assumption that all prices took time to move,[17] the new 'rationing models' describing the equilibria that would

[15] There were also important elements of disequilibrium in Patinkin (1965) but these were not presented as undermining the neoclassical synthesis. Clower's (and later Leijonhufvud's) rhetoric was very important.

[16] This list includes only authors of macroeconomic theories. Microeconomic general equilibrium theory was also affected, economists such as Arrow, Hahn, Benassy, Dreze and many others working on such models. For a survey see Drazen (1980). I have not included Leijonhufvud, whose name is frequently bracketed with Clower's in this context, for though his book (1968) did much to stimulate interest in this type of theory, he did not construct formal models in the way required by the neo-Walrasian research programme. Whilst his 1968 book was definitely Walrasian in its approach, his later work took him outside this research programme.

[17] This was explained by Clower as being the consequence of removing the artificial device of the Walrasian auctioneer.

result as long as prices were out of equilibrium. These models were formal optimizing models, specifying a new set of rules governing the interaction between agents. They defined a new equilibrium concept (fixed-price equilibrium) in terms of which the economy was analysed. This was all in accordance with the positive heuristics of the neo-Walrasian research programme.

For a few years this extension to the neo-Walrasian research programme appeared both theoretically and empirically progressive. Focusing on the failure of prices to adjust instantaneously rather than on wage inflexibility seemed to remove an anomaly in explanations of unemployment. In addition, the use of rationing models led to further successful predictions, some of which are discussed in section 5 below. These new insights, however, proved limited. More important than this, by the mid-1970s the assumption of price stickiness came to be seen as a major anomaly, and attempts were made to solve it through what turned out to be a progressive extension of the research programme.

The problem with existing theories was that variations in the level of output and employment could be explained only by assuming that prices were inflexible, an assumption which seemed inconsistent with the hard-core postulate of optimizing behaviour: if a market is out of equilibrium it is in the interests of both buyers and sellers to change the price. This hard-core assumption had to be protected by assuming that it was costly for firms to change prices, that changing prices took time and other assumptions which were *ad hoc* in the sense that they had nothing to do with either the hard core or the positive heuristics of the research programme. The response to this came in papers by Phelps (1967) and Friedman (1968) who showed how limited information could be used to explain why changes in the level of demand frequently affected output and employment. Phelps explained this using his famous 'island' parable (later taken up by Lucas). The economy consists of a number of islands and whilst workers are fully informed about prices and wages on their own island, information flows between islands are costly. If wages on one island fall workers will not know whether this reflects an economy-wide fall in wages or whether it is specific to their own island. Some workers will thus choose to become unemployed in order to search for better wages elsewhere. A fall in wages will, therefore, even if prices fall in the same proportion, lead to a fall in employment.

It is with the work of Phelps and Friedman that PH5' becomes important to the neo-Walrasian research programme: prior to this economists had not given much attention to the information available to agents. The assumption that workers have incomplete information made it possible to reconcile unemployment with the hard-core postulate of maximizing behaviour (Phelps described himself as sticking 'doggedly' to this assumption) and turned the 'anomaly' of the Phillips curve into corroborating evidence for the neo-Walrasian programme. In addition, when economists began to examine the implications of imperfect and asymmetric information and to allow for different attitudes towards risk they started to explain previously unexplained phenomena: for example, the existence of long-term labour contracts (e.g. Baily, 1974; Azariadis, 1975; Calvo and Phelps, 1977; Hall, 1980) and why employers may pay more than the market-clearing wage rate (Weiss, 1980). Anomalies have been turned into corroborating evidence for the programme.

The most widely known extension to the neo-Walrasian programme has been its extension to the formation of expectations: the theory of rational expectations. As with price stickiness, the assumption that expectations adjusted slowly in response to changes was *ad hoc*: it was part of the protective belt, required to protect the hard core. The theory of rational expectations, developed by Muth (1961) and applied to macroeconomics by Lucas (1972) showed how this anomaly could be eliminated. More important than this, however, the assumption of rational expectations opened up a new set of macroeconomic models capable of generating new predictions. Such models included not only the 'new classical macroeconomics', associated with Lucas, Sargent, Wallace, Barro and their followers, but also work such as that of Dornbusch (1976). The introduction of rational expectations was undoubtedly *theoretically* progressive. Whether or not it was *empirically* progressive is considered below.

## EVALUATING THE NEO-WALRASIAN RESEARCH PROGRAMME

### Novel facts[18]

There seems little doubt that the neo-Walrasian programme in macroeconomics has been *theoretically* progressive. It has managed to explain an increasing range of economic phenomena without resorting to an increasing number of *ad hoc* auxiliary assumptions. The critical question, however, is whether or not it has also been *empirically* progressive. This is important for two reasons. The obvious one is that we are interested not only in explanation but also in appraisal: we want to know whether the subject is developing in a satisfactory manner. The other reason is related to this. If Lakatos's methodology of scientific research programmes were an appropriate model of how scientists (including economists) behaved, we would expect economists to support progressive research programmes. Therefore, if we could show that the neo-Walrasian research programme were empirically progressive, we would have shown those economists working within the programme (the vast majority of post-war macroeconomists, if the rational reconstruction given here is appropriate) to have been behaving in a rational manner. We would thus have corroborating evidence for the adequacy of the rational reconstruction contained in section 3. As Lakatos put it, 'In the light of better rational reconstructions of science one can always reconstruct more of actual great science as rational' (Lakatos, 1971, p. 132).

The fundamental notion here is that a theoretical change is progressive if it is content-increasing: if theories explain not only the facts that they were designed to explain, but also some novel facts. It is the prediction of such novel facts that distinguishes progressive research programmes from series of *ad hoc* rationalizations. The key issue here is what constitutes a novel fact. The most clear-cut examples

---

[18] The ideas in this section are all taken from Lakatos. It is included because when I presented early drafts of this paper I was criticized *both* for paying too much attention to predictions *and* for not paying enough attention to them. I concluded that it was necessary to explain in more detail what I was trying to do.

of novel facts are, of course, facts not known when the theory is proposed: genuine *pre*dictions which turn out to be successful. Such predictions clearly provide corroborating evidence for a research programme. It is, however, necessary to broaden the definition of novel facts to include new interpretations of already-known facts and facts which were not previously explained within the research programme (Lakatos, 1970, pp. 32, 70–1). If a new theory explains the phenomena it was designed to explain and in addition explains what had previously been an anomaly, an unexplained fact or fact explicable only by some *ad hoc* auxiliary hypothesis, this can be interpreted as corroboration of the programme. When it comes to comparing two research programmes, a programme can also be corroborated if it explains facts which played no essential role in the competing programme (they may have been explained only with the aid of *ad hoc* hypotheses, or they may have been ignored as being unimportant).[19]

To show that the neo-Walrasian research programme in macroeconomics has been progressive we must, therefore, find examples of where it has successfully predicted novel facts. To do this we must do three things. (1) We must find examples of novel facts, which can be (a) predictions before the event, (b) facts that were not previously explained, (c) new interpretations of old facts or (d) facts which played no role in competing research programmes. These facts must all be facts that the theory was not specifically designed to explain. (2) We must show that these novel facts follow from the hard core and heuristics of the neo-Walrasian programme. (3) We must show that these were corroborated. Note that it is not necessary that all, or even most of, the predictions made within the neo-Walrasian programme be confirmed: rather, to quote Lakatos, 'what matters is a few dramatic signs of empirical progress' (Lakatos and Zahar, 1976, p. 179).

---

[19]    Lakatos and Zahar (1976, p. 185); cf. Zahar (1973). They argue that it was only this category of novel facts that, for many years, provided any corroborating evidence in favour of Copernicus's research programme *vis à vis* Ptolomy's.

## Alternative programmes

In appraising the neo-Walrasian research programme we must not forget the existence of alternative research programmes. In particular, it is important that any 'novel facts' we use as evidence for the programme's success do not follow equally well from the heuristics of some competing programme. A programme which is especially important here is what can best be called the 'Chicago' programme. This is important because there is such a large overlap between the two programmes. Though they overlap, however, they are not the same.[20]

The main distinguishing feature of Chicago economics is what Reder has termed 'Tight Prior Equilibrium' theory, based on the hypothesis of Pareto-optimality; namely that

> decision makers so allocate the resources under their control that there is no alternative allocation such that any one decision maker could have his expected utility increased without a reduction occurring in the expected utility of at least one other decision maker.
>
> (Reder, 1982, p. 11)

Imperfect competition, market failure and government intervention are taken to be sufficiently infrequent and have a sufficiently limited impact that the hypothesis of perfect competition provides a good approximation to the way in which markets work (Reder, 1982, p. 15).

A further difference between Chicago and neo-Walrasian economics concerns the role of formal model-building. Although many Chicago economists do construct formal mathematical models, and although much Chicago economics could be seen as also lying within neo-Walrasian economics, the construction and use of formal models does not receive the same emphasis. There is a strong tradition in Chicago economics, of which Friedman is undoubtedly the main representative, which favours simple models. Models which would be quite respectable

---

[20] It would clearly be desirable to discuss the hard core and heuristics of competing research programmes in the same detail as we have discussed those of the neo-Walrasian programme. However, because this is too large a task to perform here Reder's characterization of Chicago economics is taken as defining the programme adequately for the purposes of this paper.

Chicago economics (such as are found in most of Friedman's work) would not be seen as 'fully specified' in the sense of heuristic PH1'.[21]

## SOME NOVEL FACTS GENERATED BY THE NEO-WALRASIAN RESEARCH PROGRAMME

### The consumption function

One of the earliest examples of successful prediction in post-war macroeconomics is the life-cycle/permanent income theory of consumption, of which Friedman's *The Theory of the Consumption Function* (1957) is the outstanding example. Note that although there are substantial differences between the approaches of Chicago economists (Friedman) and non-Chicago ones (Ando and Modigliani), with the latter providing a much more formal treatment of the maximizing hypothesis, we are not attempting here to distinguish between them, accepting the generally-held view that the two theories yield substantially the same empirical predictions.

The basic facts the life-cycle theory was designed to explain were:

(a) the rough constancy of the average propensity to consume in the United States over the past half-century, as measured by time series data, despite a substantial rise in real income; (b) the rough similarity of the average propensity to consume in budget studies for widely separated dates, despite substantial differences in average real income; (c) the sharply lower savings ratio in the United States in the period after World War II than would have been consistent with the relation between income and savings computed from data for the interwar period.

(Friedman, 1957, p. 38)

---

[21] In section 5 below we consider the consumption function and the expectations-augmented Phillips curve. In both cases Friedman's contribution exemplifies the Chicago, non-neo-Walrasian approach, with the work of Ando and Modigliani (on consumption) and Phelps (the Phillips curve) representing the neo-Walrasian approach.

Friedman managed to explain not only these broad generalizations, but his theory also predicted several additional 'novel facts' concerning things such as shifts in the consumption function over time, the differences between farm and non-farm savings behaviour, inter-country differences and so on. He confronted these predictions with detailed evidence, in all cases coming to the conclusion that the data either supported his theory or were not inconsistent with it (the data were often inconclusive). Friedman claimed that

> Perhaps the two most striking pieces of evidence for the hypothesis are, first, its success in predicting in quantitative detail the effect of classifying consumer units by the change in their measured income from one year to another; and, second, its consistency with a body of data that *have not heretofore been used in analyzing consumption behavior* or, indeed, *even regarded as relevant to consumption behavior*, namely, data on the measured income of individual consumer units in successive years.
>
> (Friedman, 1957, p. 225)

The theory was developed to explain one set of data and was then used to make predictions concerning other things. Friedman and many other economists considered that these predictions were mostly confirmed. Though there are now signs of a possible movement away from the permanent income–life-cycle theory, and it is conceivable that it might at some stage be abandoned (see Gilbert, 1991), the theory was thought for many years to have been important in predicting a broad range of facts about the behaviour of consumption and income.

### Inflation and unemployment

The expectations-augmented Phillips curve as developed by Phelps and Friedman led to a number of predictions concerning the relationship between the level of aggregate demand, inflation and unemployment. The main ones were that: (a) the level of unemployment consistent with a constant inflation rate is independent of the inflation rate; (b) persistent low unemployment will lead to accelerating inflation; (c) increasing the growth rate of demand produces a short-term rise in unemployment, but in the long run produces only a rise in inflation.

The first of these predictions is difficult, if not impossible, to test conclusively because, as Friedman admitted, the 'natural' rate of unemployment is not constant. There have been numerous attempts to estimate the natural rate, but the problems are sufficiently great that it is hard to regard such work as being anything like a satisfactory test of the theory. The best we can say is that the hypothesis has not been refuted by empirical evidence. The other two, related, predictions, on the other hand, could be regarded as having been corroborated by the experience of the 1970s.[22] The predictions were first made in 1967, when inflation had started to rise, but had not yet reached levels which suggested anything substantially different from earlier experience: there was little evidence that inflation was accelerating or that the 'conventional' Phillips curve had broken down (see Figure 10.1).

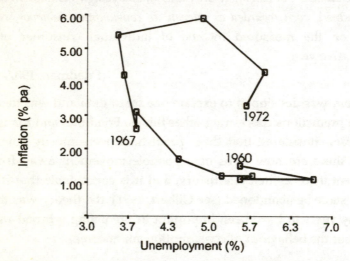

*Figure 10.1* Inflation and unemployment in the USA, 1960–72

During the late 1960s there was a large expansion of aggregate demand, due first to Kennedy's application of Keynesian policies and later to the cost of the Vietnam war. The sharp rise in inflation, without much change in unemployment, in 1968–9 could be explained in terms

---

[22]  This is when the results were first published, Friedman's 'The role of monetary policy' (Friedman, 1968) having been delivered as his Presidential Address to the AEA the previous year.

of a non-linear Phillips curve, but once this high inflation rate began to feed into expectations, the economy moved off the 1960s Phillips curve. Rising unemployment was needed in 1970–1 simply to stop inflation rising still further: even with unemployment rates comparable with those of the early 1960s inflation remained over 3%. Friedman and Phelps could well argue that these events vindicated their predictions, and that their predictions were made well in advance of events.[23]

**Models of price stickiness**

One of the problems with the consumption function and the expectations-augmented Phillips curve as examples of the neo-Walrasian research programme generating novel facts is that they do not discriminate between the neo-Walrasian and Chicago research programmes. In order to do this, therefore, we turn now to examples of predictions made by models which lie squarely within the neo-Walrasian research programme but which are clearly outside the Chicago programme. Start with rationing models. These were designed to explain the problem of Keynesian unemployment, but the logic of the simple two-market models initially discussed led naturally to a threefold classification of Keynesian unemployment, classical unemployment and repressed inflation (a logically possible fourth category was dismissed as economically uninteresting). Though these models are notoriously difficult to estimate, let alone to test, disequilibrium phenomena causing severe econometric problems, it could be argued that they were corroborated by the response of different economies to OPEC I. Labour market institutions were very different in Europe and the USA, with real wage rigidity in Europe and nominal wage rigidity in the USA. This should, if rationing models are correct, result in classical unemployment in the USA and Keynesian unemployment in Europe. Econometric evidence on real wage gaps is too tenuous to provide any firm evidence that the theory was

---

[23] We have provided data only for the years up to 1972 in order to leave aside the complications caused by the oil-price rise of 1973–4 and the productivity slowdown, confining our attention to the period when the main cause of inflation was high aggregate demand.

confirmed, but it is reinforced by evidence that European governments responded as though the problem was one of classical unemployment (they tried to reduce real wages) whilst the USA tried to deflate demand. If we assume that governments were acting rationally, this suggests that these economies were behaving in conformity with rationing theory. What makes this significant is that this was happening in circumstances that had not previously been observed, the oil shock with the simultaneous fall in productivity and deflation of aggregate demand being unlike anything that had happened before.

A more dramatic and much more conclusive example is the 'Dornbusch model' (Dornbusch, 1976). This combined the assumption of perfect foresight in financial markets (equivalent to rational expectations in the deterministic model Dornbusch was using) with sluggish price-adjustment in goods markets. His prediction was that a monetary expansion (contraction) would produce a depreciation (appreciation) of the exchange rate, which might overshoot its long-run equilibrium. The characteristic feature of Dornbusch's model, distinguishing it from previous exchange-rate models, was that flexibility and rational, forward-looking behaviour in financial markets *contributed to* instability, rather than reducing it.

As dramatic a test of this theory as one might reasonably expect to see came in the UK in 1979–80 when the newly-elected Conservative government introduced an exceptionally tight monetary policy at the same time as financial markets were becoming much more flexible. From the third quarter of 1979 (the election was in October 1979) the growth rate of both broad and narrow monetary aggregates fell sharply: after being positive in the first half of 1979 growth rates of the real money supply fell to *minus* 10% per annum in the first half of 1980.[24] Real interest rates rose very sharply. The result, as the Dornbusch

---

[24] The one exception to this pattern was sterling M3, the aggregate to which the government was paying most attention. Monetary base, M1 and the aggregates broader than sterling M3 all behaved as described here. The errant behaviour of sterling M3 may explain why the government effected such a severe recession despite policy statements which appeared to imply a 'gradualist' outlook. The severity of the monetary policy, and the mechanism whereby it affected the economy, are clearly documented in Buiter and Miller (1981).

model predicts, was a massive appreciation of sterling. Relative unit labour costs, perhaps the best measure of the real exchange rate, rose by an unprecedented 54% in two years.

There are, as always, other factors to take into account. North Sea oil was coming on stream and this would account for part of the appreciation, especially after OPEC II. However, most calculations of the 'oil premium' suggest that it was substantially below the appreciation that was observed. In addition, oil exploration had been under way since the mid-1970s and the results, though obviously subject to uncertainty, must to a substantial extent have been anticipated. Furthermore, the severity of the recession, due to a massive de-stocking as firms failed to export goods, suggests that the exchange rate had risen well above the level compatible with international competitiveness. It could be argued, therefore, that the 'Thatcher experiment' corroborated the predictions of the Dornbusch model.

## The new classical macroeconomics

The new classical macroeconomics produces such strong predictions, with such dramatic implications for government policy and presenting suitable econometric challenges that there have been numerous attempts to test them. The predictions resulting from the new classical macroeconomics include: (a) anticipated changes in aggregate demand will have no effect on real output (structural neutrality), with the corollary that only unpredictable movements in aggregate demand will affect real variables; (b) the more unpredictable is aggregate demand, the smaller is the effect on real output of any given unpredictable movement in aggregate demand. Lucas (1973) produced empirical evidence in support of the latter whilst Barro (1977, 1978; Barro and Rush, 1980) produced evidence for the former.

These predictions and the empirical evidence which seemed to corroborate them have stimulated much econometric work, with many economists coming to the conclusion that the new classical theories were not consistent with the data. For example, Gordon (1982) found that anticipated changes in aggregate demand *did* have a significant effect on real output. He reconciled this with Barro's evidence, according to which anticipated changes in the money supply had no such effects, by suggesting that the link between monetary growth and the growth rate of demand was weak. The reason for Barro's results was the traditional Keynesian notion that money had only a limited effect on aggregate demand. Other economists criticized Barro and Lucas on more technical grounds (lag lengths, the type of statistical tests they performed and so on).

The new classical assumptions have also been applied to generate other predictions. One of the most dramatic predictions concerned the consumption function, where Hall (1978) claimed that 'no variable apart from current consumption should be of any value in predicting future consumption' (Hall, 1978, p. 971). As with Lucas's and Barro's results, subsequent empirical evidence has suggested that this is not so: that other variables do affect consumption.

Finally, it is worth pointing out that the logic of the new classical theory is that there should be no business cycle. According to the new classical theory it is only unanticipated, and hence unpredictable changes in aggregate demand that cause departures from full employment. Fluctuations in real output about full-employment output should, therefore, be uncorrelated with any information available to decision-makers, a prediction which is inconsistent with the existence of a business cycle (i.e. with deviations from full-employment output exhibiting positive serial correlation). Had there been no business cycle, we can be sure that this would have been cited as corroborating evidence for the new classical programme (a part of the Chicago programme) so it seems reasonable to cite the existence of a business cycle as evidence against it.[25] Lucas and others have, of course, attempted to explain why there is a business cycle, but the assumptions they introduce to do this are essentially *ad hoc*.

[25]  See Okun (1980) for a discussion of new classical theories of the cycle and the evidence against them.

## IS THE NEO-WALRASIAN PROGRAMME IN MACROECONOMICS PROGRESSIVE?

The first thing to look for is predictions before the event, for, although it is not necessary that predictions be of this type, there can be no doubt that these constitute corroborating evidence. Due to the nature of economics such predictions are inevitably hard to obtain – until a new circumstance has arisen economists often have no incentive to construct a theory capable of generating predictions. Furthermore, once a prediction has been made, behaviour may change in response to this prediction so as to ensure that it is never tested.

Two predictions before the event have been cited above: the Friedman–Phelps prediction of the consequences of sustained high aggregate demand in the late 1960s, and Dornbusch's prediction of the consequences of a severe monetary shock in a world of floating exchange rates, mobile capital and rational expectations. Doubts have been expressed about both, but it can nonetheless be argued that these have been dramatically corroborated.

Broadening our use of the term prediction to include predictions of anything that the theories concerned were not designed to predict, we have the example of Friedman's theory of the consumption function, designed to explain a few basic facts, but which explained a large number of related facts. To this could be added numerous instances of neo-Walrasian theories explaining other phenomena they were not designed to explain. Indeed, it could be argued that the main feature of neo-Walrasian economics, too obvious to need documenting, is its ability to generate and explain apparently disparate phenomena in terms of maximizing behaviour.

There is, however, a serious problem here, connected with the question of what constitutes the relevant theory. Take an example. Dixit (1978) uses a rationing model, of the type used by Barro, Grossman, Malinvaud *et al.* to analyse the problem of the balance of trade. He managed to explain in terms of this theory 'facts' about the relationship between the government deficit and the balance of trade which were essentially *ad hoc* assumptions (believed to be empirically justified) in another research programme (the so-called 'New Cambridge' theory).[26] The issue here is whether this constitutes an example of disequilibrium macroeconomics, designed to explain the problem of Keynesian unemployment in a closed economy, successfully generating predictions in an area that it was not intended to cover; or whether we have to regard Dixit's model as a new model designed to explain the balance of trade. At another level, could the whole of neo-Walrasian *macro*economics be regarded as generating predictions from a theory aimed at explaining something very different (whatever neo-Walrasian *micro*economics is about)? We might wish to examine assumptions used in different neo-Walrasian models in detail to determine when we have a 'new' theory and when we have simply an application of an old theory, but we are in the end faced with a subjective decision about what constitutes a new model.[27] We thus have to make a subjective decision as to whether a prediction has been generated from a model designed to explain something else, or whether it has been generated by a purpose-built one. To criticize neo-Walrasian economics we focus on theoretical novelties; to defend it we focus on the fact that many theories are 'essentially' the same.

There is also the issue of how neo-Walrasian economics compares with other competing, and possibly overlapping, programmes – in particular, of what can be claimed *vis à vis* the Chicago programme. The overlap between these two programmes is so large that to a certain extent they stand or fall together. The examples cited in section 5, however, suggest that there is a strong case for claiming that neo-Walrasian macroeconomics remains progressive in a way that Chicago *macro*economics (we are making no comment on Chicago *micro*economics) does not. There are two sides to this. On the one hand, important predictions from the non-Chicago part of neo-Walrasian

---

26  The thesis was that a change in the government deficit would, in the short run, cause the balance of trade to change by an equal and opposite amount. The New Cambridge explanation used the accounting identity that the sum of sectoral deficits must be zero together with the assumption that the private sector deficit was approximately constant. The latter assumption was believed to have empirical support, but there was no theoretical rationale for it.

27  A related point is made, in a very different context, in Chapter 2.

economics have been successful. On the other hand, the dramatic predictions made within the new classical macroeconomics have not been confirmed.

## CONCLUDING REMARKS

In this paper I have viewed contemporary macroeconomics from a Lakatosian perspective for two reasons. The first is to provide another case study which can be used in evaluating the relevance of Lakatosian ideas for economics. This is one reason why Lakatosian ideas have been applied relatively rigidly: we need to see how far we can push them before they cease to work. Here, the main conclusion to emerge from the paper is that the rational reconstruction of macroeconomics since Keynes, provided in this chapter, fits the facts very well. There are the problems of pre-test bias and of having fewer observations than we would like. In addition, we have not explored the alternatives to the neo-Walrasian programme adequately. On the other hand, the fact that we can reconstruct the period's 'great (macroeconomic) science' as rational can be taken as corroborating the Lakatosian perspective.[28] Furthermore, the key feature of the neo-Walrasian programme as described here is its stress on rational behaviour. This is something that most of the theorists concerned would immediately acknowledge as a key assumption underlying their work and underlying post-war economic theory. In addition, possibly the most common defence of neo-Walrasian economics (from practitioners, not methodologists) is that 'it works'. By this economists usually have in mind something akin to the Lakatosian criterion for a progressive research programme: that their theories provide a source of new predictions, a significant number of which turn out to be correct. The Lakatosian perspective can thus be defended on the grounds that it is in accordance with the way economists see their work.[29]

[28] I have let the conclusions stand as they were when the chapter was first published in 1991. Now I would be a little more guarded in my support for a Lakatosian methodology, though still arguing that a Lakatosian perspective can be revealing. See Backhouse (1994c).

[29] I am grateful to Harry Collins for drawing my attention to this issue.

The second reason for adopting a Lakatosian perspective is to appraise contemporary economics. I am assuming that the superstructure of economic theory needs an empirical justification, and that Lakatos's methodology provides a possible way of doing this. Here, the conclusion to emerge from the paper is that the neo-Walrasian research programme appears to be both theoretically and empirically progressive. By way of a postscript it is worth noting a corollary to the argument advanced here. This concerns 'monetarism' and 'Keynesianism'. These are often presented as two rival research programmes. According to our interpretation of post-war macroeconomics, however, the much of the debate between monetarism and Keynesianism emerges as a debate within the neo-Walrasian programme.[30] This would explain why Keynesian and monetarist theories have developed in such similar ways during the post-war period.[31] The very great changes which have taken place in macroeconomics since 1970 should, according to this interpretation, be seen not in terms of the replacement of one research programme with another but in terms of a shift of attention within a larger research programme.

[30] It is not, of course, entirely within neo-Walrasian economics. We might wish, for example, to think in terms of a 'National Bureau' research programme, dominated by Wesley Clair Mitchell, having heuristics that are very different from those of the neo-Walrasian programme. Friedman's work would fit into such a programme much better than into the neo- Walrasian programme.
[31] This is argued in more detail in Chapter 8.

# Part IV

# Rhetoric and macroeconomics

# Chapter 11

# Rhetoric and implicit methodology in Friedman's macroeconomics*

## INTRODUCTION

Milton Friedman is a paradoxical figure. He is undoubtedly one of the leading figures in post-war macroeconomics, with a reputation as an aggressive and powerful debater capable of holding the attention of a wide audience. His essay on 'The methodology of positive economics' (1953) was, for many economists, one of the few methodological works they ever read. His work on the consumption function and the expectations-augmented Phillips curve have become widely accepted. Though Keynesian theories have stubbornly persisted, his views on money, inflation and monetary policy are no longer seen as those of an idiosyncratic outsider, but have become securely established in the mainstream of macroeconomic thought. Despite these achievements, however, Friedman remains an outsider. Though he is in certain respects a classic 'Chicago' economist (in the sense of Reder, 1982) his methodological views are unorthodox, for he distrusts elaborate theories in a manner strongly reminiscent of Alfred Marshall. His empirical work bears little resemblance to contemporary applied economics, exhibiting an extreme distrust of multiple regression techniques which have become, for most economists, the dominant statistical technique. Furthermore, despite the popularity of his essay on

*   I wish to thank Tony Dudley-Evans, Daniel Hammond, Willie Henderson and Abraham Hirsch for helpful comments on earlier versions of this chapter. None of them is responsible for the resulting product.

methodology, this essay has been vehemently criticized by specialists on methodology.

Part of the work necessary to understand Friedman has been undertaken by Hirsch and de Marchi (1986, 1990) who argue that his methodology is profoundly unorthodox, in a way that few commentators have been patient enough to understand. Their argument is that to understand his methodology one has to look at the way he does his economics. When they do this they find strong evidence for a Deweyan methodology, not previously recognized, they argue, because of the Popperian perspective from which most commentators approached his methodological writings.

This chapter approaches the paradox of Friedman from a different perspective: it considers what can be learned from the way he argues the case for the quantity theory of money. This is a fascinating issue, for despite the enormous influence Friedman's writing has had, his writing has frequently infuriated his opponents. Thus Tobin once referred to Friedman's 'propensity in professional debate to evade by verbal quibbling the responsibility and the credit for the characteristic propositions of "monetarism" associated with his name' (Tobin, 1970, p. 329). Johnson accused him of 'scholarly chicanery' (quoted in Gordon, 1974, p. 158). Hendry and Ericsson complain of 'the failure of Friedman and Schwartz to present statistical evidence pertinent to their main claims' (Hendry and Ericsson, 1991, p. 32). The list could be continued.

The question of the relationship between Friedman's rhetoric and the rest of his work is also interesting from a meta-methodological point of view. McCloskey (1983, 1986) has argued that we need to distinguish between economists' 'explicit' and 'implicit' attitudes to economic discourse (often referred to as the 'official' and 'unofficial') (see, for example, 1983, p. 484; 1986, p. 5). The explicit methodology is what one finds in writings on methodology, and in teaching new students. The implicit methodology, on the other hand, has to be sought by examining their work. Here we have a choice. We can, following Hirsch and de Marchi, examine an economist's statements concerning methodology in the light of what he or she actually does when doing economics (and *vice versa*). Alternatively, following McCloskey, we can start by considering their rhetoric, in the sense of looking at the way they argue: the way they seek to persuade each other. The view implicit in McCloskey's work (his analysis of economists such as Muth, Samuelson and Fogel) is that examining rhetoric reveals the way economists are thinking and working (their implicit rhetoric), for otherwise it would make little sense to use unofficial rhetoric as the basis for a critique of official methodology in the way that he does. Thus where Hirsch and de Marchi would argue that we need to 'see through' an economist's rhetoric if we are to understand his or her work, McCloskey asks us to 'see through' his or her explicit statements on methodology. The case of Friedman helps us to evaluate these competing claims.

## FRIEDMAN'S RESTATEMENT OF THE QUANTITY THEORY

The aim of Friedman's 'The quantity theory of money: a restatement' (1956) was to persuade economists to take the quantity theory seriously. Given that this chapter was published only three years after 'The methodology of positive economics', in which he argued the case for testing economic theories only by their assumptions, and given the conventional interpretation of that essay, we would expect his arguments to emphasize, perhaps to the exclusion of all other types of argument, the predictive success of the quantity theory. That is, we might expect it to conform to the criteria that McCloskey has termed 'modernism' (McCloskey, 1983, pp. 484–5). What we in fact find is very different indeed.

(1) He appeals to the authority of a non-mainstream ('aberrant') oral tradition:

> Chicago was one of the few academic centers at which the quantity theory continued to be a central and vigorous part of the oral tradition throughout the 1930s and 1940s, where students continued to study monetary theory and to write theses on monetary problems.
>
> (Friedman, 1956, p. 51)

This oral tradition is 'alive and vigorous' (Friedman, 1956, p. 67) and has 'nurtured' essays (Friedman, 1956, p. 52).

(2) Friedman is explicit in advocating not a testable theory but an 'approach', or point of view: something which cannot be written down precisely, for two reasons. The first is that flexibility (vagueness?) is an important part of the tradition.

> To the best of my knowledge, no systematic statement of this theory as developed at Chicago exists. And this is as it should be, for the Chicago tradition was not a rigid system, an unchangeable orthodoxy, but a way of looking at things.
>
> The purpose of this introduction is not to enshrine – or should I say, inter – a definitive version of the Chicago tradition. To suppose that one could do so would be inconsistent with that tradition itself.
>
> (Friedman, 1956, p. 52)

The second reason why the theory is not written down precisely is that it is incomplete. (a) Even if the supply of money is fixed (which should 'help' the quantity theory), the demand for money equation (expressed in its 'usual quantity theory form' (Friedman, 1956, p. 58), 'is not sufficient to determine money income'. (b) Even if we assume 'the most favourable conditions' for the quantity theory so that it can explain money income, it still says nothing about how changes in money income are reflected in changes in real output and prices (Friedman, 1956, pp. 61–2).

(3) At what might be considered one of the crucial points in his argument,[1] Friedman makes claims not about the quantity theory, but about what 'the quantity theorist' 'accepts', 'regards' and 'holds'.

> The quantity theorist accepts the empirical hypothesis that the demand for money is highly stable ...

> The quantity theorist ... also regards it [the demand function for money] as playing a vital role in determining variables that he considers of great importance for the analysis of the economy as a whole ...

---

[1]    The points made in the quotations here have frequently been cited by commentators seeking to sum up Friedman's views of the quantity theory.

The quantity theorist also holds that there are important factors affecting the supply of money ...

(Friedman, 1956, pp. 62, 63)

The emphasis is on opinions and beliefs rather than on proof or demonstration.

(4) He appeals to the judgement of his (economist) readers.

There is an extraordinary stability and regularity to such magnitudes as income velocity that cannot help impressing anyone who works extensively with monetary data.

Almost every economist will accept the general lines of the preceding analysis on a purely formal and abstract level, although each would doubtless choose to express it differently in detail.

One cannot read Lerner's description of the effects of monetary reform in the Confederacy of 1864 without recognizing that ...

(Friedman, 1956, pp. 67, 62, 64)

He does not, however, define what he means by 'general lines', 'on a purely formal and abstract level' or 'detail'.

(5) He uses the metaphor of eating at the point where one might expect him to refer to demonstration or proof. 'The proof of this pudding is in the eating; and the essays in this book [*Studies in the Quantity Theory of Money*] contain much relevant food, of which I must mention three juicy items' (Friedman, 1956, p. 64). This is the same metaphor as is used at the beginning of the chapter where he writes that his essay is 'an attempt to convey the flavor of the oral tradition' (Friedman, 1956, p. 52). It is consistent with his almost 'biological' view of the oral tradition as 'nurturing' essays.

(6) When it comes to expounding the theory of the demand for money, the central part of the chapter, Friedman adopts an approach similar to that adopted in mainstream macroeconomics. Pages 52–8 contain little that is unconventional, though Friedman introduces some distinctive twists into the argument, such as the introduction of the human/non-human capital distinction. On pages 58–60 a more novel approach is adopted to the demand for money by businesses, but his

conclusion is that such considerations will not affect the form of the money demand function.[2]

There are, however, some arguments which make sense in 'modernist' terms.

(7) The essays in the book are claimed to 'add to our tested knowledge about the characteristics of the demand function for money' (Friedman, 1956, p. 64). In discussing three examples, however, he provides good examples of methods that could be seen as Kuhnian 'normal science' or of changes in a Lakatosian 'protective belt': income is redefined as 'permanent income'; the line between money and other assets (between which 'there is no hard-and-fast line' (Friedman, 1956, p. 65) is redefined; the whole expected pattern of price movements is replaced by the rate of change expected at the moment. The problems such adjustments pose for the notion of testing theories are not explored.

(8) He responds to the charge that there are so few numerical 'constants' or empirical regularities in economics.

> The field of money is the chief example one can offer in rebuttal: there is perhaps no other empirical relation in economics that has been observed to recur so uniformly under so wide a variety of circumstances as the relation between substantial changes over short periods in the stock of money and prices; the one is invariably linked with the other and is in the same direction; this uniformity is, I suspect, of the same order as many of the uniformities that form the basis of the physical sciences
>
> (Friedman, 1956, p. 67)

Though conceding that velocity of circulation is not a constant, he implies that there is 'a stability and regularity in monetary relations', and the essays in the book make 'an important contribution toward extracting this stability and regularity, toward isolating the numerical "constants" of monetary behaviour' (Friedman, 1956, p. 67).

---

2    It is worth noting that his dismissal of distinctions between 'active' and 'idle', and 'transactions' and 'speculative' balances (page 61) is a direct attack on the way demand for money functions were frequently expounded, such distinctions being a feature of Keynes's theory, both in the *Treatise on Money* (1930) and in *The General Theory* (1936).

Friedman's arguments are thus, with some exceptions, neither those of 'modernism' nor even a Popperian process of conjecture and refutation. He is advocating not a specific, refutable theory, but a position of approach which is neither rigid nor refutable. Whatever the similarities between his theory and orthodoxy, he portrays his position as standing apart from the mainstream of macroeconomic theory.

## FRIEDMAN'S DEBATE WITH TOBIN OVER MONEY AND THE BUSINESS CYCLE

### Tobin's attack

Tobin starts by summarizing what he takes to be Friedman's main argument:

> Milton Friedman asserts that changes in the supply of money $M$ (defined to include time deposits) are the principal cause of changes in money income $Y$. In his less guarded and more popular expositions, he comes close to asserting that they are the unique cause.

> (Tobin, 1970, p. 301; 497)

He goes on to argue that Friedman and his associates have marshalled 'an imposing volume of evidence', which falls into three categories: historical case studies; reduced form regressions;[3] and evidence on timing. It is with the last of these that Tobin's paper is concerned: he wishes to make a general point about 'the dangers of accepting timing evidence as empirical proof of propositions about causation' (Tobin, 1970, p. 303; 498).

---

[3]    The regressions involved are ones such as $\Delta Y = a_0 + a_1 \Delta M$, or $\Delta Y = b_0 + b_1 \Delta I$, where $Y$ is nominal income, $M$ the money supply, and $I$ investment. The former equation supports Friedman's position, the latter a Keynesian position (according to which income changes in response to changes in investment rather than changes in the money supply). They are called reduced form equations, because both are simple equations summarizing a relationship that can be deduced from a more complicated model. Tobin's reference to this type of evidence is alluding to the controversy discussed on page 129.

Because his main point is about evidence from the timing of cycles in money and income, Tobin prefaces his models with a discussion of Friedman's views. He notes that Friedman recognizes the inconclusive nature of timing evidence.

> Friedman himself says, 'These regular and sizeable leads of the money series are suggestive of an influence running from money to business but they are by no means decisive'.
>
> (Tobin, 1970, p. 302; 498)

He then outlines Friedman's reasons for concluding that 'it is not easy to rationalize positive conformity with a lead as reflecting supply response [i.e. money responding to changes in income]' (Friedman, quoted in Tobin, 1970, p. 302; 498).[4] This quotation is very important, for what Tobin proceeds to do is to show, using two simple models (an 'ultra-Keynesian' model and a 'Friedman's' model) not only that is it possible (and presumably 'easy') to rationalize this piece of timing evidence as reflecting a supply response, but also that the ultra-Keynesian model explains all of Friedman's empirical evidence better than does his 'Friedman' model.

> I shall show that the ultra-Keynesian model – in which money has no causal importance whatsoever – throws up observations which a superficial believer in *post hoc ergo propter hoc* would regard as more favourable to the idea that money is causally important than does Friedman's own model. What is even more striking and surprising is that the ultra-Keynesian model implies cyclical timing patterns just like the empirical patterns that Friedman reports, while the Friedman model does not.
>
> (Tobin, 1970, p. 315; 510)

After expounding the two models and working out their implications for the timing of changes in money and income, Tobin concludes,

---

[4]    At the end of his article, Tobin quotes another sentence from Friedman, which says something similar, but looking at it the other way round: 'An inverse relation with money lagging would be much easier to rationalize in terms of business influencing money than of money influencing business' (quoted in Tobin, 1970, p. 315; 510).

*Every single piece of observed evidence that Friedman reports on timing is consistent with the timing implications of the ultra-Keynesian model. ... This evidence actually contradicts his own 'permanent income' theory and lends support to the ultra-Keynesian model.*

(Tobin, 1970, p. 315; 510)

Finally, Tobin argues that Friedman upholds two, mutually inconsistent, positions: his permanent-income theory has clear, strong implications, but has important limitations which Friedman recognizes; elsewhere he adopts a more conventional position, according to which money affects income gradually, operating via interest rates, asset prices, saving and investment.

### Friedman's reply

In his reply Friedman does not dispute Tobin's results. What he disputes is what he describes as Tobin's 'thoroughly misleading impression' of his conclusions (Friedman, 1970b, p. 318). He focuses on Tobin's claim that he regards changes in the supply of money as being the *principal* causes of changes in income. His arguments are worth considering in detail.

(1) He accuses Tobin of being unscholarly in giving no documentary evidence for this view ('Elementary canons of scholarship call for documentation of such statements', Friedman, 1970b, p. 318).[5]

(2) He denies having made this assertion, but admits that 'it does give the right flavor of my views, and I have no wish to quibble over the wording' (Friedman, 1970b, p. 319).[6] He has thus accused Tobin as being unscholarly whilst admitting that Tobin was essentially correct.[7]

(3) He accuses Tobin of being unscientific in using an imprecise form of words: 'What does "principal" cause mean?' Friedman suggests that to be a principal cause, something must account for 'more of the

[5]  He also criticizes Tobin's statement concerning his more popular writings, but this is a side-issue.

[6]  In interpreting this remark it is useful to remember Friedman's extensive use of metaphors associated with food and taste in his restatement of the quantity theory.

[7]  Compare the remark to which Friedman takes exception with the statement that is quoted on page 195 below from Section 1 of his monetary framework.

variance of money income than any other single cause'. Having defined 'principal cause' in this way he tears it to pieces: if there were enough causes (i.e. over 100), money might be more important than any other cause, and yet explain only 1% of the variance of money; and if the money supply were kept constant, it would explain none of the variance (Friedman, 1970b, p. 319). Note that Friedman had, in the previous paragraph, said that he had no wish to 'quibble over wording'. Note also that though Friedman considers the term 'principal cause' imprecise, he himself uses terms such as 'important', 'substantial', 'broadly predictable', 'decisive evidence', 'senior partner', 'equal partner' and 'the major direction of influence' (Friedman, 1970b, pp. 319, 321). Note also that he was content to give the 'flavor' of the quantity theory.

(4) Tobin explicitly recognized that Friedman acknowledged the problems involved in using evidence from timing to infer causation. Friedman, however, dismisses these remarks by implying that their purpose was to suggest that Tobin's paper was not intended as a criticism of his views. Since they fail to do this ('no fair-minded reader of his [Tobin's] paper can come away with any other impression than that the paper is intended as a criticism of my views' (Friedman, 1970b, p. 320) they are, presumably, of no consequence. Having dismissed Tobin's arguments on this point, Friedman is then free to make the point himself: recognition of the problems involved with using lags thus becomes a point that Friedman can use against Tobin.

(5) He argues that his research on timing was done for reasons other than establishing causation (Friedman, 1970b, p. 322).

(6) He criticizes the 'un-Keynesian' demand for money function in Tobin's ultra-Keynesian model. Tobin's model is thus contradicted by the facts (Friedman, 1970b, p. 325).[8]

---

[8]   This seems very much like criticizing Tobin's model on the grounds that it is based on an unrealistic assumption. Yet the main contention of Friedman's 'Methodology of positive economics' (cited on the same page) was that the realism of a theory's assumptions was irrelevant: all that mattered was a theory's conclusions.

(7) He argues that his demand for money function was never intended as a complete model, and that it needs to be supplemented by other things.

(8) He concludes that Tobin's claims about timing are right, but that his reasoning is not. Ending on a different note, he argues that he has departed from his general rule of not replying to criticism because of his 'great respect and admiration for James Tobin's scientific ability and because this article is thoroughly out of character. Unlike most of his work, it is imprecise, inaccurate and misleading' (Friedman, 1970b, p. 327).

## Tobin's rejoinder

Tobin points out that despite what he calls Friedman's 'pained indignation' (Tobin, 1970, p. 328), Friedman agrees with the main points of his paper. Throughout his brief rejoinder he stresses their agreement. Apart from criticizing (in a footnote) a minor technical point made by Friedman, his only criticism is of his 'propensity in professional debate to evade by verbal quibbling the responsibility and the credit for the characteristic propositions of "monetarism" associated with his name' (Tobin, 1970, p. 329).

## Interpretation

This debate appears, at first sight, to be concerned with a single, well-defined issue: the validity of Friedman's evidence on timing as evidence for a causal connection running from money to income. Given that the method of creating counter-examples is a well-established way of disproving a theory, it would be natural to expect the debate to take the form of disputes over the validity of the counter-example. This does happen in that Friedman argues that Tobin's money-demand function renders his model inadmissible as a counter-example, a view with which Tobin takes issue. Friedman, however, takes the debate further than this: he disputes Tobin's interpretation of his purpose in producing evidence on timing; and he raises the methodological issue of whether or not it is right to take specific assumptions to their logical conclusion, arguing instead for the defence of an incompletely defined theory, not amenable to formal disproof, and of which only the 'flavour' can be given. Tobin sees such arguments simply as means of evasion rather than as methodological issues to be taken up.

## THE DEBATE OVER FRIEDMAN'S MONETARY FRAMEWORK

Throughout the 1960s Friedman was criticized on the grounds that though he was amassing a vast quantity of empirical evidence, he had failed to provide any theoretical framework on which his conclusions could be based. He responded to this in two articles, in 1970 and 1971, in which he outlined his 'Theoretical framework for monetary analysis'. A revised version of material from these articles was reprinted, together with critical comments by Karl Brunner and Allan Meltzer, James Tobin, Paul Davidson and Don Patinkin, and Friedman's response to his critics as *Milton Friedman's Monetary Framework: a Debate with his Critics* (Gordon, 1974).[9] Though it is widely considered that this debate led nowhere, there are some interesting points to note about the way Friedman conducted his argument.

(1) His *starting point* is to defend the quantity theory as supported by empirical evidence:

> It has probably been 'tested' with quantitative data more extensively than any other set of propositions in formal economics – unless it be the negatively sloping demand curve.

> Both its acceptance and its rejection have been grounded basically on judgements about empirical regularities.

> (Friedman, 1974, p. 1)

He then moves on to the theoretical framework which is the main subject of his paper. However, he returns to empirical evidence later on, using empirical arguments, not theoretical ones, as evidence for what he considers to be his theoretical framework's chief defect: its failure to explain lags and turning points (Friedman, 1974, pp. 46–7).

(2) He appeals to the authority of the community of 'professional' economists:

---

[9] For a detailed discussion of this debate, see Backhouse (1993a).

Until the past three decades, it [the quantity theory] was generally supported by serious students of economics, those whom we would today term professional economists, and rejected by laymen.

(ibid.)

The success of the Keynesian revolution that caused economists to reject it, but 'Only recently it has experienced a revival so that it once again commands the adherence of many professional economists' (ibid.).

The authority of the community of economists is also used as an argument against what he takes to be Keynesian theory:

As a result of both experience and further theoretical analysis, there is hardly an economist today who accepts Keynes's conclusion about the strictly passive character of $k$ [the ratio of money to nominal income], or the accompanying conclusion that money (in the sense of the quantity of money) does not matter, or who will explicitly assert that $P$ is 'really' an institutional datum that will be completely unaffected even in short periods by changes in $M$.

(Friedman, 1974, p. 20)

He is thus claiming that virtually the whole profession, past and present, supports his point of view.

(3) He makes rather an important, though in some respects puzzling, distinction between what he terms the analytical and the empirical levels of a theory.

On an analytical level it [the quantity theory] is an analysis of the factors determining the quantity of money the community wishes to hold; on an empirical level, it is the generalization that changes in desired real balances (in the demand for money) tend to proceed slowly and gradually or to be the results of events set in train by prior changes in supply, whereas, in contrast, substantial changes in the supply of nominal balances can and frequently do occur independently of any changes in demand. The conclusion is that substantial changes in prices or nominal income are almost invariably the result of changes in the nominal supply of money.

(Friedman, 1974, p. 3)

One reason for arguing that this distinction between the analytical and the empirical levels, which we discuss in more detail below, is important is that he returns to it when he responds to Tobin's attempt to define the quantity theory as involving the neutrality of money.

> Tobin gives six alternative meanings of 'the long run quantity theory'. One of them ... can be regarded as corresponding to the 'analytical' level in my statement. None of them corresponds to the 'empirical' level ...
>
> (Friedman, 1974, p. 145)

After this remark, he turns to the question of why communication between them is so difficult.

(4) When challenged on details of particular theories, Friedman gives way very easily. (i) Friedman had tried to argue, on the basis of his 'common model' (essentially an IS–LM model) that provided it was 'seldom capable of being approximated by -∝' (Friedman, 1974, p. 138). When Tobin disputed this by performing some standard exercises with the model, Friedman accepted the criticisms, and shifted his ground, bringing in dynamic questions concerned with the government budget constraint. (ii) When Tobin worked through the implications of Friedman's 'third approach' model, concluding that it was 'bizarre' (Friedman, 1974, p. 82) Friedman argued simply that Tobin was using the model in a way that he had not intended: he did not question the conclusions Tobin drew concerning the model. This is similar to his response to Brunner and Meltzer's criticisms, where he simply replied that his model was not intended to do everything. (iii) When Tobin pointed out that Keynesian models did not assume constant prices, Friedman 'reinterpreted' his phrase 'institutional datum' to mean 'exogenous', a clear modification of his previous position.

(5) In contrast with this willingness to abandon specific theoretical statements, Friedman goes to great lengths to defend the historical setting of the quantity theory. There are two aspects to this. On the one hand, he is concerned to place his own work in the context of a continuing Chicago tradition, of which his own work gives the 'flavor', which has its roots in the nineteenth-century quantity theory. On the other hand, he is not prepared to accept that his approach is in any way

Keynesian, even going so far as to point out the quantity theory origins of Keynes's own work. This spirited defence of his interpretation of doctrinal history in the face of Patinkin's barrage of detailed historical evidence, contrasts with his ready concessions to Tobin, and raises doubts concerning his statement that,

> In writing this article, I did not intend to engage in doctrinal history and did not express any such intention. I made no attempt to present a comprehensive survey of either the quantity theory or the Keynesian theory. I used references to earlier writers as expository devices to bring out analytical points rather than for their own sake.
>
> (Friedman, 1974, p. 133)

(6) He suggests that the reason he is being misunderstood is that his methodology is Marshallian, whilst that of Tobin and Patinkin is Walrasian (1974, pp. 145–6, 161). This question of methodology is considered below.

## FRIEDMAN'S METHODOLOGY IN THE LIGHT OF HIS RHETORIC

### The 'official' versus the 'unofficial' rhetoric

Friedman is best known for his 'methodology of positive economics'. If we were to adopt a conventional reading of this essay, whether 'instrumentalist' or 'Popperian', we should expect Friedman's defence of his theory to involve providing evidence for the success of its predictions, perhaps with additional evidence concerning its simplicity, elegance and fruitfulness. Such an expectation is reinforced by remarks made during this controversy, such as his being concerned to provide an analytic defence of the quantity theory, and his comment about his tendency to push arguments to their logical conclusions (both quoted above).

What we find, however, appears to be completely different. Friedman is very concerned to establish that his work forms part of a continuing, dissenting tradition (associated with Chicago). Furthermore, despite his claim to be concerned primarily with analytic issues, given the extent of his concern with this issue, it is virtually impossible to infer that it is a matter of more than historical importance: that it is somehow an important part of his defence of the quantity theory. Similarly, his determination (and this does not seem too strong a word) to find closer links between his approach and the traditional quantity theory than between his theory and Keynes's, makes it natural to see him as defending his theory by an appeal to authority – the authority of a centuries-old tradition. He attaches great significance to the terminology used: the quantity theory label matters greatly, for he is not content to be labelled as either a radical innovator (he accepts that he has made some innovations) or a post-Keynesian. A similar interpretation can be placed on his claims that certain ideas are almost universally accepted by economists, despite the fact that his critics, who between them clearly represent the views of many economists, would not agree. He would appear to be appealing to what McCloskey describes as 'the lore of academe'.

In contrast with his spirited defence of claims involving history and the interpretation of texts, he gives way, as was pointed out above, comparatively easily on matters involving purely analytical issues. This reinforces the view that history is something to which he attaches great importance. It would thus be natural to infer that historical arguments are more persuasive than analytical ones, and to interpret this as revealing that, in McCloskey's terms, Friedman's 'implicit rhetoric' is very different from his 'explicit methodology'.

## The methodology 'implicit' in Friedman's rhetoric

Because Friedman's work (notably his permanent income theory of consumption, his stress on rationality and maximizing behaviour, and his expectations-augmented Phillips curve) has so much in common with that of mainstream economists, and because his 'Methodology of positive economics' is so widely cited as representing a widely-held methodology, there is a continual temptation to regard him as a conventional, neoclassical economist. However, a close examination of the way in which he defends the quantity theory makes it clear that such a view is *profoundly* mistaken. Several aspects of his approach are worth mentioning.

1  His preference for simple theories. This is more than simply a personal preference, but is an integral feature of his methodology.
2  His frequent retreat to defending theories as partial explanations, and to stop short of providing a more general model that integrates different ideas.
3  His willingness to take up any ideas that support his position, showing little concern to investigate their implications for other parts of his theory.
4  His emphasis on an approach rather than on a specific theory.
5  His very loose use of the notion of Walrasian general equilibrium.

Though Friedman quite correctly describes certain of these aspects of his work (notably 1, 3 and 5) as Marshallian, they are remarks that could equally easily have been made about Mitchell, whose theoretical eclecticism, his preference for partial explanations which could be built up, very loosely, into an overall account of economic phenomena, and his belief that no single theory could ever account for the complexity of the real world, made him very critical of neoclassical theory. As such they underlie much of the work undertaken in the National Bureau for Economic Research, under the aegis of which Friedman's research was undertaken. The similarity between Friedman's and Mitchell's approaches is disguised by Friedman's having, in a way not true of Mitchell, made so many theoretical contributions that proved capable of integration within mainstream economics, and by Friedman's commitment to a theory of individual maximizing behaviour, something to which Mitchell took great exception.

## FRIEDMAN'S RHETORIC IN THE LIGHT OF HIS METHODOLOGY

### Friedman as a Deweyian pragmatist[10]

An alternative route involves starting with Friedman's methodology, seeking to find a coherent methodological position that is consistent

10    As will be obvious, this section is based on Hirsch and de Marchi (1990).

both with his explicit statements on methodology and with the way he pursued his economic research. This is an approach that, prior to Hirsch and de Marchi's work, had not been followed. The interpretation of Friedman's 'Methodology of positive economics' (1953) centred on whether his stress on the importance of predictions as the test of a theory should be seen as evidence for instrumentalism, or of a Popperian approach. The relative merits of these two interpretations are of little importance compared with what these interpretations both have in common: namely that they involve making the assumption that Friedman did not, in practice, follow the methodological prescriptions laid down in his famous essay on methodology. His work, as is well known, contains a strong inductive element, yet at the same time he is committed to working within what many would see as an unfalsifiable framework of perfect competition and utility maximization (the Chicago element in his work).

The key to unlocking Friedman's methodology, according to Hirsch and de Marchi, is to recognize that his methodology is not Popperian. The relevant feature of Popper's methodology here is that for him methodology is concerned simply with the appraisal of theories: the contexts of discovery and justification are rigorously separated. For Friedman, on the other hand, argue Hirsch and de Marchi, this is not so. For him methodology is concerned with the process of inquiry, not simply with the justification of theories. He regards theory choice as involving judgement, not just rules that can be articulated; he regards the results of past inquiries as important in helping us formulate criteria for judging theories; he is concerned to test for the truth of theories rather than with falsification. Friedman's very un-Popperian view, consistent with all his empirical work, is that theories must arise out of a close familiarity with the facts. Empirical investigation is important in deriving a theory, not simply for evaluating it. This explains works such as *The Monetary History of the United States* (1963), a work that makes no sense for an orthodox, or a Popperian theorist, for in that book he was not looking to falsify any theory: indeed, one might argue that the basic theory underlying that book was not falsifiable. When one has a theory that is well grounded in the facts, and which has worked on numerous occasions in the past, the appropriate response to an anomaly is not to see it as a falsification, but as a sign that the theory needs modification. Such attitudes are in no way Popperian, yet neither are they instrumentalist, for great importance is attached to theories: theories are far more than simply mechanisms for generating predictions. What of Friedman's notorious argument about the virtues of unrealistic assumptions? Hirsch and de Marchi argue very convincingly that we must interpret Friedman's arguments as those, not of a philosopher, but of a working economist with little interest in philosophy. Against such a background it is natural to interpret 'realism' as meaning 'plausibility'. Introspection was unreliable. Thus, in contrast to orthodox methodologists, Friedman argued that it was important to work back from observations to assumptions or premises. Only in this way could theory have an empirical basis. What he rejected was the notion that theories could be empirically grounded by virtue of their being based on commonly-held generalizations. Economists should adopt an 'outside' view of behaviour, not relying on introspection or shared common-sense. Such a view is remarkably coherent, though unorthodox. It has much in common with the approach of Mitchell, well-established as methodologically heterodox, who founded the National Bureau, under the aegis of which Friedman undertook most of his work. It is compatible with Friedman's oft-repeated claim to be a Marshallian. Hirsch and de Marchi, however, for reasons we cannot explore here, characterize it as Deweyian.

## Methodology and practice

From a meta-methodological point of view the significant feature of the Hirsch and de Marchi interpretation is that it succeeds in making sense of Friedman's explicit methodology by looking very carefully at the way he practised economics, both before and after his well-known essay. It is a perspective on Friedman's methodology that is reinforced by the analysis of Friedman's rhetoric undertaken in sections 2 to 5 above, but an analysis of his rhetoric would have given few, if any, clues. It is an interpretation that would not have suggested itself without a close analysis of the way he actually pursued his economic inquiries, and without attempting sympathetically to make sense of his methodological statements in the light of this.

This raises the question of how, if Friedman's essay does in fact describe his actual practice, his methodological position could have remained so obscure and misunderstood. Why was he prepared, when questioned, to make statements that implied a Popperian influence? The answer has to be sought in his being a working economist, not a 'professional' methodologist or philosopher of science. He never succeeded in articulating his methodology adequately, for he was not equipped to do so. When viewed unsympathetically, and in a context different from that in which it was derived, his methodological pronouncements seemed at best naive and at worst incoherent.[11] His failure to articulate his methodological position was, it could be argued, one reason why critics accused him of verbal quibbling instead of seeing that he was making a methodological point.

## CONCLUSIONS

### Friedman as a heterodox economist

In this paper we have outlined two approaches to the problem of understanding Friedman's methodology. Both of these lead unambiguously to the conclusion that, methodologically, Friedman is heterodox, in the tradition of Marshall, Mitchell and his colleagues in the National Bureau. To anyone who has read Friedman's appreciative remarks on Mitchell (Friedman, 1950), and who takes seriously his defence of the Marshallian approach to economics,[12] such a conclusion should not be surprising. This, however, is not the conventional view of Friedman. There are several reasons for this.

1 His methodological essay, if read through Popperian spectacles, looks like a clear, bold, if philosophically naive version of

---

[11] Thus Mäki, on the basis of Friedman's essay on methodology, has suggested that one interpretation of Friedman is as an ally of Feyerabend, ready to use whatever methodology suits his purposes (Mäki, 1986, pp. 139–40).

[12] See Hirsch and de Marchi (1990) for a discussion of this point.

falsificationism, quite compatible with Samuelson's 'operationalism' (1947) or the version of 'positive economics' later popularized by Lipsey (1964).

2   Post-war economics has been characterized by a preoccupation with theory, with formal econometrics increasingly being the means whereby theories are related to empirical data. Thus when viewing Friedman's work, economists have normally focused on his theoretical work, to the exclusion of his empirical work. His correlations, and even his monetary history, have tended to be dismissed, as Koopmans dismissed Mitchell's work, as 'measurement without theory' (Koopmans, 1947).[13] Where his empirical work has been noticed (for example his analysis of the causes of the depression of 1929–32) it has been easy to see this as methodologically separate from work on economic theory (to see it as economic history).

3   Friedman has never been able to articulate his methodology adequately. What should have been explanations of methodological differences with his critics came across as confused argument, evasion and verbal quibbling.

The analysis of Friedman's rhetoric carried out in sections 2 to 5 could be read in a number of ways. It could be seen as confirming either the conclusion reached by Hirsch and de Marchi, that Friedman is best seen as a Deweyian pragmatist; or it could be taken as confirming Mäki's conclusion that Friedman uses whatever methodological arguments suit his rhetorical purposes.[14] In either case, it emerges that, methodologically, Friedman is far from orthodox.

### The role of rhetorical analysis

Our discussion of Friedman is also helpful in evaluating the relative merits of the two approaches to methodology discussed in section 1,

---

13   See, for example, his exchange with Tobin, discussed in section 3 above.

14   Mäki also argues that there are pragmatic elements in Friedman's methodology, but the aspect of pragmatism that he focuses on is the social construction of knowledge. He does not explore the idea, emphasized by Hirsch and de Marchi, that methodology is about the process of inquiry rather than simply the justification of theories.

and explored at greater length in section 6. For many economists, McCloskey's analysis may go far enough. Off-the-cuff remarks are made concerning methodology, which have no real bearing on the methods actually pursued by the economists concerned. One might conjecture that this will be particularly true of economists whose only activity is 'normal science' in Kuhn's sense. However, for others, and Friedman is surely one, such an approach does not get us very far. Our analysis of Friedman's rhetoric establishes some very important features of his methodology, but these hardly amount to more than clues. Crucially, analysing rhetoric is very different from analysing what he does as an economist. If we are to speak of implicit methodology, it is the methodology implicit in practice, not rhetoric, that we should be looking for. These are not the same thing.[15] Rhetoric *may* reveal methodology, but there is an equally strong case for arguing that rhetorical analysis should rather be used as a check on our interpretation of an economist's methodology. Of course, economists' methodological pronouncements should not be taken at face value, and an analysis of rhetoric may be revealing (this far we go with McCloskey), but, at least in the first instance, we should be looking for an interpretation that renders an economist's practice consistent with his or her stated views on methodology.[16]

[15]  It may be that a case could be made for basing an analysis of implicit methodology simply on rhetoric could be based on an *extreme* relativist–constructivist view of economic knowledge. If the view were taken that there were no empirical constraints on knowledge whatsoever, attempts to discover the truth could play no possible role in persuasion, and hence persuasion would be everything. Discovering the truth and successful persuasion would be synonymous.

[16]  This conclusion has something in common with Stigler's principle of textual exegesis (1965).

# Chapter 12

# Rhetoric and persuasion in macroeconomics: a comparison of Muth and Leijonhufvud

## INTRODUCTION

Donald McCloskey (1986) has drawn attention to the importance of the rhetorical devices used by economists, arguing that they are much more complex than most writing on the methodology of economics would lead one to expect. He takes as two of his main examples Muth's 'Rational expectations and the theory of price movements' (1961) and Fogel's *Railroads and American Economic Growth* (1964), claiming that the undoubted success of these works owed much to the rhetorical devices employed by their authors. A major problem with his arguments is that he neglects the vital question of why economists find certain arguments persuasive, and hence he fails to address the issue of how important the rhetorical devices he points out really are.

The aim of this chapter is to explore these issues using two examples taken from contemporary macroeconomics. It will be argued that whilst the factors McCloskey cites may be important in determining the initial impact of a new work, there are other, more important, criteria which determine which ideas survive, and which are discarded. The examples chosen are Muth's theory of rational expectations (one of McCloskey's examples) and Leijonhufvud's work on Keynesian economics. Both works appeared during the 1960s and, at least for a while, had a significant impact on macroeconomics. Beyond that there are major differences.

1  Muth's work was slow to be recognized, whereas Leijonhufvud made an immediate impact.
2  Muth provided a concept that has been used to transform the subject, whereas Leijonhufvud's ideas have fallen into comparative oblivion.
3  Muth published a short, comparatively simple, article, Leijonhufvud a big, complicated book.
4  Muth was not trying to transform macroeconomics, Leijonhufvud was.

In short, Muth's work had enormous unintended consequences, whilst Leijonhufvud attempted a revolution, but failed. These differences are important because to establish the importance of rhetoric it is necessary to consider failure as well as success.

The success of his ideas means that the story of Muth, rational expectations, the new classical and new Keynesian macroeconomics is now so well known that it does not need to be told here.[1] In contrast, Leijonhufvud's story is now relatively unknown and needs telling in more detail.

## MUTH

The main point of Muth's 'Rational expectations and the theory of price movements' is the notion that expectations should be rational: that expectations should take account of all information that is available when the expectations are formed. We shall call this the weak version of rational expectations. To formulate an economic theory, however, this is not enough. We need to make assumptions about the information agents have at their disposal. A natural case to consider here is that in which agents know the true model which is generating the data: they know as much as it is possible for them to know. This leads to what may be called the strong version of rational expectations: that 'expectations are the same as the predictions of the relevant economic theory' (Muth, 1961; quoted in McCloskey, 1986, pp. 92–3).

---

1    It is sketched in Chapters 8, 9 and 10.

As McCloskey has shown, Muth uses a number of arguments to support this thesis. In his paper it is not simply a matter of reporting results, nor do the techniques by which he tries to persuade fit easily into the modernist methodological mould. Muth's statement that 'the only real test ... is whether theories involving rationality explain observed behaviour better than alternative theories' (quoted in McCloskey, 1986, p. 94) is part of Muth's rhetoric, not a statement about what others found persuasive about his article. The real arguments, McCloskey claims, are aesthetic, involving comparisons between information and ordinary goods. Such arguments are persuasive only amongst a certain circle. Knowledge is social rather than individual.

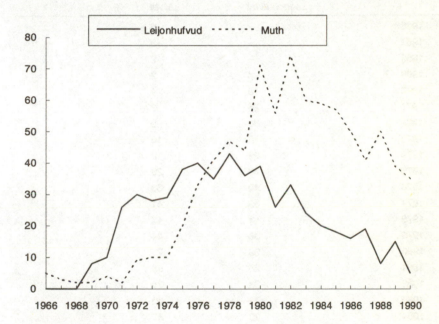

*Figure 12.1* Citations of Muth (1961) and Leijonhufvud (1968)
*Source:* as Table 12.1.

Though McCloskey is undoubtedly correct in much of what he says, there is a puzzle. Despite all the rhetorical devices involved, Muth's article was, for a long time, largely *un*persuasive. As Table 12.1 and Figure 12.1 show, until 1972 it was never cited more than five times in a year. From the mid-1970s there was a rapid growth in the popularity of the article until it was cited over seventy times in 1980 and 1982. McCloskey's explanation is that 'the paper took a long time to be recognised as important because it was badly written' (McCloskey, 1986, p. 88). His comparison with the ideas of Galileo, Poincaré, Einstein and Keynes, all of whom could write well, is not persuasive: surely the success of their ideas depended on far more than their literary style. To explain why Muth's article was ultimately so persuasive, and also why it was unpersuasive for so long, we have to look not simply at Muth's rhetoric, but at the content of macroeconomic theories.

*Table 12.1* Citations of Muth (1961) and Leijonhufvud (1968)

|        | Leijonhufvud | Muth |
|--------|--------------|------|
| 1966   | –            | 5    |
| 1967   | –            | 3    |
| 1968   | –            | 2    |
| 1969   | 8            | 2    |
| 1970   | 10           | 4    |
| 1971   | 26           | 2    |
| 1972   | 30           | 9    |
| 1973   | 28           | 10   |
| 1974   | 29           | 10   |
| 1975   | 38           | 20   |
| 1976   | 40           | 33   |
| 1977   | 35           | 41   |
| 1978   | 43           | 47   |
| 1979   | 36           | 44   |
| 1980   | 39           | 71   |
| 1981   | 26           | 56   |
| 1982   | 33           | 74   |
| 1983   | 24           | 60   |
| 1984   | 20           | 59   |
| 1985   | 18           | 57   |
| 1986   | 16           | 50   |
| 1987   | 19           | 41   |
| 1988   | 8            | 50   |
| 1989   | 15           | 39   |
| 1990   | 5            | 35   |

*Source: Social Science Citation Index.* The figures on Muth for 1966–82 are taken from McCloskey (1986, p. 87).

The concept of rational expectations is usable in any area of economics for almost all behaviour depends in some way on expectations of the future. It was, however, macroeconomics where the concept had its greatest impact, the reason for this being that in the early 1970s a number of economists, of whom the most important was Lucas (a colleague of Muth's at Chicago), showed how the assumption of rational expectations could be used, along with certain other assumptions, to overturn many widely accepted notions. The assumptions that Lucas made were: (1) the absence of money illusion – uniform changes in the price level will affect behaviour only when they are unanticipated; (2) prices adjust to ensure continuous market clearing; (3) the strong version of rational expectations. Using these assumptions Lucas was able to show a number of things. The first was that only unanticipated monetary policy will affect the level of economic activity. Anticipated monetary changes will merely affect the price level, leaving behaviour unaffected. In addition, he showed that traditional models (ones which neglected price expectations) might fit data generated by what he claimed was the true model (involving such expectations). The problem for traditional models was that if monetary policy were changed so too would the parameters of the traditional models. This result, widely known as the 'Lucas critique', means that it is inappropriate to use traditional models as a basis for designing monetary policy.

Once we accept that the main impact of Muth's work was in this area, there is no problem in explaining why his ideas were neglected for a decade. The Phillips curve was, in 1960, still new theory of inflation, this being the year when Samuelson and Solow's widely read article on its implications for policy making was first published. Econometric evidence during much of the 1960s suggested that there might be a stable relationship between unemployment and inflation, albeit one which depended on certain other variables such as union power. As the inflation rate was low and fairly predictable inflationary expectations were not seen as a problem – indeed Samuelson and Solow mentioned the possibility that a change in inflationary expectations would shift the Phillips curve, but did not attach great importance to this. It was towards the end of the 1960s that inflation became a greater problem, and Friedman and Phelps showed the implications of inflationary expectations for the Phillips curve. To do this they assumed that expectations responded with a lag to actual inflation. Their conclusion was that monetary policy could affect economic activity only in the short run. The result was intense econometric activity, resulting in numerous estimates of expectations-augmented Phillips curves.

It was against this background that Lucas took up Muth's notion of rational expectations, thus transforming macroeconomics. The work of Friedman and Phelps, together with the developments in the economy which had by then caused the traditional Phillips curve to break down, had placed inflationary expectations at the head of the macroeconomic agenda. Rational expectations, in addition to being attractive on what McCloskey dubs aesthetic grounds, solved a pre-existing puzzle: it could not be ignored.[2]

One of the striking features of this episode is the extent to which the concept of rational expectations has become widely accepted, even by 'Keynesian' economists who remain unconvinced by Lucasian arguments about the scope for macroeconomic policy. Economists such as Tobin, Solow and Hahn have come to accept the concept of rational expectations as an essential modelling tool. Their objections to the work of Lucas and his associates are associated with the other assumptions they combine with rational expectations: the assumption that markets are always in equilibrium is seen as a much more problematic assumption, not consistent with observed behaviour.

## LEIJONHUFVUD'S THESIS

### On Keynesian Economics and the Economics of Keynes

The thesis of Leijonhufvud's *On Keynesian Economics and the Economics of Keynes* was that the prevailing orthodoxy misrepresented Keynes's economics: that 'Keynes' theory is quite different from the "Keynesian" income–expenditure theory' (Leijonhufvud, 1968, p. 8). There was, he

[2]   See Chapters 8 and 10.

argued, substantial agreement that macroeconomic debate should be conducted using a static, simultaneous equation model such as Hicks proposed in 1937. Once the decision was taken to adopt such a framework it followed that unemployment equilibrium had to arise from wage rigidity, a liquidity trap or insufficient investment demand, *even though none of these explanations was accepted by Keynes*. Keynes's economics simply did not fit into this framework. Leijonhufvud, however, went much further than this – he provided an interpretation of Keynes's economics within the framework of Walrasian general equilibrium theory.[3]

According to Leijonhufvud, Keynes made four crucial departures from the classical theory.

1  He dispensed with the Walrasian auctioneer. In the absence of any auctioneer, trade takes place at disequilibrium prices, with the result that transactors face quantity constraints, Clower's 'dual decision hypothesis' (Clower, 1965) becomes relevant, and as a result excess demands fail to transmit the right signals.

2  He reversed the Marshallian ranking of price and quantity adjustment speeds. Where Marshall had assumed prices adjusted more rapidly than quantities, Keynes assumed the reverse. Leijonhufvud went so far as to claim,

> Keynes's 'long struggle to escape' seems primarily to have been a struggle with the dynamics of the Marshallian period analysis.
>
> (Leijonhufvud, 1968, p. 53)

3  He assumed inelastic expectations. This was the basis for Keynes's speculative demand for money. This is central not because it provided the reason for the liquidity trap, but because inelastic expectations can cause an 'intertemporal disequilibrium' through causing asset prices to be inappropriate. The argument was that inelastic expectations caused the relative price of money and bonds to be wrong. Because bonds and capital were aggregated this

---

[3]  As this was understood in the 1960s. Whether 'Walrasian economics' as it is commonly understood is 'the economics of Walras' is another issue. See Van Daal and Jolink (1993).

implied that the price of capital was too low, with the result that investment was too low for full employment.

4  He did not aggregate over investment and consumption goods (as is necessary to obtain a conventional aggregate production function) because had he done so it would not have been possible to have an imbalance in the prices of output and capital goods. By assuming an aggregate production function, economists were ruling out the source of disequilibrium that was fundamental to Keynes's economics.

However, though he provided a new way of thinking about macroeconomics, Leijonhufvud's arguments were largely critical in the sense that he did not show how an alternative to conventional macroeconomic models could be constructed. His main positive suggestion about how Keynesian problems might be modelled is that

the 'post-Keynesian' development of cybernetics as an inter-disciplinary field studying communication and control in complex dynamic systems may provide valuable suggestions for economists interested in exploring the 'revolutionary' approach to monetary theory towards which Keynes was groping.

(Leijonhufvud, 1968, p. 48)

Later on he elaborates on this, focusing on the unclear mix of statics and dynamics in conventional theory:

What is required, I believe, is a systematic investigation, from the standpoint of the information problems stressed in this study, of what elements of the static theory of resource allocation can without further ado be utilized in the analysis of dynamic and historical systems.

(Leijonhufvud, 1968, pp. 400–1)

There is also the suggestion that we might 'go back to Hayek' in order to get ideas as to how this might be done.[4] Beyond this there is nothing.

---

4    The full quotation is 'If one must retrace some steps of past developments in order to get on the right track – and that is probably advisable – my own preference is to go back to Hayek. Hayek's Gestalt-conception of what happens during business cycles was much less

## The reception of Leijonhufvud's ideas

The most enduring legacy of Leijonhufvud's work is arguably the literature, both macro- and microeconomic, on equilibrium with rationing. Barro and Grossman (1971, 1976) developed a model where quantity rationing and the resulting spillover effects created the possibility of equilibria with unemployment but zero excess demand in all other markets. During the 1970s such models were extended, the most widely-known probably being those of Malinvaud (1977) and Muellbauer and Portes (1978). On the microeconomic side there were the models of Drèze and Benassy (see Drazen, 1980). Such models, however, owed as much to the influence of Clower (1965) and Patinkin (1965) as to Leijonhufvud.[5] In such models the 'Marshallian' ranking of adjustment speeds was reversed and trade took place at disequilibrium prices, but otherwise they owed little to Leijonhufvud. Leijonhufvud himself never followed this route.

Though the most widespread reaction was arguably to ignore most of the details of Leijonhufvud's thesis, virtually all the steps in his argument were questioned. It was argued that wage stickiness was more important to Keynes's economics than Leijonhufvud had claimed (Grossman, 1972; Jackman, 1974; Bliss, 1975b; Brothwell, 1975; Backhouse, 1982); that his thesis on the aggregative structure of the *General Theory* was wrong (Froyen, 1976); and that his thesis on the ranking of adjustment speeds was not correct (Backhouse, 1980).

Perhaps more interesting, Leijonhufvud himself changed his view dramatically (1974, 1976). He began to argue that he had been wrong to interpret Keynes through the perspective of Walrasian economics. Keynes was a Marshallian and, therefore, using arguments that do not make sense within a Walrasian framework.

(Continued from previous page)
sound than Keynes's. As an unhappy consequence, his far superior work on the fundamentals of the problem has not received the attention it deserves' (Leijonhufvud, 1968, p. 401). The works he cites are Hayek's essays 'Economics and knowledge', 'The use of knowledge in society' and 'The meaning of competition'.
[5]    Though it was not as widely noticed as Barro and Grossman's work, Solow and Stiglitz (1968), which came before Leijonhufvud's book, contained a very similar model.

The Marshallian ground rules of his [Keynes's] analysis will not accommodate a still shorter Hicksian 'fix-price market day'.

(Leijonhufvud, 1974, p. 169)

Not only did Keynes not reverse the Marshallian ranking of price and quantity adjustment speeds, but he could not have done so.

Leijonhufvud continued to see a difference between Keynes's economics and the 'Keynesian' economics of the neoclassical synthesis, but saw the issues rather differently. The central issue, he claimed, was 'the co-ordination of economic activities', Keynes's theory being a denial of 'the orthodox presupposition that the economic system "naturally" and "automatically" works to co-ordinate economic activities' (1976, p. 91). He described as a 'red herring' the task of 'analytically isolating the atypical assumption or assumptions of Keynes's theory that were responsible for its "unemployment equilibrium" implications' (ibid., p. 94), the task to which his earlier work had been a major contribution. Instead, he suggested that the problem of coordination failures needed to be analysed in terms of a dynamic process analysis; that there is a 'corridor' around full employment within which the economy may be self-equilibrating; and that maximization may be an inappropriate way of modelling behaviour.

More significant than these detailed arguments, however, is Leijonhufvud's claim that the difficulties lie at the 'presuppositional level' – that Keynes's achievement can be analysed only in terms of 'an informal and improvised meta-language', not in terms of a formal model (1976, p. 82).

The analytical devices and routines of the neo-Walrasian general equilibrium theory and Keynesian theory will not 'mix'.

(Leijonhufvud, 1976, p. 103)

Leijonhufvud's interpretation of Keynes's economics focused on the effectiveness of price signals. Keynes, he contended, had tried to show how unemployment could arise even if price signals worked – even if prices responded to excess demands. This was in contrast with the orthodox interpretation of Keynesian economics which implies that unemployment arises because price signals are ineffective: wage rigidity, the liquidity trap and insufficient investment demand all prevent price signals from working to restore full employment.

## LEIJONHUFVUD'S RHETORIC

In contrast with Muth's article, Leijonhufvud's *On Keynesian Economics and the Economics of Keynes* was an immediate success. The pattern of citations, shown in Table 12.1, shows a substantial interest in the book throughout the 1970s, diminishing only in the 1980s.[6] The book exhibits a number of rhetorical features that can easily be used to explain its initial success.

1 It presented a bold, paradoxical thesis, clearly expressed in its title, that 'Keynesian economics' as economists then understood it was not the economics of Keynes. Taking as his example a passage in which Klein had argued that Keynes did not really understand what he had written, Leijonhufvud was very critical of contemporary interpretations of Keynesian economics:[7]

> The impression of Keynes that one gains from such comments is that of a Delphic oracle, half hidden in billowing fumes, mouthing earth-shattering profundities whilst in a sense-less trance – an oracle revered for his powers, to be sure, but not worthy of the same respect as that accorded the High Priests whose function is to interpret the revelations.
>
> (Leijonhufvud, 1968, p. 35)

2 Like Keynes's *General Theory*, it was a long and difficult book.
3 Though he used not a single equation, Leijonhufvud demonstrated an apparent familiarity with the technical details of both general

6   Part, though not all, of the difference is that Leijonhufvud (1968) was a book. Many of the very early citations are to reviews.
7   Note that Leijonhufvud himself comes close to such an interpretation of Keynes when he writes that 'Keynes's apparatus did not serve to communicate his ideas accurately' (Leijonhufvud, 1968, p. 400).

equilibrium theory and the theory of aggregation.[8] His paradoxical claims could not simply be ignored.

4  The book was filled with new concepts which had a clear intuitive meaning, even though their theoretical content was not worked out: economics without the auctioneer; a reversal of adjustment speed rankings; inter-temporal disequilibrium. It was ideas such as these, as much as the technical arguments contained in the book, which accounted for its success. Thus Bliss, in providing one of the first critiques of Leijonhufvud's work, contended that

> there are serious deficiencies in his arguments, which when they amount to more than rather general speculation are sometimes quite simply wrong.
>
> (Bliss, 1975b, p. 203)

At the same time he said of the book:

> it inspires students. ... I have shared, and continue to share, some of the infectious enthusiasm to which the book gives rise.
>
> (ibid.)

Commenting on Bliss's paper, Blaug endorsed this reaction:

> Leijonhufvud's book was well received. Indeed, it was too well received: it was swallowed whole, despite the fact that its central message is uncertain, its style of exposition subtle to the point of being obscure, and its target more or less the whole of received macroeconomics.
>
> (Bliss, 1975b, p. 213)

## CONCLUSIONS

Comparing Muth and Leijonhufvud helps put McCloskey's claims about the importance of Muth's rhetoric in perspective. If we focus simply on the delayed acceptance of Muth's ideas and the rapid success of Leijonhufvud's, it is not totally implausible to suggest that the

---

[8]  Cf. McCloskey (1986) on Fogel.

difference had something to do with differences in style. The way arguments are presented does matter. It is difficult, however, to go much further than this. One might wish, perhaps, to suggest that Muth's scientistic rhetoric was, in the long run, more effective than Leijonhufvud's 'old fashioned' literary style, but this creates a puzzle about why Leijonhufvud's book had such a big initial impact.

No such puzzles are raised by more conventional accounts[9] of what happened to macroeconomics during this period. Interest in Leijonhufvud's book was so great because economists saw that there were problems with conventional theories of unemployment and his ideas opened up the possibility of a new way of thinking about markets and why coordination failures might arise. When it became clear that the only formal models that were going to arise from Leijonhufvud's perspective were fix-price 'disequilibrium' models, interest waned for a variety of reasons.

1  The events of the 1970s meant that economists came to be concerned with issues (in particular the dynamics of inflation, unemployment and exchange rates) with which disequilibrium models were not equipped to deal. High inflation made fix-price models seem very unrealistic.

2  By the late 1970s disequilibrium models were seen as posing few theoretical challenges, the main issues being by then understood. In contrast, the concept of rational expectations was raising important and challenging technical problems.

3  At the beginning of the 1970s disequilibrium economics seemed to many economists a way of providing Keynesian economics with a more rigorous microeconomic foundation, for it was retaining the assumption of individual maximizing behaviour, but taking account of additional constraints on behaviour. Fix-price models, however, soon came to be seen as denying the assumption of rational, maximizing behaviour. Imperfect competition, asymmetric information and transactions costs were seen as better ways forward.

9  See, for example, Chapters 8, 9 and 10.

The interpretations of post-war macroeconomics provided in Chapters 8 and 10 have no difficulty in explaining why Muth's influence rose at the expense of Leijonhufvud's. There may, as McCloskey has correctly pointed out, be a large gap between economists' methodological statements and the reasons why their work is found persuasive. Economic theories are not accepted and rejected according to naive falsificationist criteria. This does not mean, however, that it is pointless to look for a logic underlying the evolution of economic ideas. The commitment to rationality which led economists progressively to remove the 'free parameters' from Keynesian theory, together with the policy challenges posed during the 1970s, can easily explain what happened to macroeconomic theory during this period.

Taking the argument a bit further, the story discussed in this chapter could be fitted into a Lakatosian framework. 'Disequilibrium macroeconomics' can be seen as a research programme, with a hard core of individual maximizing behaviour, quantity rationing and spillover effects. Around 1970 the programme appeared, at least to many economists, theoretically and empirically progressive. 'Dropping the auctioneer' and analysing markets as being in disequilibrium raised the possibility of explaining phenomena previously thought inexplicable. When it became clear that the research programme was not leading anywhere, and when alternative, more progressive research programmes (the new classical, and later new Keynesian programmes) appeared, it was abandoned. Rhetoric should be examined, but it provides a much poorer explanation of why economists found the ideas of Leijonhufvud and Muth persuasive when they did.

# References

Allett, J. (1981) *New Liberalism: the Political Economy of J. A. Hobson*. Toronto: University of Toronto Press.

Ando, Albert, and Modigliani, Franco (1965) 'The relative stability of monetary velocity and the investment multiplier', *American Economic Review* 55, pp. 693–728.

Attfield, C. L. F., Demery, D., and Duck, N. W. (1985) *Rational Expectations in Macroeconomics: An Introduction to Theory and Evidence*. Oxford: Basil Blackwell.

Azariadis, C. (1975) 'Implicit contracts and underemployment equilibria', *Journal of Political Economy* 83, pp. 1183–202.

Backhouse, Roger E. (1980) 'Fix-price versus flex-price models of macroeconomic equilibrium with rationing', *Oxford Economic Papers* 32, pp. 210–23.

Backhouse, Roger E. (1982) 'Price flexibility and Keynesian unemployment in a macroeconomic model with quantity rationing', *Oxford Economic Papers* 34, pp. 292–304.

Backhouse, Roger E. (1983) *Macroeconomics and the British Economy*. Oxford: Martin Robertson.

Backhouse, Roger E. (1985) *A History of Modern Economic Analysis*. Oxford: Basil Blackwell.

Backhouse, Roger E. (1992) 'The constructivist critique of economic methodology', *Methodus* 4(1), pp. 65–82.

Backhouse, Roger E. (1993a) 'The debate over Milton Friedman's theoretical framework: an economist's view', *Economics and Language*, edited by Willie Henderson, Tony Dudley-Evans and Roger Backhouse. London: Routledge.

Backhouse, Roger E. (1993b) 'Rhetoric and methodology', in R. F. Hébert (ed.) *Perspectives on the History of Economic Thought* 9. Aldershot: Edward Elgar.

Backhouse, Roger E. (1994a) *Economists and the Economy*, second edition. New Brunswick, NJ: Transaction.

Backhouse, Roger E. (ed.) (1994b) *New Directions in Economic Methodology*. London: Routledge.

Backhouse, Roger E. (1994c) 'The Lakatosian legacy in economic methodology', in Backhouse (1994b).

Bagehot, W. (1896) *Lombard Street (1873)*, tenth edition. London.

Baily, M. N. (1974) 'Wages and employment under uncertain demand', *Review of Economic Studies* 41, pp. 37–50.

Barro, R. J. (1977) 'Unanticipated money growth and unemployment in the United States', *American Economic Review* 67, pp. 101–15.

Barro, R. J. (1978) 'Unanticipated money, output and the price level in the United States', *Journal of Political Economy* 86, pp. 549–80.

Barro, R. J., and Grossman, H. I. (1971) 'A general disequilibrium model of income and employment', *American Economic Review* 61, pp. 82–93.

Barro, R. J., and Grossman, H. I. (1976) *Money, Employment and Inflation*. London and New York: Cambridge University Press.

Barro, R. J., and Rush, M. (1980) 'Unanticipated money and economic activity', in S. Fischer (ed.) *Rational Expectations and Economic Policy*, National Bureau of Economic Research. Chicago: Chicago University Press.

Bazerman, Charles (1989) *Shaping Written Knowledge*. Madison: University of Wisconsin Press.

Blaug, Mark (1980/1992) *The Methodology of Economics*. Cambridge: Cambridge University Press.

Blaug, Mark (1985) *Economic Theory in Retrospect*, fourth edition. Cambridge: Cambridge University Press.

Blaug, Mark (1990) 'On the historiography of economics', *Journal of the History of Economic Thought* 12(1), pp. 27–37.

Blaug, Mark (1991a) 'Introduction' to *The Historiography of Economics* (Pioneers in Economics, Volume 1). Brookfield, VT, and Aldershot: Edward Elgar.

Blaug, Mark (1991b) 'Second thoughts on the Keynesian revolution', *History of Political Economy* 23, pp. 171–92.

Blinder, Alan (1987) 'Keynes, Lucas and scientific progress', *American Economic Review* 77, pp. 130–6.

Bliss, C. J. (1975a) *Capital Theory and the Distribution of Income*. Amsterdam: North-Holland.

Bliss, C. J. (1975b) 'The reappraisal of Keynes's economics: an appraisal', in M. Parkin and A. R. Nobay (eds) *Current Economic Problems*. Cambridge: Cambridge University Press.

Bliss, C. J. and Stern, N. (1982) *Palanpur: the Economy of an Indian Village*. Oxford: Oxford University Press.

Brainard, W. C., and Cooper, R. N. (1975) 'Empirical monetary macro-economics: what have we learned in the last 25 years?' *American Economic Review* 65, pp. 167–75.

Brothwell, J. F. (1975) 'A simple Keynesian's response to Leijonhufvud', *Bulletin of Economic Research* 27(1), pp. 3–21.

Brown, Vivienne (1993) 'Decanonizing discourses' in *Economics and Language*, edited by Willie Henderson, Tony Dudley-Evans and Roger E. Backhouse. London: Routledge.

Buiter, W., and Miller, M. (1981) 'The Thatcher experiment: the first two years', *Brookings Papers on Economic Activity*, pp. 315–79.

Calvo, G., and Phelps, E. S. (1977) 'Employment-contingent wage contracts', in K. Brunner and A. Meltzer (eds) *Stabilization of the Domestic and International Economy*, Carnegie-Rochester Series in Public Policy, 1977, pp. 160–8.

Cantillon, R. (1755) *Essai sur la Nature du Commerce en Générale*. Translated by H. Higgs. London, 1932.

Casson, M. (1983) *The Economics of Unemployment*. Oxford: Martin Robertson.

Champernowne, D. G. (1936) 'Unemployment, basic and monetary: the classical analysis and the Keynesian', *Review of Economic Studies* 3, pp. 201–16.

Clark, J. M. (1923) *The Economics of Overhead Costs*. Chicago: Chicago University Press.

Clark, J. M. (1934) *Strategic Factors in Business Cycles*. New York: National Bureau of Economic Research.

Clarke, P. (1990) 'Hobson and Keynes as economic heretics', in M. Freeden (ed.) *Reappraising J. A. Hobson: Humanism and Welfare*. London: Allen and Unwin.

Clower, Robert W. (1965) 'The Keynesian counter–revolution: a theoretical appraisal', in F. H. Hahn and F. Brechling (eds) *The Theory of Interest Rates*. London and Basingstoke: Macmillan.

Coats, A. W. (1967) 'Sociological aspects of British economic thought (ca. 1880–1930)', *Journal of Political Economy* 75, pp. 706–29.

Coats, A. W. (1969) 'Is there a "structure of scientific revolutions" in economics?', *Kyklos* 22, pp. 289–96.

Coats, A. W. (1984) 'The sociology of knowledge in the history of economics', *Research in the History of Economic Thought and Methodology* 2. Greenwich, CT and London: JAI Press.

Colander, David (1990) *Why Aren't Economists as Important as Garbagemen?* Armonk, NY, and London: M. E. Sharpe.

Collins, Harry (1985) *Changing Order: Replication and Induction in Scientific Practice*. London: Sage.

Coppock, D. J. (1953) 'A reconsideration of Hobson's theory of unemployment', *Manchester School* 21, pp. 1–21.

Corry, Bernard (1975) 'Should economists abandon HOPE?' *History of Political Economy* 7(2), pp. 252–60.

Davis, J. R. (1971) *The New Economics and the Old Economists*. Ames, IA: Iowa State University Press.

Dasgupta, A. K. (1985) *Epochs of Economic Theory*. Oxford: Basil Blackwell.

De Marchi, Neil (1988) 'Popper and the LSE economists', in Neil de Marchi (ed.) *The Popperian Legacy in Economics*. Cambridge: Cambridge University Press.

De Marchi, Neil, and Blaug, Mark (1991) *Appraising Economic Theories: Studies in the Methodology of Research Programmes*. Aldershot: Edward Elgar.

Diamond, Peter A. (1984) *A Search Equilibrium Approach to the Micro Foundations of Macroeconomics*. Cambridge, MA: MIT Press.

Dixit, A. K. (1978) 'The balance of trade in a model of temporary equilibrium with rationing', *Review of Economic Studies* 45, pp. 393–404.

Domar, E. (1946) 'Capital expansion, rate of growth and employment', *Econometrica* 14, pp. 137–47.

Dorfman, J. (1949) *The Economic Mind in American Civilization, vol. 3*. New York: Viking.

Dornbusch, R. (1976) 'Expectations and exchange rate dynamics', *Journal of Political Economy* 84, pp. 1161–76.

Dow, S. C. (1985) *Macroeconomic Thought*. Oxford: Basil Blackwell.

Dray, W. H. (1985) 'Narrative versus analysis in history', *Philosophy of Social Science* 15, pp. 125–45.

Drazen, A. (1980) 'Recent developments in macroeconomic disequilibrium theory', *Econometrica* 48, pp. 283–306.

Fish, S. (1980) *Is There a Text in this Class?* Cambridge, MA: Harvard University Press.

Flemming, J. S. (1973) 'The consumption function when capital markets are imperfect', *Oxford Economic Papers* 25, pp. 160–72.

Fogel, R. W. (1964) *Railroads and American Economic Growth*. Baltimore: Johns Hopkins.

Friedman, Milton (1950) 'Wesley C. Mitchell as an economic theorist', *Journal of Political Economy* 58, pp. 463–95.

Friedman, Milton (1953) 'The methodology of positive economics', in M. Friedman (ed.) *Essays in Positive Economics*. Chicago: Chicago University Press.

Friedman, Milton (1956) 'The quantity theory of money: a restatement', in M. Friedman (ed.) *Studies in the Quantity Theory of Money*. Chicago: Chicago University Press.

Friedman, Milton (1957) *The Theory of the Consumption Function*. Princeton: Princeton University Press.

Friedman, Milton (1959) 'The demand for money: some theoretical and empirical results', *Journal of Political Economy* 67; reprinted in Friedman (1969).

Friedman, Milton (1963) *The Monetary History of the United States*. Princeton: Princeton University Press.

Friedman, Milton (1968) 'The role of monetary policy', *American Economic Review* 58, pp. 1–17.

Friedman, Milton (1969) *The Optimum Quantity of Money and Other Essays*. London: Macmillan.

Friedman, Milton (1970a) 'A theoretical framework for monetary analysis', *Journal of Political Economy* 78, pp. 193–238. Reprinted in Gordon (1974).

Friedman, Milton (1970b) 'Money and income: post hoc ergo propter hoc?: Comment', *Quarterly Journal of Economics* 84, pp. 318–27.

Friedman, Milton (1974) 'Comments on the critics', in Gordon (1974).

Friedman, Milton, and Schwartz, Anna J. (1963) *A Monetary History of the US, 1861–1960*. Princeton: Princeton University Press.

Friedman, Milton, and Meiselman, David (1963) 'The relative stability of monetary velocity and the investment multiplier in the United States, 1897–1958', in Commission on Money and Credit *Stabilization Policies*. New York: Prentice-Hall.

Froyen, R. T. (1976) 'The aggregative structure of Keynes's *General Theory*', *Quarterly Journal of Economics* 90, pp. 369–87.

Gerrard, B. (1988) 'Keynesian economics: the road to nowhere?' in J. Hillard (ed.) *J. M. Keynes in Retrospect*. Aldershot: Edward Elgar.

Gide, C., and Rist, C. (1909) *A History of Economic Doctrines*. Translated by R. Richards, 1917. London: Harrap.

Gilbert, C. (1991) 'On demand analysis and consumption analysis as tests of theories of methodology', in de Marchi and Blaug (1991).

Gordon, Robert J. (1974) *Milton Friedman's Monetary Framework*. Chicago: Chicago University Press.

Gordon, Robert J. (1982) 'Price inertia and policy ineffectiveness in the United States, 1890–1980', *Journal of Political Economy* 86, pp. 971–87.

Gordon, S. (1973) 'The wage fund controversy: the second round', *History of Political Economy* 5, pp. 14–35.

Grossman, H. I. (1972) 'Was Keynes a "Keynesian"? A review article', *Journal of Economic Literature* 10, pp. 26–30.

Haberler, G. (1943) *Prosperity and Depression* (1936), third edition. Geneva: League of Nations.

Hacking, Ian (1983) *Representing and Intervening.* Cambridge: Cambridge University Press.

Hall, R. E. (1978) 'Stochastic implications of the life cycle-permanent income hypothesis: theory and evidence', *Journal of Political Economy* 86, pp. 971–87.

Hall, R. E. (1980) 'Employment fluctuations and wage rigidities', *Brookings Papers on Economic Activity,* 1980(1), pp. 91–124.

Hall, R. E. (1982) 'Monetary trends in the United States and the United Kingdom: a review from the perspective of the new developments in monetary economics', *Journal of Economic Literature* 20, pp. 1552–6.

Hands, D. Wade (1990) 'Second thoughts on "Second thoughts": reconsidering the Lakatosian progress of *The General Theory*', *Review of Political Economy* 2, pp. 69–82.

Hands, D. Wade (1992) Review of Weintraub (1991a). *Economic Journal* 102, pp. 953–8.

Hansen, Alvin H. (1953) *A Guide to Keynes.* New York: McGraw-Hill.

Hansen, Alvin H. (1964) *Business Cycles and National Income,* second edition. London: Allen and Unwin.

Harcourt, G. C., and Hamouda, O. F. (1988) 'Post-Keynesianism: from criticism to coherence?' *Bulletin of Economic Research* 40, pp. 1–33.

Harrod, R. F. (1937) 'Mr Keynes and traditional theory', *Economica* 5, pp. 74–86.

Harrod, R. F. (1939) 'An essay in dynamic theory', *Economic Journal* 49, pp. 14–33.

Harrod, R. F. (1956) 'Walras: a re-appraisal review article', *Economic Journal* 66, pp. 307ff.

Hart, Oliver D. (1982) 'A model of imperfect competition with Keynesian features', *Quarterly Journal of Economics* 97, pp.109–38.

Hendry, David, and Ericsson, Neil (1991) 'An econometric analysis of UK money demand in *Monetary Trends in the United States and the United Kingdom* by Milton Friedman and Anna Schwartz', *American Economic Review* 81(1), pp. 8–38.

Hicks, John R. (1937) 'Mr Keynes and the "classics": a suggested interpretation', *Econometrica* 5, pp. 147–59.

Hicks, John R. (1939) *Value and Capital*. Oxford: Oxford University Press.

Hicks, John R. (1967) 'Monetary theory and history – an attempt at perspective', in *Critical Essays in Monetary Theory*. Oxford: Oxford University Press.

Hicks, John R. (1974) *The Crisis in Keynesian Economics*. Oxford: Basil Blackwell.

Hirsch, Abraham, and de Marchi, Neil (1986) 'Making a case when a theory is unfalsifiable: Friedman's *Monetary History*', *Economics and Philosophy* 2(1), pp. 1–22.

Hirsch, Abraham, and de Marchi, Neil (1990) *Milton Friedman: Economics in Theory and Practice*. Brighton: Harvester Wheatsheaf.

Hobson, J. A. (1900) *The Economics of Distribution*. New York: Macmillan. Reprinted by A. M. Kelley, 1972.

Hobson, J. A. (1904) *The Problem of the Unemployed*, Second edition. London: Methuen. First edition, 1896. Reprinted in Hobson (1993).

Hobson, J. A. (1906) *The Evolution of Modern Capitalism*. London: Walter Scott.

Hobson, J. A. (1910) *The Industrial System*. London: Longmans Green. Reprinted in Hobson (1993).

Hobson, J. A. (1913) *Gold, Prices and Wages*. London: Methuen. Reprinted 1973, New York: Augustus M. Kelley.

Hobson, J. A. (1930) *Rationalisation and Unemployment*. London: Allen.

Hobson, J. A. (1933) 'Underconsumption: an exposition and a reply', *Economica* 13, pp. 402–17. Reprinted in Hobson (1993).

Hobson, J. A. (1993) *A Collection of Economic Works*. Bristol: Thoemmes Press.

Howitt, Peter (1986) 'The Keynesian recovery', *Canadian Journal of Economics* 19, pp. 626–41.

Hutchison, Terence W. (1937) *The Significance and Basic Postulates of Economic Theory*. London: Macmillan.

Hutchison, Terence W. (1953) *A Review of Economic Doctrines, 1870–1929*. Oxford: Oxford University Press.

Hutchison, Terence W. (1978) *On Revolutions and Progress in Economic Knowledge*. Cambridge: Cambridge University Press.

Hutchison, Terence W. (1981) *The Politics and Philosophy of Economics*. Oxford: Basil Blackwell.

Jackman, R. (1974) 'Keynes and Leijonhufvud', *Oxford Economic Papers* 26, pp. 259–72.

Jones, R. (1833) *An Essay on the Distribution of Wealth*. New York: Kelley and Millman, 1956.

Keynes, John Maynard (1913) Review of *Gold, Prices and Wages* by J. A. Hobson, *Economic Journal* 23. Reprinted in Keynes (1971–83), volume XI.

Keynes, John Maynard (1930) *A Treatise on Money*, 2 volumes. London: Macmillan. Reprinted in Keynes (1971–83), volumes V and VI.

Keynes, John Maynard (1936) *The General Theory of Employment, Interest and Money*. London: Macmillan. Reprinted in Keynes (1971–83), volume VII.

Keynes, John Maynard (1937) 'The general theory of employment', *Quarterly Journal of Economics* 51, pp. 209–23.

Keynes, John Maynard (1971–83) *The Collected Writings of John Maynard Keynes*, 30 volumes. London: Macmillan.

Klamer, Arjo, and Colander, David (1990) *The Making of an Economist*. Boulder, San Francisco and London: Westview Press.

Koopmans, T. C. (1947) 'Measurement without theory', *Review of Economics and Statistics* 29, pp. 161–72.

Kuhn, Thomas (1970) *The Structure of Scientific Revolutions*. Chicago: Chicago University Press. First edition, 1962.

Lakatos, I. (1970) 'Falsification and the methodology of scientific research programmes', in I. Lakatos and A. Musgrave (eds) *Criticism and the Growth of Knowledge*. Cambridge: Cambridge University Press. Reprinted in Lakatos (1978).

Lakatos, I. (1971) 'History of science and its rational reconstructions', in R. C. Buck and R. S. Cohen (eds) P.S.A. 1970 *Boston Studies in the Philosophy of Science*, 8. Dordrecht: Reidel. Reprinted in Lakatos (1978), pp. 102–38.

Lakatos, I. (1978) *The Methodology of Scientific Research Programmes: Philosophical Papers, Volume I*. Cambridge: Cambridge University Press.

Lakatos, I., and Zahar, E. G. (1976) 'Why did Copernicus's programme supersede Ptolomy's?', in R. Westman (ed.) *The Copernican Achievement*. Los Angeles: University of California Press. Reprinted in Lakatos (1978), pp. 168–92.

Layard, P. R. G., Nickell, S., and Jackman, R. (1991) *Unemployment: Macroeconomic Performance and the Labour Market*. Oxford: Oxford University Press.

Leijonhufvud, Axel (1974) 'Keynes's employment function: comment', *History of Political Economy* 6, pp. 164–70.

Leijonhufvud, Axel (1968) *On Keynesian Economics and the Economics of Keynes*. Oxford: Oxford University Press.

Leijonhufvud, Axel (1976) 'Schools, "revolutions" and research programmes in economic theory', in S. J. Latsis (ed.) *Method and Appraisal in Economics*. Cambridge: Cambridge University Press.

Leontief, Wassily A. (1937) 'Implicit theorizing: a methodological criticism of the Cambridge school', *Quarterly Journal of Economics*, 51; reprinted in W. A. Leontief, *Essays in Economics*, volume 1. Oxford: Basil Blackwell, 1966.

Leontief, Wassily (1971) 'Theoretical assumptions and non-observed facts', *American Economic Review* 61; reprinted in W. A. Leontief, *Essays in Economics*, volume 2. Oxford: Basil Blackwell, 1977.

Lipsey, Richard G. (1960) 'The relationship between unemployment and the rate of change of money wage rates in the UK 1862–1957: a further analysis', *Economica* 27, pp. 1–31.

Lipsey, Richard G. (1964) *Introduction to Positive Economics*. London: Weidenfeld.

Lucas, R. E. (1972) 'Expectations and the neutrality of money', *Journal of Economic Theory* 4, pp. 103–24.

Lucas, R. E. (1973) 'Some international evidence on output-inflation trade offs', *American Economic Review*, 63, pp. 326–34.

Lucas, R. E. (1976) 'Econometric policy evaluation: a critique', in *The Phillips Curve and Labour Markets* (Supplement to *Journal of Monetary Economics*), edited by K. Brunner and A. H. Meltzer.

Lucas, R. E. (1979) 'After Keynesian macroeconomics', *Federal Reserve Bank of Minneapolis Quarterly Review* 3(2). Reprinted in R. E. Lucas and T. J. Sargent (eds) *Rational Expectations and Econometric Practice*. London: George Allen and Unwin, 1981.

Maes, I. (1988) 'Did the Keynesian revolution retard the development of portfolio theory', *Banca Nazionale del Lavoro Quarterly Review*, 151, pp. 407–21.

Mäki, Uskali (1986) 'Rhetoric at the expense of coherence: a reinterpretation of Milton Friedman's methodology', *Research in the History of Economic Thought and Methodology* 4, pp. 127–43.

Mäki, Uskali (1993) 'Two philosophies of the rhetoric of economics', in W. Henderson, T. Dudley-Evans and R. Backhouse (eds), *Economics and Language*. London: Routledge.

Malinvaud, E. (1977) *The Theory of Unemployment Reconsidered*. Oxford: Basil Blackwell.

Marris, Robin (1991) *Reconstructing Keynesian Macroeconomics: a Desktop Simulation*. Aldershot: Edward Elgar.

Marshall, A. (1920) *Principles of Economics* (1890), eighth edition. London.

Marshall, A., and Marshall, M. P. (1979) *The Economics of Industry*. London.

McCloskey, Donald N. (1983) 'The rhetoric of economics', *Journal of Economic Literature* 21, pp. 481–517.

McCloskey, Donald N. (1986) *The Rhetoric of Economics*. Brighton: Wheatsheaf Books.

McCloskey, Donald N. (1988) 'Thick and thin methodologies in the history of economic thought', in Neil de Marchi (ed.) *The Popperian Legacy in Economics*. Cambridge: Cambridge University Press.

McCloskey, Donald N. (1990) *If You're So Smart: The Narrative of Economic Expertise*. Chicago: Chicago University Press.

Meade, J. E. (1937) 'A simplified model of Mr Keynes's system', *Review of Economic Studies* 4, pp. 98–107.

Mill, J. S. (1844) *Essays on Some Unsettled Questions of Political Economy*. Reprinted Bristol: Thoemmes Press, 1992.

Mirowski, Philip (1987) Review of Backhouse (1985). *Journal of Economic Literature* 25(4), pp. 1858–9.

Mirowski, Philip (1988) 'Shall I compare thee to a Minkowski–Ricardo–Leontief–Metzler matrix of the Mosak–Hicks type?' in Arjo Klamer, Donald N. McCloskey and Robert M. Solow (eds) *The Consequences of Economic Rhetoric*. Cambridge: Cambridge University Press.

Mirowski, Philip (1990) *More Heat than Light*. Cambridge: Cambridge University Press.

Mitchell, W. C. (1913) *Business Cycles*. New York: Burt Franklin.

Mitchell, W. C. (1927) *Business Cycles: The Problem and Its Setting*. New York: National Bureau of Economic Research.

Modigliani, Franco (1944) 'Liquidity preference and the theory of interest of money', *Econometrica* 12, pp. 45–88.

Morishima, M. (1977) *Walras's Economics*. Cambridge: Cambridge University Press.

Muellbauer, J. and Portes, R. (1978) 'Macroeconomic models with quantity rationing', *Economic Journal* 88, pp. 788–821.

Mummery, A. F., and Hobson, J. A. (1889) *The Physiology of Industry*. London: John Murray. Reprinted in Hobson (1993).

Muth, J. F. (1961) 'Rational expectations and the theory of price movements', *Econometrica* 29, pp. 315–35.

Nemmers, E. E. (1956) *Hobson and Underconsumption*. Amsterdam: North-Holland.

Newbery, D. M. G., and Stiglitz, J. E. (1981) *The Theory of Commodity Price Stabilization*. Oxford: Oxford University Press.

O'Brien, D. P. (1975) *The Classical Economists*. Oxford: Oxford University Press.

Okun, A. M. (1980) 'Rational-expectations-with-misperceptions as a theory of the business cycle', *Journal of Money, Credit and Banking* 12, pp. 817–25.

Passmore, John (1965) 'The idea of a history of philosophy' *History and Theory*, 1964–5, Beiheft 5, pp. 1–32.

Patinkin, D. (1956) *Money, Interest and Prices*. New York: Harper and Row.

Patinkin, D. (1962) *Money, Interest and Prices*, second edition. New York: Harper and Row.

Patinkin, D. (1965) *Money, Interest and Prices*. Evanston, IL: Row, Peterson and Co.

Patinkin, D. (1982) *Anticipations of the General Theory?* Oxford: Oxford University Press.

Perlman, M. (1980) 'Orthodoxy and heterodoxy in economics: a retrospective view of experiences in Britain and the USA', *Zeitschrift für National-ökonomie* 37, pp. 153–64.

Phelps, E. S. (1967) 'Phillips curves, expectations of inflation and optimal unemployment over time', *Economica* 34, pp. 254–81.

Phillips, A. W. (1958) 'The relation between unemployment and the rate of change of money wage rates in the United Kingdom 1861–1957', *Economica* 25, pp. 283–99.

Pigou, A. C. (1927) *Industrial Fluctuations*. London: Macmillan.

Pigou, A. C. (1929) 'The monetary theory of the trade cycle', *Economic Journal* 39, pp. 183–94.

Pigou, A. C. (1933) *The Theory of Employment*. London: Macmillan.

Popper, Karl R. (1983) *Realism and the Aim of Science*. London: Hutchinson.

Reder, Melvin W. (1982) 'Chicago economics: permanence and change', *Journal of Economic Literature* 20(1), pp. 1–38.

Remenyi, J. V. (1979) 'Core and demi-core interaction: toward a general theory of disciplinary and interdisciplinary growth', *History of Political Economy*, 11, pp. 30–63.

Richmond, W. (1978) 'John A. Hobson: economic heretic', *American Journal of Economics and Sociology* 37, pp. 283–94.

Robbins, Lionel (1932) *An Essay on the Nature and Significance of Economic Science*. London: Macmillan. Second edition, 1935.

Rogin, Leo (1956) *The Meaning and Validity of Economic Theory*. New York: Harper.

Rorty, Richard (1980) *Philosophy and the Mirror of Nature*. Oxford: Basil Blackwell.

Rorty, Richard (1984) 'The historiography of philosophy: four genres', in R. Rorty, J. B. Schneewind and Q. Skinner (eds) *Philosophy in History*. Cambridge and New York: Cambridge University Press.

Rorty, Richard (1991) *Objectivity, Relativism, and Truth*. Philosophical Papers, Volume I. Cambridge: Cambridge University Press.

Rorty, Richard, Schneewind, J. B., and Skinner, Quentin (1984) 'Introduction' to *Philosophy in History*. Cambridge: Cambridge University Press.

Ross, Dorothy (1991) *The Origins of American Social Science*. Cambridge: Cambridge University Press.

Sachs, J. D. (1979) 'Wages, profits and macroeconomic adjustment', *Brookings Papers on Economic Activity* 1979(2), pp. 269–319.

Samuelson, Paul A. (1939) 'Interaction between multiplier analysis and the principle of acceleration', *Review of Economics and Statistics* 21(2), pp. 75–8. Reprinted in American Economic Association, *Readings in Business Cycle Theory*. Homewood, IL: Richard D. Irwin, 1951.

Samuelson, Paul A. (1947) *Foundations of Economic Analysis*. Harvard: Harvard University Press.

Samuelson, Paul A. (1955) *Economics*, third edition. New York and London: McGraw-Hill.

Samuelson, Paul A. (1987) 'Out of the closet: a program for the Whig history of economic science', *History of Economics Society Bulletin* 9(1), pp. 51–60.

Samuelson, Paul A., and Solow, Robert M. (1960) 'Analytical aspects of anti-inflation policy', *American Economic Review* 50, pp. 177–94.

Sargent, T. J. and Wallace, N. (1982) 'The real bills doctrine versus the quantity theory: a reconsideration', *Journal of Political Economy* 90, pp. 1212–36.

Schabas, Margaret (1991) *A World Ruled by Number: William Stanley Jevons and the Rise of Mathematical Economics*. Princeton: Princeton University Press.

Schabas, Margaret. (1992) 'Breaking away: history of economics as history of science', *History of Political Economy*, 24(1), pp. 187–203.

Schumpeter, J. A. (1954) *History of Economic Analysis*. New York: Oxford University Press.

Sidgwick, H. (1883) *Principles of Political Economy*. London: Macmillan.

Solow, Robert M., and Stiglitz, Joseph E. (1968) 'Output, employment and wages in the short run', *Quarterly Journal of Economics* 82, pp. 537–60.

Sraffa, P. (1960) *Production of Commodities by Means of Commodities*. Cambridge: Cambridge University Press.

Stark, Werner (1944) *History of Economics in Relation to its Social Development*. London: Kegan Paul, Trench and Trubner.

Stigler, George J. (1965) 'Textual exegesis as a scientific problem', *Economica* 32. Reprinted in G. J. Stigler (ed.) *The Economist as Preacher and Other Essays*. Oxford: Basil Blackwell, 1982.

Stone, Lawrence (1979) 'The revival of narrative: reflections on a new old history', *Past and Present* 85, pp. 3–24.

Thornton, Henry (1802) *An Enquiry into the Nature and Effects of the Paper Credit of Great Britain*. Edited with an Introduction by F. A. Hayek. London: Allen and Unwin, 1939.

Tobin, James (1970) 'Post hoc ergo propter hoc', *Quarterly Journal of Economics* 84, pp. 301–17. 'Rejoinder', pp. 328–9.

Tobin, James (1987) *Policies for Prosperity: Essays in a Keynesian Mode*, ed. Peter M. Jackson. Brighton: Wheatsheaf Books.

Van Daal, Jan, and Jolink, Albert (1993) *The Equilibrium Economics of Léon Walras*. London: Routledge.

Vint, John (1994) *Capital and Wages: A Lakatosian History of the Wages Fund Doctrine*. Aldershot: Edward Elgar.

Walker, Donald (1988) 'Ten major problems in the study of the history of economic thought', *HES Bulletin* 10(2), 1988, pp. 99–115.

Walker, Donald (1992) 'Comment on Margaret Schabas's "Breaking away": history of economics as history of science', *History of Political Economy*, 24(1), pp. 243–5.

Walker, F. A. (1876) *The Wages Question*. London.

Walker, F. A. (1889) *Money, Trade and Industry* (1879). London.

Walker, F. A. (1896a) *Political Economy* (1885), third edition. New York.

Walker, F. A. (1896b) *International Bimetallism*. New York.

Walras, L. (1874) *Elements of Pure Economics*. Translated by W. Jaffé. London: George Allen and Unwin, 1954.

Weintraub, E. R. (1979) *Microfoundations*. Cambridge: Cambridge University Press.

Weintraub, E. Roy (1985) *General Equilibrium Analysis: Studies in Appraisal*. Cambridge: Cambridge University Press.

Weintraub, E. Roy (1989) 'Methodology doesn't matter, but the history of thought might', *Scandinavian Journal of Economics*; reprinted in Seppo Honkapohja (ed.) *The State of Macroeconomics*. Oxford: Basil Blackwell, pp. 263–79.

Weintraub, E. Roy (1991a) *Stabilizing Dynamics: Constructing Economic Knowledge*. Cambridge: Cambridge University Press.

Weintraub, E. Roy (1991b) 'Allais, stability and Liapunov theory', *History of Political Economy* 23(3), pp. 383–96.

Weintraub, E. Roy (1992) 'Thicker is better: comment on Backhouse', *Methodus* 4(2), pp. 53–7.

Weintraub, E. Roy (1994) 'After Mirowski, what?', *Non-Natural Social Science: Reflecting on the Enterprise of More Heat than Light*, Annual supplement to *History of Political Economy* 25, pp. 300–2.

Weiss, Andrew (1980) 'Job queues and layoffs in labour markets with flexible wages', *Journal of Political Economy* 88, pp. 526–38.

Wicksell, K. (1894) *Interest and Prices*. Translated by R. F. Kahn, 1934. London: Macmillan.

Wright, A. L. (1956) 'The genesis of the multiplier theory'. *Oxford Economic Papers* 8, pp. 181–93.

Young, W. (1987) *Interpreting Mr Keynes: The IS–LM Enigma*. Cambridge: Polity Press.

Zahar, Elie (1973) 'Why did Einstein's programme supersede Lorentz's? (I)', *British Journal for the Philosophy of Science* 24, pp. 95–123.

# Index